SOCIAL CASEWORK
A Behavioral Approach

SOCIAL CASEWORK
A Behavioral Approach

Arthur Schwartz
and
Israel Goldiamond

with
Michael W. Howe

Columbia University Press
New York and London, 1975

Library of Congress Cataloging in Publication Data

Schwartz, Arthur.
  Social casework.

  Bibliography: p.
  Includes index.
  1. Social casework. I. Goldiamond, Israel,
1919–   joint author. II. Howe, Michael W., joint
author. III. Title. [DNLM: 1. Behavior. 2. Social
service.   HV43 S399s]
HV43.S34   361.3   75-2298
ISBN 0-231-03778-3

CONTENTS

WITHDRAWN

Contents

Contents vii

PREFACE

This book is the result of a fortuitous academic request. As part of a continuous search for new modalities of treatment and research, I developed a course called "Alternate Approaches to the Helping Process." I approached Israel Goldiamond in the autumn of 1969 and asked him to give a guest lecture on operant methods to my class. The conversation ended with his presenting me with a key to an office in his clinic and an offer to train me in the approach. Goldiamond never did give that guest lecture, but he did teach me the principles of the approach, I attended his classes and seminars, and he supervised me in my clinical work with clients at his laboratory.

This affiliation was formalized by my receiving a joint appointment in the Department of Psychiatry of the University of Chicago. I have experimented with and worked with the model described in this book in a number of additional settings, such as a clinic for sexual dysfunctioning and marriage counseling (which I codirect with R. Taylor Segraves, M.D., Ph.D.), a home for the aged, a laboratory school, a home and hospital for disturbed children, and a student mental health clinic. Furthermore, through the cooperation of the faculty of the School of Social Service Administration of the University of Chicago, I started what is probably the first track in applied behavior analysis in a school of social work in the United States. The track offers both courses and field work at both the master's and the doctoral level.

My feeling, based on twenty years of practice, research, and teaching in the field of social work, is that the model offers a great deal that is useful for current social work practice. We are still developing and expanding the model, even entering into areas not previously considered "behavioral," such as the cognitive and affective aspects of social casework. The work I am doing in the marital counseling clinic, and the theoretical work done jointly with Jarl E. Dyrud, M.D., director of clinical services, will be reported in the near future. Dr. Dyrud has long been investigating the interfaces of the psychoanalytic and behavioral approaches, and has encouraged and enriched the work that formed the basis of this book.

Many people, both directly and indirectly, helped us with the writing of this book. Rachel Marks, Samuel Deutsch Professor Emeritus of the School of Social Service Administration, gave us a great deal of initial encouragement and aid. She also introduced us to John Moore, our editor from Columbia University Press, who has been extremely generous with his time and constructive criticism. Dean Harold Richman, of the School of Social Service Administration at the University of Chicago, aided the writing of this book by his encouragement, praise, and provision of resources for the typing and editing of the book, as well as time for me to work on the book. Juanita Brown-El and Lew Flagg assisted by providing us with the willing hands to help convert a scribbled manuscript into typed drafts. Mrs. Margaret Tafel edited the draft at several stages and helped compile the index; her expertise and constructive criticism were invaluable. Mrs. Dorothy Swart of Columbia University Press also edited the book with great care. My wife, Ruth, whose interest in the approach led her to return to school, helped revise the manuscript from her perspective as a student in this behavioral sequence. Dr. Daniel X. Freedman, and other members of the Department of Psychiatry (mentioned by Israel Goldiamond below), were very encouraging and helpful.

There were many others who helped over the long writing of this book; it is impossible to list them all. To all these people who helped, named and unnamed, our heartfelt gratitude.

Just a final note: this book is a joint effort of the two authors, Arthur Schwartz, a social worker, and Israel Goldiamond, a psychologist and a pioneer in the application of operant psychology to therapy. While both authors collaborated on the book, Chapter 3, by Goldiamond, represents the essence of his "self control" or "constructional" approach which we have here applied to social casework. Chapter 7, the concluding chapter, is primarily the work of Arthur Schwartz. Michael Howe, as a graduate student, helped with the original planning of the book and the gathering of background material until the pressure of his studies prevented him from participating in the actual writing of the book.

While we express gratitude to all these people, responsibility for the contents lies, of course, exclusively with the two authors.

Arthur Schwartz

For the past twenty years I have been concerned with extending the laboratory precision of experimental psychology, in which I was trained, to research on human problems of social relevance. In this regard, the operant research tradition, in which the investigator acts as a change agent in the context of scientific discovery, is exemplary. When we add to this the fact that the operant approach employs the classical experimental design of long-term treatment of single subjects, and that, in contrast to many other behaviorist traditions, it does not summarily reject concepts such as thinking and feeling (rather, questions their explanatory use), it becomes a model of choice.

In 1968, Dr. Jarl E. Dyrud, a close colleague for the past five years, and I came to the University of Chicago upon the initiative of Dr. Daniel X. Freedman, chairman of the Department of Psychiatry. With his support I proceeded to establish and direct an animal and human laboratory-clinic. Using the operant rationale, I developed and supervised a clinical delivery system in the context of a larger research program. Dr. Dyrud became clinical director of the Department of Psychiatry and, later, its associate chairman. He and Dr. E. R. Uhlenhuth, director of the Out-Patient Department, were supportive in numerous ways. The clinic is one of the constituent units of O.P.D. Research support has been provided by the State of Illinois Department of Mental Health and the Division of Biological Sciences of the University of Chicago. These colleagues and institutions made the program possible.

I am also grateful to the many students and residents who worked with me in testing the applicability of the procedures described in Chapter 3 of this book, and illustrated in Chapters 4 and 5. The participating students have been undergraduates in the College; graduate students in education, human development, psychology (both clinical and experimental), and social service administration; and students in the Medical School, as well as residents in psychiatry.

Major credit must also be given to the patients, who bore with us in filling out the numerous logs required and who, by their records and progress toward mutually agreed-upon goals, showed what parts of the delivery system were functioning properly and which required revision. Their records serve the same purpose that a cumulative record does in the laboratory. The procedures and delivery system are still in process of change in what is an ongoing exploration, even as are the various courses I have been teaching the past twenty years on behavior analysis and its extensions. The delivery system and methods are being extended to new areas and populations which are beyond the scope of this book.

In late 1970 I was seriously injured in an automobile accident and was hospitalized for eight months. During that period, several students and faculty members pitched in to keep the laboratory and related courses going. I am profoundly grateful to them, and especially to Mrs. Lucie Hughes, my secretary, who always advised people to "hang loose" while she saw to it that all the wheels kept turning.

Among the supportive faculty colleagues during this period was Dr. Arthur Schwartz, who participated in the program during the years 1969–72. When I returned from the hospital, he persuaded me that it was extremely important that the rationale and delivery system be communicated to social caseworkers to introduce them to the approach, and be stated in a manner consonant with their interests and concerns about behavior analysis. This rationale was also to be extended to providing overviews of other approaches and introduction to basic terminologies as they are currently used, so that social caseworkers might then pursue further study on their own. This book is the outcome of that collaboration. Since that time, Dr. Schwartz has initiated a behavioral track in the School of Social Service Administration.

There are at present numerous approaches vying for consideration, many of which are effective. It has always been my belief that what the field needs most critically is data on the explicit procedures used and their demonstrated relation to outcomes and theory. The effort described has been so directed. Numerous patients with varying diagnoses have been treated. They have required different programs and analyses. These specific results and their general implications for practice, research, and understanding of individual and social behavior were considered beyond the scope of this book. They are to appear in other works which are in progress (they were unfortunately interrupted by the accident and its aftermath) or are in press.

Israel Goldiamond

SOCIAL CASEWORK
A Behavioral Approach

one

INTRODUCTION AND OVERVIEW

Why another book on social casework, when the past few years have been characterized by a virtual outpouring of new books on social casework? Because in this book we present an empirically and procedurally oriented model for casework, a model based on what is popularly called "behavioristic psychology." This book presents an overview of the procedures and the findings of the newly burgeoning behavioristic approaches, including behavior modification, and also presents a model for casework which, we believe, combines the concerns of the humanistically oriented practitioner with the precision of the operant investigator.

The model calls for the precise specification and definition of problems, change goals, and intervention procedures. This specification not only heightens understanding between worker and client, it also facilitates research, evaluation, and accountability essential for the development of an empirically oriented discipline of casework.

Most books on casework have concentrated primarily upon the intrapsychic and have neglected or underemphasized the social environment. In this volume we shall amplify and facilitate the analysis of the environments that influence the behaviors of man.

Many social workers have reacted negatively to the terms "behaviorism" and "behavior modification," but there are many kinds of behaviorism, just as there are many kinds of "dynamic" orientations.

Behaviorism in this book is based on the systematic study and analysis of man as the proper study of casework. Man is observed in interaction with—both influencing and being influenced by—his total environment: the physical environments of his surrounding world; the physical environments of his own biological being and inheritance; the social environments, comprising his family, his groups, and his society; in short, man in the full context of his relationships to himself and his environment. As such, this approach encompasses a principle long held sacred in social work—viewing the total man, viewing the "individual-in-the-situation." Thus it parallels the familiar study-diagnosis-treatment model, and, as in the more traditional approach, the phases are not mutually exclusive; they occur sequentially but tend to overlap considerably.

The analysis of clinical observations, the terminology employed, the problem focus and the problem definition, and the method(s) of intervention vary considerably among the traditional and the differing operant approaches. We shall emphasize the analysis and modification of observable behavior, and of the observable environmental framework of the individual—his total life picture. The emphasis is on observables. Thoughts and emotions are considered, but through an examination of the behaviors, and their environmental contexts, in which the thoughts and emotions occur. Similarly, history is also considered but defined in terms of past behavior-environmental relations. Both behavior and environmental contingencies can be observed, measured, and changed. Central to behavior analysis, and to the focus of this book, is the examination and change of the relationship of the behavior of the individual to relevant environmental factors—the contingencies.

Client problems are viewed as problems in social functioning; that is, problems of clients involved in relationships that maintain behaviors that have undesirable effects, or are preventing the individual from obtaining desirable effects, desirable to him or others as they affect him. We are not advocating blind adherence to the status quo, nor is it always advisable to help people "adapt" to the social system. Moreover, if a social system is lacking or deficient in any way, and nearly all social systems evidence some deficits, then the operant approach lends itself well to work toward changing that system, as well as toward helping the client with his individual problem.

We believe that the issue currently dividing the field of social work—whether the main thrust of its efforts should be helping the individual or changing the system itself—posits an artificial dichotomy. True, much goes on that can be described as system failure. However, this translates into the human suffering of individuals. Systems do not become depressed, suicidal, hungry. Systems are concepts, but human beings, whose sufferings are very real and very painful, are the recipients of a system's functioning.

The intervention model in this book addresses problems of both the individual and the system or, more precisely, problems of the interaction of the two. We shall elaborate on the individual-system dichotomy in the final chapter.

Similar to other approaches, the behavioral caseworker ascertains with the client the goals they can work toward and where the client is at the beginning of the intervention. Together they spell out his problems and the environmental variables affecting his problems. They establish a baseline. However, in contrast to many other current approaches, the spelling-out is explicit rather than implied.

They then formalize the working relationship in a written contract which specifies the goals of the interventions and the methods that the worker and client will use together to achieve these goals. This contract, which is based on mutual agreement, can be revised by mutual agreement but never unilaterally by the worker.

By working with the client to develop approaches and procedures that he can use to understand and change his own behavior within the context of his environments, we hope that he is equipped with an approach that he can carry out of the casework situation and use in his life. Although worker and client develop the techniques together, *he* uses them to "control" his own life, to enhance his self-direction and his future. The interventions are carried out within the context of a warm, helping, interpersonal relationship. This is a far cry from the popular stereotypes of a mechanistic behaviorism and but one of the many misconceptions that we hope to dispel in this book.

A GENERAL OUTLINE OF THIS BOOK

First, we shall briefly outline the major behavioristic treatment approaches. They can be roughly categorized into three general orientations: the classical or Pavlovian; the mediating or modeling; and the operant or Skinnerian approach that underlies the model in this book. We shall explain the general principles of operant conditioning and then explain in detail the model in this book—a model developed by Goldiamond (1974) and based on the operant principles of "self control." We shall present two case histories, one in great detail and the other in a more summarized form.

We shall then briefly present an overview of therapeutic approaches based on the Pavlovian and the mediating (modeling) paradigms, because these techniques have applicability in their own right for some kinds of therapeutic problems and because the reader will undoubtedly encounter them in his reading. We shall, in the final chapter, spell out in detail some of the commonalities and some of the differences, endeavor to clear up some misconceptions and answer some questions, and then predict future developments in social casework.

The authors believe that operantly oriented social work has not only much proven value, but also much promise for the development of future intervention models. While the contributions of applied behavior analysis include many that are new and innovative, they also include many points of agreement as well as disagreement with more traditional models. Social workers can choose these points of disagreement as occasion for future battles, or can seize them as the entering points for a dialogue that could lead to development of future practice models that could combine the best elements of the current and yet-to-be-developed approaches. The authors see this book as a step toward development of more effective models of intervention.

WAYS OF LOOKING AT BEHAVIOR

Behavior, and the principles assumed to underly behavior, can be considered as complicated phenomena. For years, social scientists have been debating the *determinants,* or the *whys,* of people's behaviors. Such debates have included the heredity-versus-environment discussions, the historical-versus-situational arguments, and so forth. In such instances, differing determinants are considered the causes, or why an individual does as he does. Unfortunately, the attempted resolution is more often through debate rather than scientific exploration, or to attention to the various meanings which can be assigned to the word "cause." No effort will be made to resolve these intellectual conflicts, or to propose still another elaborate theory.

Even though individuals are not equal in their genetic endowments, and their reflexes differ, much (if not most) of their behavior affects the environment, which in turn affects the behavior, in a continual interaction of mutual influence. Environments, from the family to the larger society and social system, place demands upon people and shape their actions. These social influences specify the norms that define some behavior as prosocial, and other behavior as undesired or antisocial. These norms vary, of course, from society to society. In America, for example, it is the height of bad taste to snap one's fingers at a waiter to get his attention, yet this behavior is perfectly acceptable in Spain. The requirements of behavior shift not only from society to society but from situation to situation within each society. Fighting behavior in a child is considered by the school (but not necessarily by classmates) to be out of place in the classroom situation, yet may be highly in place (so far as the school is concerned) for that same child in the streets. Since behaviors interact with the environment, they are continually modified by new demands placed upon people by new or changed environmental circumstances (or conditions, or new environments). Examples of this kind of modification may be seen in the new behaviors demanded upon entering from high school into college, and those demanded upon entering professional training. In fact, part of the responsibility or function of these new environments is to train the individual in those role behaviors that not only help the individual to function effectively in that new environment but are also necessary for that environment—or institution—to survive. This process is called "socialization."

Behavior and its environmental contexts are the focus of applied behavior analysis, the major thrust of this book. Although people often come for help because they feel unhappy, no one ever was sent to a mental hospital merely because he was unhappy. Feelings of unhappiness may also be approached along a number of dimensions of behavior-environment relations. The feeling of unhappiness may be a sign or signal that in certain environments the individual may experience behavioral deficits or behavioral excesses. The individual may already have these behaviors, but they occur at a too low rate, that is, infrequently in contexts where more is required. He may talk in class, but not frequently enough; hence the therapeutic task is to increase the frequency of this behavior. He may have, as the fighting boy, some behaviors that occur too frequently in the classroom but that should not be eliminated. He should continue to fight, perhaps, but he needs to learn to discriminate those situations in which fighting is helpful to him from those in which fighting is not.

Emotions are also extremely important, but their relation to behavior can be viewed within a behavior-environment framework, as was unhappiness. By now, there is a good deal of evidence that if an individual is helped to change his relation to his controlling environmental contingencies (through his behavior), or through its consequences, then changes in feelings can follow, as well as changes in attitudes (Festinger, 1964). The research on desegregation, for example, supports this view. One can talk to whites, adults or children, about loving their black neighbors, and their attitudes will not change, but research and demonstration projects in which black children became integrated into classrooms have shown that, as a result, there were attitudinal and cognitive changes.

An unemployed individual may have a very poor self-image.

If he is helped to get a job he considers worth while (which may include teaching him new skills), then, as a result of his working, being self-supporting, and so on, his self-image will improve.

Applied behavior analysis, which is backed by a growing body of evidence, concentrates on behavior-environment relationships first, and then attitudes (feelings) will change, rather than the other way around. Behaviors, and the environmental contingencies controlling those behaviors, are the targets of intervention activities.

ORIENTATIONS TO BEHAVIORISM

It is important for the reader to know that there is no single approach, no single uniform body of knowledge and techniques, that is known as "behavior modification." That branch of the helping processes called "behaviorist" is characterized by many schisms. Krasner (1971) lists at least fifteen "streams" or "schools" of behaviorist therapy.[1] Part of the confusion and

[1] We have used a three-way classification to categorize behavioristic orientations. Although Krasner (1971) cited fifteen, we believe that some of these differences are more relevant to the historian of psychology than to the practitioner. In a recent article on the behavioral modification approach in social work, Thomas (1970) cites the following "schools": (1) the operant; (2) the respondent; (3) the personalistic, whom he describes as "behaviorally oriented personality theorists whose practice is informed by personality assessments and theory"; (4) the cognitive-symbolic, who not only use the A-B-C concepts but "emphasize the role of such factors as cognitive and symbolic mediation and vicarious conditioning"; (5) the specialized practitioners who utilize primarily one behavioral technique, such as systematic desensitization. Thomas calls a sixth group the "eclectic." These are not only the most numerous, but they have three subclassifications: (a) the behavioral eclectic, who uses many different techniques and is analogous to the general practitioner in medicine; (b) the broad-spectrum eclectic, who uses behavioral techniques and more "conventional therapeutic techniques"; and (c) the "sociobehavioral eclectic" (Thomas's orientation), who uses empirically based techniques from a variety of behavioral, psychological, and sociopsychological theories. "This approach has the most promise for social work, for it embraces contribution to direct ser-

the extreme emotionalism that characterize much of the negative reaction to behaviorism arises because most social workers either are not aware of, or do not sufficiently appreciate, the various "splits" that characterize contemporary behaviorism, or assign to all approaches the properties of one or more.

One of their problems may be found in the adjective "behavioral," which has become a very popular term these days. The caseworker may pick up a book called *A Behavioral Approach to Parental Quandaries,* or some such title, and discover that the author has merely substituted the "new" terms "problem behaviors" or "target behaviors" or "maladaptive behaviors" for the more familiar "symptom" or "presenting problem" or "complaint." He will find that the author is not really saying much that is new.

The behaviorist orientation is not uniform or monolithic. Behavior modifiers or behavior therapists use different procedures and rationales. One behavior therapist will try to help a patient to do something that the patient seems incapable of doing, by first asking him to relax, and then asking him to *imagine* a scene somewhat removed from his fantasied anxiety. Then the therapist will gradually "zero in" on a scene (a target scene) which evokes the patient's anxiety. The therapist is operating on a rationale that states that the removal of the anxiety *underlying* the fear will eliminate the fear.

A second behavior modifier or behavior therapist may have the patient *observe* someone who is evidencing the target behavior, because he believes that the most expeditious way of learning adaptive behavior is by observing and imitating others.

A third behavior modifier or behavior therapist may ask the patient to *perform* a behavior somewhat removed from the ultimate behavior the client wishes to evidence. The therapist may himself (or have others) immediately reward this behavior, and then consistently reward behavior that more and more resembles the desired behavior. Thus, there is a progression of

vice (meeting selected criteria) from all relevant behavioral science disciplines and from practice in social work as well as in other helping professions" (Thomas, 1971, pp. 1227–28).

behaviors which gradually zero in on the rewards available for the target behavior (the desired behavior). This therapist is operating on the rationale that the problem behavior that occurs is related not so much to the underlying anxiety as it is to the consequences of that undesired behavior in the present life situation of the client.

The first behaviorist utilized techniques based on the classical or Pavlovian or respondent conditioning approach. The orientation of the second was the so-called "process" or "mediating" view popularly associated with Albert Bandura. The third utilized the operant conditioning orientation based on the work of B. F. Skinner and his disciples. As presented, of course, these are ideal types and are oversimplifications of the many procedures used by these three schools. There are commonalities among these three approaches, as well as important differences. This book is based primarily upon the operant, or instrumental, or Skinnerian type of conditioning.[2] We shall examine each of these major orientations briefly.

THE RESPONDENT (CLASSICAL OR PAVLOVIAN) CONDITIONING ORIENTATION

This is the orientation that underlies the earliest behaviorist approaches and is probably the best known. It is generally the conditioning model thought of by the average person when the term "behaviorist" is used.

In the respondent model, the events preceding a particular pattern of behavior are viewed as governing that behavior. Accordingly, behavior is in response to stimuli which elicit behavior. An antecedent stimulus elicits a response, and the response is under the control of that antecedent stimulus. This formulation gives us the familiar $S \rightarrow R$ (stimulus-produces-a-response) designation, often called the "SR formulation."

[2] For more detailed and extended accounts of the various behavioral approaches, there are several excellent volumes available. We particularly recommend Kanfer and Phillips (1970), Bandura (1969), and the now classic and still relevant programmed text by Holland and Skinner (1961).

When *S* (stimulus) occurs or is presented under appropriate conditions, *R* (behavior, or response) will occur or will be produced.

Many of us are familiar with the work of the Russian physiologist Pavlov, who observed that if one rang a bell, or sounded a tone, or shined a light (and so forth), either just before or simultaneously with the presentation of food to a dog, the dog would later salivate when he heard the bell or the tone or saw the light by itself. In the terminology of the laboratory, the food which produces the salivation is called an "unconditioned [3] stimulus." The salivation at the presentation of the food itself is called an unconditioned response. The entire food-salivation relationship is called an unconditioned reflex. The bell (or light or tone) that acquires the property of producing the salivation, by pairing with the unconditioned stimulus, is called the conditioned stimulus. The salivation at the occurrence of the bell (or tone or light) by itself is called a conditioned response. The entire bell→salivation relationship is called a conditioned reflex, or a stimulus-response relation.

In the above process, an existent reflex is used to establish a new reflex. Once it is established, the bell→salivation reflex may then be used to establish new, or higher order, conditioning. However, for the conditioned reflex to be continued (for the dog to continue to salivate at the tone alone), the unconditioned stimulus (food) must occasionally be presented. Otherwise, the dog will not continue to salivate when he hears the tone, and the conditioned response (or the stimulus-response sequence) will no longer be present. This process is called "extinction."

In the Pavlovian conditioning scheme the response is dependent upon the presence of a prior stimulus (conditioned or unconditioned); the response follows a stimulus, and the strength, the speed, the very presence of the response, depend upon the presence, strength, and other aspects of the stimulus. In other words, the stimulus *must* be present for the response to occur. Hence, the Pavlovian paradigm is often called a "re-

[3] The reader may occasionally see the term "unconditional" as an alternative translation for "unconditioned," and "conditional" for "conditioned."

spondent" or type *S* (as in stimulus) or an "involuntary" or "classical" conditioning. Pavlov ascribed the relation to neurological processes, and he elaborated theories to account for the experimental evidence of respondent conditioning. This stimulus-response orientation (which has been developed considerably since Pavlov's time) is the majority view in Europe, and it is reflected in the early writings of the English behaviorist social workers (Jehu, 1967; Jehu *et al.,* 1972). It also undergirds the writings of the most prolific American Pavlovian therapist, Joseph Wolpe, and his "reciprocal inhibition" therapies, particularly systematic desensitization and assertive counterconditioning (Wolpe, 1958, 1969).

Among other respondent therapies are the implosive therapy of Stampfl; the various aversive treatments, such as conditioned reflex treatment for alcoholism and homosexuality; and the early conditioned reflex approaches of Andrew Salter. The Pavlovian stimulus-response model is also the basis of much of the "sex therapies" of Masters and Johnson. Applications and examples of these and other therapeutic approaches based primarily upon a Pavlovian or respondent conditioning paradigm will be discussed briefly in Chapter 6.

THE OPERANT (CONSEQUENTIAL) ORIENTATION

In the operant approach of B. F. Skinner and his followers, the probability of occurrence of some behavior pattern is viewed as being governed primarily by its *consequences.* We may salivate (a response) at the sight of a box (conditioned stimulus) of peanuts (unconditioned stimulus); this is a conditioned reflex, according to the Pavlovian scheme. However, our behavior of reaching (a response) into the box (a stimulus) is governed by the consequences of getting a peanut (a reinforcing stimulus, according to the operant orientation). We continue to reach only so long as the reaching has the consequences of providing us with peanuts (has a reinforcing consequence), *or* until we do not want any more peanuts (we are satiated). The likelihood of reaching for the peanuts is governed by the consequences (getting the peanuts), *not* by the sight of the box. The reinforcing stimulus (the peanuts) keeps the behavior (reaching) going.

If reaching would no longer produce food, then the antecedent stimulus, the box, would have no control over behavior. The box *by itself* will not keep the behavior going. The relationship of the box to behavior is not such that the box *alone* elicits reaching, as a tone would a knee jerk in the classical stimulus-response relation. The box is a *discriminative stimulus.* It sets the occasion for the reaching response only when the reinforcing stimulus, food, is contingent on reaching. The response, or behavior, is called "operant" behavior because the behavior *operates* (has an effect) on the environment; the behavior has consequences (here, obtaining food). The behavior is governed by the effects it produces. This kind of behavior is also called "instrumental" behavior (it serves as an "instrument" which gets something), or type *R* (as in response dependent, rather than stimulus dependent, such as the classical model). Some writers also call it "voluntary," but this is not valid, for people are often unaware of the consequences involved, or even (sometimes) of what they are doing.

The Differences between Pavlovian and Operant Conditioning. Much of the current misunderstanding of, and antagonism toward, contemporary behaviorism may be based on lack of understanding of the very important theoretical and procedural differences between the Pavlovian and Skinnerian models of behavior and on lack of understanding of the models themselves. It is essential that the reader understand these differences; for, while the models overlap in some ways, the differences have led to development of markedly different therapeutic techniques.

The main differences lie in the ways in which behavior is defined, the behavior/environment relationship, the ways in which change occurs, and the use of the term "conditioning" itself, which has resulted in a good deal of confusion.

In the Pavlovian model, behaviors are thought of as being controlled by their antecedents. A stimulus *elicits* a response.

For example, a puff of air against the eye will produce an eye-blink. This is a simple stimulus-response function. New relations are acquired ("conditioned") through repeated pairings with established relations.

In the Skinnerian view, certain behaviors are considered as being primarily dependent upon the *consequences* of those behaviors to the actor. Some consequences will result in an increase or repetition of the behavior; some will not. The future rate, or frequency, or form of that behavior will be governed by the consequences attached to the behavior under those conditions. Unlike the Pavlovian conditioning, in which behavior is defined as a relationship between a prior stimulus and an ensuing response, in operant conditioning behavior depends upon the relationship between the behavior and the consequences. Thus changes in behavior can be produced by changing environmental contingencies.

THE VICARIOUS, OR SOCIAL LEARNING, ORIENTATION

Bandura, one of the major social learning theorists, states that behavior can be acquired without the response component of either the Pavlovian or the Skinnerian approach (Bandura and Walters, 1963; Bandura, 1969). For example, a child can learn to do something by merely watching someone else do it. He may also learn consequential relations simply by observation alone. For example, a child who sees another child being punished for stepping out of line in school may stay in line thereafter. He is affected vicariously; he has learned by observing others. In the field of behavior modification this approach has been given major impetus by Bandura, who has developed procedures for changing patterns of behavior through *modeling.* As the name suggests, "people are deliberately instructed to observe and to reproduce either the behavior exemplified by others or an imaginatively reconstructed role" (Bandura, 1969). Techniques of modeling and imitation may be used in programs to produce enduring behavioral and emotional changes.

The model is also called "mediational," since what is considered learned is not any set of specific $S{\rightarrow}R$ (or $R{\rightarrow}S$) relationships, but "imaginal and verbal representations of modeling stimuli" (Bandura, 1969). These representations can then be utilized in a variety of different stimulus situations, and can mediate between these stimuli in a specific situation and the responses that then occur. Bandura, who distinguishes between learning and performance in the role assigned to consequential reinforcement, states that, since learning can occur vicariously, the behavior-consequence relationship may not be necessary for *learning.* However, reinforcement may be important in producing or maintaining the *performance* of the behavior. A subject may learn a response, but if there is "nothing in it" (there is no reinforcement), he simply may not make that response (Baer and Sherman, 1964).

Modeling procedures have great potential for use by social caseworkers. Showing a person how to do something, or exposing him to successful models that he may imitate, may eliminate the necessity for extended discussion. Role-playing, as a technique, may be viewed within this vicarious learning orientation. The procedures developed by Bandura and others in this tradition have made the application of these techniques, such as role-playing, more precise and have facilitated the evaluation of their effects. Further elaboration of social learning, and examples of work done within this orientation, may be found in Chapter 6.

SIMILARITIES AMONG THESE THREE APPROACHES

There are some important commonalities among these three approaches. The first is that all three have their roots in experimental laboratory research, which includes investigations using animals. When an animal performs in a laboratory, concepts such as "insight" cannot be used to attribute causality to the animal's behavior. The equivalent of "insight" is the describable relationship between the procedures used by the experimenter, the specifically defined conditions, and the results he obtained. Similarly, behavioral models have incorporated empirically based procedures. The client's behavior is best understood in relation to the events controlling the situation. If the conditions under which a client experiences concern can be appropriately altered, so too can the distressing experience. This is the applied analysis of behavior and the basis for the procedures in this book.[4] Application of the behavioral approaches requires the definition of the current clinical problem, the desired outcome of the treatment program, and the treatment procedures themselves, in specific, observable, measurable, and reproducible terms.

This does not mean that operant procedures are cut-and-dried or mechanistic. On the contrary, as will be seen, considerable ingenuity is often required in developing interventions. Furthermore, the approaches require very careful attention to the behaviors of the individual client. The therapist is actively involved. Moreover, operant casework takes place within the context of an interpersonal relationship. The competent and caring programmer, like the competent and caring therapist, is sensitive to his client first and to his theory second. Furthermore, the field utilizes explicit contracts between two mutually consenting participants and deals with a number of problems from the simple to the complex. Before examining the model of this book, however, we must examine in greater detail the principles of operant behavior that underlie that model.

---

[4] This framework can also include modeling and imitation techniques, as will be discussed in Chapter 6. While we have stressed differences among the three major orientations, in practice the differences tend to blur, so that behaviorists of one persuasion will use techniques from another. This blurring often also applies to theoretical explanations.

two

THE OPERANT
(CONSEQUENTIAL) MODEL

Operant behavior is governed by its consequences (C). The antecedent events (A), which seem to control behavior (B), exert their influence not automatically but because they set the occasion whereby some behavior will be reinforced and some behavior will not be reinforced. The antecedent factors (A) and the behavior (B) are both functionally defined, related to, and dependent upon, the consequences (C).

In operant formulations, discussion of behavior is focused on the *relationship* of the consequence to the behavior, rather than on what follows the behavior. This relationship of behavior to its consequences and the relation of the behavior to the antecedent conditions under which this behavior occurs is called a "contingency relation" and is the basic building block of operant analysis. The critical element in a contingency relation is that certain consequences are contingent on certain behaviors under certain circumstances. The focus is on these contingency relationships.

Procedural definition of the specified relations of behavior to its ecology (which is the relation of behavior to the events that both follow and precede it and to its setting) is the basis of a technology of behavior with an explicit language and a method of helping based on this technology. This technology can be transmitted with a minimum of ambiguity and misunderstanding from one person to another. In light of this new procedural definition, the following discussion examines the events that follow behavior that influence behavior.

THE ECOLOGY OF CONSEQUENCES

REINFORCEMENT PROCEDURES

A consequence may be either something that is presented or something that is taken away or postponed. A behavior may be followed either by the (contingent) presentation of an event or by the (contingent) withdrawal of an event. Either relationship may subsequently *increase* the rate of that behavior. The differences, the presentation or the withdrawal (or postponement) of the event, are a procedural distinction that differentiates the two kinds of reinforcement. Regardless of the nature of the behavior, the first is called "positive" reinforcement; the second is called "negative" reinforcement. In both cases, behavior is increased or, if it is already at a high level, it is maintained. The terms "positive" and "negative" do not mean "good" or "bad" or "desirable" or "undesirable," but refer simply to behavior maintenance by presentation or withdrawal of an event.

Positive Reinforcement. When a response is followed by the presentation of an event and the rate of behavior rises, the procedure is called "positive reinforcement." For example, a child may say "Da-da," and his mother may pat him on the head. If the child continues to repeat "Da-da," then patting him on the head is a positive reinforcer. Or, if the child throws a temper tantrum and his mother stops ignoring him and becomes attentive, her attention would be classified as a positive reinforcer if the child began to have temper tantrums when he wanted her attention. In each case, the mother's action following the behavior positively reinforced it, for it increased the rate of that behavior. We might note that one of the child's behaviors was "good" (desirable) and one of the behaviors was "bad" (undesirable). The word "positive," once again, refers not to any feeling state, to any moral position, or to any progressive movement, but only to the effects of the presentation of a contingent event.

Negative Reinforcement. There is another kind of reinforcement. One may observe that when a behavior occurs an event may be withdrawn or terminated or postponed, and the rate of the observed behavior then increases. For example, a mother wants her teen-age daughter to clean her room; the daughter, like many teen-age girls, does not clean the room. The mother may begin to nag and harangue the daughter. The daughter, to stop the mother's nagging (an aversive stimulus), will clean her room. The room-cleaning behavior is maintained by the removal of the nagging, which will return if she discontinues her room-cleaning behavior. This procedure is "negative reinforcement." It is the procedure by which we stop at red lights. As long as we continue to stop, we will not receive a traffic ticket, nor will we be hit by cross traffic; thus such law-abiding behavior is maintained by the nonoccurrence of something aversive or, stated otherwise, by the presentation of something aversive when we do not so behave.

There are two classes of negative reinforcement: escape and avoidance. When a response terminates an ongoing event, it is *escape behavior* (Skinner, 1953). When a response postpones the onset of an event, it is *avoidance behavior* (Skinner, 1953). An example of escape behavior would be the child who cleans his room to forestall an event—the aversive words of his parent. An example of avoidance behavior would be the child who responds to the parent's statement in order to eliminate an *oncoming* event: "If you don't clean up your room by the time your father comes home, you're in for trouble." The child cleans his room to avoid aversive consequences when his father gets home.

Whether maintained by the presentation or by the withdrawal of an event, these procedures are classified as reinforcement because the subsequent rate of the response (behavior) increases under these conditions. Here, too, the terms "positive" and "negative" relate only to the effects of the occurrence or elimination of a consequent event. Both—positive reinforcement (the presentation of an event) and negative reinforcement (the elimination of an event)—are reinforcement procedures. Both are defined by the *increase* in the rate of behavior when a consequence (presentation or withdrawal) is contingent.

PUNISHMENT

In operant terminology, punishment is a procedure which decreases the frequency of the behavior. There are two types of punishment. In one type, an aversive stimulus follows the behavior. If a child says a rude word and his mother strikes him, and the rate of saying rude words in her presence decreases, the mother has punished the child.

In the other type, punishment can be the *removal* of a stimulus in the environment. For example, if the child says rude words, the mother may take away his ice cream or some other goody. If taking away the ice cream (a nonaversive stimulus) causes the rate of rude-word-saying behavior to go down, the procedure is called "punishment." In either event, the consequences of the procedures are the same. Both of these procedures are called punishment, as they produce a decrease in the rate of a continuing undesirable behavior. If, in either of those instances, behavior had increased rather than decreased, the procedure would *not* be defined as punishment, even though in the first instance the mother struck the child, and in the second, she took away his ice cream. Punishment is defined by its effect on behavior and *not* by the intent of the person administering the procedure (here, the mother).

Negative reinforcement is often confused with punishment because these words, as they are commonly used, have a meaning that is not the same as that of precise operant usage. In operant terminology, "reinforcement" means the maintenance or raising of a rate of behavior, while "punishment" refers to the decrease of the rate of behavior. "Positive" and "negative" again refer to the presentation or withdrawal of a stimulus. Thus negative reinforcement is a procedure that *reinforces* by removing an aversive stimulus, while both forms of punishment lower rates of behavior. These might, by analogy to reinforcement, be called positive punishment (by presenting an aversive stimulus) and negative punishment (by removing a desired stimulus). The most common usage is to refer to both these procedures simply as *punishment* (Azrin and Holz, 1966).

Both reinforcement and punishment, in varying forms, are widely used in everyday life. They obviously are effective under many conditions, or their use would not be so widespread. Neither procedure was invented by behaviorists, for not everyone who rewards or who punishes to get the effects he desires is practicing behaviorism or behavior modification—certainly not in a planful way. Investigators in behavioral laboratories have been trying to ascertain the conditions under which both reinforcement and punishment procedures work, and there have been efforts to apply this knowledge to alleviate human distress. In the "self control" model in this book we oppose the use of punishment (or negative reinforcement, both aversive procedures). In addition to the moral arguments, to be discussed further in this Chapter and in Chapter 7, both present problems for casework. The caseworker who uses negative reinforcement or punishment to persuade the client to follow her advice (withdraws her nagging when the client follows advice or chastises the client when he does not) would probably not keep her clients in therapy long enough to help them (in the voluntary setting, of course). The abuses of clients in nonvoluntary settings such as prisons, relief-distributing agencies, and others are well-known (Goldiamond, 1974). One obvious ethical injunction is that clients who come for treatment are already suffering, and we certainly do not want to increase the suffering, even if it is for their "eventual own good" as *we* might define it. In any event, we do not recommend punitive procedures as a method of eliminating nondesirable behaviors or negative reinforcement as a method of maintaining desirable behaviors.

EXTINCTION

Another possible relationship of behavior to consequences is *extinction.* Extinction occurs when behavior no longer has an effect on its environment; in other words, when behavior which had been either reinforced or punished now has no consequence contingent on it. The consequent event is no longer available. If a pattern of behavior has previously been reinforced, the rate of current responding may ultimately drop. If the behavior had previously been punished, the rate of current responding may ultimately increase. Both procedures are called "extinction."

An important difference between extinction and the previously discussed procedures is that extinction is not defined by a contingency. It is not the withdrawal of reinforcement or punishment contingent on behavior. Extinction is the *absence* of a contingency that was once in effect, regardless of the behavior.

To sum it up, behavior may be followed by the presentation of an event or by the withdrawal of an event. The presentation or withdrawal of an event may affect the rate of behavior in one of four ways: (1) A response may be followed by the presentation of an event and the rate of behavior rises. This procedure is called *positive reinforcement.* (2) A response may be followed by the withdrawal of an event and the rate of behavior rises. This procedure is called *negative reinforcement.* (3) A response may be followed by the presentation of an event and the rate of behavior decreases. This procedure is called *punishment.* (4) A response may be followed by the withdrawal of an event and the rate of behavior decreases. This procedure is also called *punishment. Extinction* refers to behavior that was once either reinforced (positively or negatively) or punished, but no longer has a consequence (is neither reinforced nor punished).

SUPERSTITIOUS BEHAVIOR (ACCIDENTAL CONDITIONING)

Not all behavior is intentionally programmed. There is also the phenomenon called "accidental conditioning," "adventitious conditioning," or "superstitious behavior."

Sometimes we may engage in behavior that we think is consequential, but the relationship is arbitrary. For example, a basketball player may shoot a ball and, just before it goes through the hoop, he may snap his fingers. There is really no relationship between the scoring and the immediately preceding behavior. However, the finger snapping is likely to occur again, for this behavior, which is quite common, is called "superstitious behavior" (Skinner, 1953) that has been adventitiously reinforced and may be maintained on an intermittent schedule. If this spurious relationship is called to the player's attention, he may justify the finger snapping by saying it limbers his fingers, or he may give some other seemingly rational reason for what is really superstitious behavior.

SCHEDULES

Another dimension of the contingency relationship is called the "schedule." A schedule relates the availability of a consequence to a number of responses or to a rate of responding. It may also specify the interval between delivery of consequences or specify the class of responses which will result. It is essential to understand the variation in the rates of behavior that these schedules produce during the acquisition and the extinction of behavior. As different schedules generate different rates of behavior and different patterns during extinction, no functional assessment of human behavior is complete without an assessment of the schedule that is in operation.

When a behavior produces an effect every time, this is called a "continuous schedule of reinforcement" (abbreviated in the literature as CRF). When an effect occurs less than every time, it is an "intermittent schedule of reinforcement." The effect can occur only after a fixed number of responses, or it can be contingent on a response that occurs only after a fixed period of time passes.

The time of delivery of consequence can also vary, as can

the number of responses required. In addition, the consequences can be contingent upon certain rates of behavior (producing a certain amount, either high or low, within a fixed period of time).

Generally speaking, and oversimplifying, behaviors on continuous schedules will extinguish more quickly than those scheduled on an intermittent basis. In particular, behaviors reinforced on variable schedules are particularly resistant to extinction. We stress this now, and will elaborate later, for extinction is one of the most misunderstood procedures in the operant literature. "Just ignore it and it will go away" will work only if you ignore *every* occurrence, and then do so for a very long time. If you first ignore and then pay attention even once, you are producing a variable schedule, and the behavior might continue for a long time and, in some instances, even increase.

A number of different schedules have been studied in both the laboratory and the natural setting. Generally, there are two major types of schedules: simple and complex. A simple schedule is one that is presented singly, by itself, not in combination. A complex schedule is any combination of two or more simple schedules. There are five major types of complex schedules: multiple, mixed, second order, concurrent, and conjunctive.[1]

FREQUENCY SCHEDULES

The first simple schedule is a frequency schedule. In the frequency schedule the individual must perform either a designated number or an average number of responses to be reinforced. If the requirement is only one response, this is the *continuous schedule of reinforcement* (CRF), mentioned earlier. This schedule is usually employed to establish or teach a particular response. The rate of behavior is steady and high, once established. Under extinction, a response maintained on this schedule will initially tend to increase in rate but will then go down very rapidly. For example, if a baby were picked up every time he cried, and then the mother stopped picking him up, the

[1] For a discussion of complex schedules the reader is referred to Ferster and Skinner (1957), among others, if he wishes to pursue this topic further.

baby would first intensify his crying, but would soon stop if he were not picked up. (We are not advocating not picking up babies; this is merely an illustration of a point.)

The second frequency schedule is the *fixed ratio schedule,* in which the individual must perform a certain specified or consistent number of responses to be reinforced. This type of schedule generates fairly high rates of responding. Characteristic of the schedule is a brief pause which occurs after the reinforcement is presented (postreinforcement pause). The pause increases in duration with each increase in the ratio requirement. For example, the pause in writing behavior that follows turning in a long term paper is longer than such a pause after turning in a smaller assignment.

During extinction, responding diminishes over time. The rate of responding tends to remain the same, but the amount of behavior (each time) tends to diminish and the patterns become farther and farther apart. The worker on piece rates is on a fixed ratio schedule; that is, reinforcement comes after a fixed amount of work has been completed. He is paid after he has produced so many units (has picked so many boxes of berries, for example) without regard to how long it takes to complete a unit. Each unit represents a fixed number of responses.

A third frequency schedule is the *variable ratio schedule,* in which a varying frequency of response is required for reinforcement to be presented; the number of responses required varies, but it varies around a predetermined mean. Variable ratio schedules maintain high sustained rates of behavior, and the pattern of responding during extinction generates many responses. The behavior of gamblers feeding slot machines in Las Vegas is a good example of variable ratio schedules.

INTERVAL SCHEDULES

The second major type of simple schedule is the *temporal schedule.* In a temporal schedule, reinforcement is available again only after a period of time has elapsed since the last delivery. The response must then be emitted for reinforcement to be presented. The major kinds of temporal schedules are fixed interval schedules, in which the interval is fixed, and variable interval schedules, in which the interval varies about some mean.

In a *fixed interval schedule,* a specified or fixed period of time must elapse between the presentation of one reinforcement and the availability of another. This schedule produces low over-all rates of responding. Each interval begins with no responding, which gradually increases until reinforcement is presented. This characteristic of the fixed interval schedule is known as a "scallop." The longer the interval between the reinforcements, the longer the scallop. During extinction the rate of responding is initially high, and it decreases slowly. An occasional scallop usually follows, but farther and farther apart. An example of fixed interval schedules may be found in the studying behavior of students, which rises dramatically just before the end of the term, before final examinations. The bill-passing behavior of Congress is also on a fixed interval schedule, low in the winter and rising dramatically just before summer vacations, when congressmen go home to see their constituents, and just before elections (Weisberg and Waldrop, 1972).

A second kind of temporal schedule is the *variable interval schedule.* In this schedule there is an inconsistent interval of time that must elapse between reinforcements. A fairly low but steady rate of behavior is maintained. During extinction the low rate gradually tapers off. As in the variable ratio, extinction will take a long time. Variable interval schedules are not seen as frequently in humans as in animals. An example is the soldier who receives letters from his girl friend irregularly. He will continue to report for mail call for many days without receiving a letter.

RATE SCHEDULES

A third major type of simple schedule is the *rate schedule.* In a rate schedule the individual must emit a certain number of responses per unit of time in order for reinforcement to be presented, as in the case of the assembly-line worker. Among the chief types of rate schedule are the *differential reinforcement of low rates,* in which only responses that occur at a specified low rate are reinforced temporally, and the *differential reinforcement of high rates,* in which high rates of responding must be attained to receive reinforcement. The reason that industrial workers often slow their rates of output (a self-imposed DRL) is their fear that management will set increasing norms (a management-imposed DRH). These schedules are complex, and differ procedurally; their only commonality is their influence on rate.

Differential Reinforcement of Other Behavior.   Another   rate schedule is the *differential reinforcement of other behavior.* In this schedule, reinforcement is given for any other behavior than the target behavior. A simple example may be seen when a mother showers attention on her infant when he is doing anything other than sucking his thumb. Reinforcement is presented when the child goes to the chair, crawls toward the playpen, rolls over, cries, does anything but suck his thumb. His mother has not punished or forbidden thumb sucking; she has differentially reinforced him for any behavior other than thumb sucking.

SCHEDULES OF REINFORCEMENT AND EXTINCTION

Different schedules of reinforcement produce different patterns of *extinction.* If one is trying to help a client, it is crucial to determine the schedule of reinforcement on which his behavior has been reinforced. Generally, behavior that has been variably reinforced (whether on an interval or a ratio basis) is more resistant to extinction. That is, if the behavior has *not* been reinforced on some regular basis, an occasional reinforcement is sufficient to keep the behavior going, to maintain the behavior. Behavior that has been reinforced every time it occurs (CRF) generally will extinguish more quickly than behavior that has been intermittently reinforced, and behavior regularly reinforced will extinguish more quickly than behavior which has been irregularly reinforced. In practically all simple schedules, however, there will be an initial increase in the rate of behavior upon the initiation of extinction.

If a child has been given a toy every time he cries for it (a CRF), and the mother tries to extinguish that behavior by withholding the toy when he cries for it, the child may first increase the rate of his crying. The increase may continue, but, if there is no reinforcement forthcoming, the crying may eventually die out. Usually in cases like this an irate parent will report that "not giving him the toy just makes it worse," and, of course, she is right, but only for a limited time. Extinction by itself can be a hazardous procedure. If the mother "gives in" and reinforces after, say, the tenth time the child cries, then she has shifted reinforcement to an intermittent basis and the behavior can become even more difficult to eliminate through extinction. In desperation, she may then strike the child. Hitting the child because he cries may quiet him for a short while (and this can be reinforcing to the mother), but he will usually start crying again soon, and in all likelihood louder than before (Keller and Schoenfeld, 1950).

Extinction by itself is a cumbersome and inefficient procedure. The preferable procedure is to help build into the child's repertoire other behaviors which produce his desired outcome. For example, the mother could be taught to provide the toy when he asks for it verbally, and to set the conditions which increase the likelihood that he do so. She might, for instance, read stories to him in which a person asks for things, and then get a "let's pretend" game going in which her child pretends to be that person. She would then provide the toy instantly, and with enthusiasm.

ANTECEDENT EVENTS

Behavior in relation to its consequences is only part of the ecology that influences human behavior. We also respond to events that precede behavior. Such events are called *antecedent* events. Responses to antecedent stimuli may differ, not only from individual to individual, but also for the same individual in different settings or at different times. This is not accidental. People respond differentially to a variety of antecedent conditions, since for each person there may be different consequences attached to the same sets of behaviors. In order to understand people and their behavior more fully, assessment is required of the functional relation of the antecedent, as well as the consequential, events to behavior and the settings in which these transactions occur.

When there are different consequences attached to behavior in the presence of certain stimuli, these stimuli are defined as *discriminative stimuli*. The important idea here is that not all stimuli are discriminative stimuli, but only those coupled with consequences for the behavior involved. When one responds to stimuli which are linked to consequences, and does not respond to stimuli when there is no linkage to consequences, this differential responding is called "discrimination."

As an example, consider a child whose mother is in the room but is not paying any attention to him; she is reading the paper. The child then throws a temper tantrum, and the mother stops reading the paper and gives him attention. However, when his father is in the room reading the paper, and the child throws a temper tantrum, the father ignores him; nothing happens. Tantrum behavior is being reinforced by the mother's attention but not by the father (during paper-reading time). In technical terms, the mother's opening the paper is an antecedent event or discriminative stimulus that sets the occasion for reinforcement of a particular response (temper tantrums). The father's opening the paper is an antecedent event in whose presence the response (temper tantrum) will not be reinforced. When a child throws a temper tantrum in the presence of the mother, but not in the presence of daddy, then that child is discriminating between antecedent events or discriminative stimuli; the behavior of temper tantrums can be said to be under the *stimulus control* of the mother.

STIMULUS CONTROL

Discriminative events can be viewed and evaluated only in terms of the consequences of the behavior. An inappropriate discrimination is one that is dysfunctional in terms of its consequence. For example, a storekeeper needs a tall clerk to reach high shelves, but hires a short one because he is the son of a friend. He has discriminated on the basis of friendship rather than business need, and he may be creating problems for himself.

There are many problems that arise in a clinical situation that involve such inappropriate discrimination by the client. Therefore, it is important to know how to establish, sharpen, or eliminate discriminative control. Discriminative events must be considered within the entire ecology of behavior, but in particular with the conditions that the discriminative events set for the consequences of behavior.

Instructional and Abstractional Stimulus Control. Behavior may also be under the control of other kinds of discriminative stimuli. For example, if a child is instructed to substitute "er" sounds for "oi" sounds in words such as "word," "bird," "heard," and so forth, and is reinforced for so doing (rather than being called a sissy by his friends), and then applies this rule to other words appropriate to this category, his behavior is said to be under the control of *instructional discriminative stimuli* (Goldiamond, 1966). Instructional control is effective discriminative control if it is paired with reinforcement. The child may speak the old way on the street, where different consequences hold. Instructional control is to be distinguished from simple instructions, which may not be linked to consequences, and may therefore "go in one ear and out the other."

A related kind of control is *abstractional control* (Goldiamond, 1966). In abstractional control, the individual learns by himself (he abstracts the guiding "rule" by himself). In the case of the child mentioned, he may never have been instructed in the pronunciation taught by the school. The teachers may be under instruction not to tell the children how to speak; the child is to learn for himself. But they nod when he uses their form of speech, and so on. Eventually his behavior may come under such control. This illustrates the procedure of abstractional control. Note that the outcome of both instructional and abstractional control may be identical, but the procedures are different. The difference lies in the fact that instructional control uses instructions *before* the child's entry into the behavior-consequence relationship, while in abstractional control the abstraction occurs *as a result of, or during,* the behavior-consequence relationship. Therefore, one might save time by using instructions rather than abstractions, but there are other consequences for doing so. Because an instruction is given does not mean that this particular instruction will be followed or even be understood by different people. Some individuals will respond better than, or differently from, others to instructions, while for some people, depending upon the circumstances, abstraction makes for better and more permanent learning.

In a counseling session, a caseworker may suggest, advise, or instruct a client to behave in a particular manner (an instructional procedure). The caseworker may *prompt* a client to engage in a particular set of behaviors and, after they occur, to "figure things out for himself" (an abstractional procedure). The goals may be the same, but there are some conditions under which instruction may be an effective method, and there are other conditions in which it may not. The question which a caseworker must continually ask in the therapeutic situation is: "What are the conditions for *this* particular client in which instruction will be the effective method of intervention?" or, "What are the conditions with *this* particular client in which he should abstract from the environment?" The answers will be different for each client; for each client will have his own history of reinforcement, his own set of life experiences, his own repertoire of behaviors, and his own set of goals and problems. It is the caseworker's task to ascertain these repertoires and determine the best procedures to attain the stated goals.

POTENTIATING VARIABLES

A consequence may either increase or decrease the frequency of a response, but all events that follow behavior do not necessarily influence that behavior. Some consequences are "meaningful" (potent); others are not. For example, most of us would be quite happy with an annual income of $50,000 and might take an unpleasant job for this kind of salary; a millionaire would not. The contingent event, the consequences of behavior (here, money) must be meaningful to the individual. More technically, a consequence must be made potent as a reinforcer—it must be potentiated (Goldiamond and Dyrud, 1967b; Goldiamond and Thompson, 1966).

It is obviously relatively simple to make food delivery a potent consequence for a pigeon, especially in a laboratory. One simply deprives the pigeon of food for a certain period of time (being careful not to overdo the deprivation and starve the bird). Deprivation of food will make food a reinforcer for that hungry pigeon; the pigeon will work for food. Similarly, deprivation of attention will make a child crave attention, and he may do all kinds of things, even "pesky" things, to get it. There are procedures other than deprivation which can make an event reinforcing. Walking through the woods all day will make food potent, and the advertiser hopes that his commercials will do so, too. The procedures which make an event a potent consequence are not always available, and some (food deprivation), while possibly available, may be ethically and morally undesirable.

SATIATION

Conversely, behavior may decrease as a function of continued presentation of a reinforcing consequence. A decrease in behavior, under these conditions, is called "satiation." Satiation depotentiates the reinforcing consequence—it makes it less effective.

A particular event may be potentiated as a reinforcing consequence by deprivation or depotentiated by the procedure of satiation. Needless to say, what is reinforcing for one pattern of behavior may not be for another. The operant analysis or functional analysis of behavior is a study of an individual in interaction with his environment. Although general laws of behavior may be formulated, to utilize the operant approach in the complex situation, behavior under observation must be individualized. Cleaning up her room may be potentiated for a teenager if her allowance depends on it and she has no other source of income. If she is baby-sitting regularly and has enough money to meet her current needs, she is "satiated," and her allowance is depotentiated as a reinforcing consequence for doing her chores.

Potentiating variables may be related to the concept of motivation. One may say that an individual is motivated (or not motivated) to engage in some behavior or other. However, motivation is often difficult to pin down. It can be a rather imprecise way of explaining that behavior has consequences. However, the consequences can be observed, and changes in rate of behavior can be observed.

One can *speculate* on why a child would write on the walls or hit other children, or one can *observe* the consequences that a child's behavior produces when he does these things. The child may run around the room because there is a payoff of mother's attention. Students go to graduate school because of the payoff of knowledge or a degree, bringing entrance into a profession, a higher salary, and the like. In fact, students can be kept working on a number of lengthy and tedious tasks for a very long time. Such students can be called "highly motivated"; the students, especially near the end of a long period of graduate studies, may not agree. It can also be said that the ultimate reinforcer of a degree is highly potent. The student without a degree may not be able to get a good job. The degree can provide status, money, and so forth. Education per se is seldom potent in its own right.

The approach of dealing with the observable ecology has enormous theoretical and practical advantages over the nonobservable, speculative, and difficult-to-define concepts currently employed in practice, such as "motivation."

Similarly, operant reasoning applies to many concepts of pathology. Some children with learning difficulties may be considered to be poorly motivated. One may question, however, whether or not the potential reinforcer has been sufficiently potentiated. Is lack of ability to read, or lack of a desire to learn to read, necessarily a sign of early trauma or early pathology? Or can one reasonably state that a child in a slum neighborhood, with old textooks, in a school with broken windows, may actually be reacting appropriately when he sees no visible reason to want to learn, especially if he sees that, eventually, for an adult, there is no payoff for this kind of behavior, that is, no payoff for this learning? If education is not made potent as a reinforcer, as leading to a better job and a better life, then the problem is social and certainly not in the realm of individual pathology. Certainly education and learning to read are made highly potent for middle-class children, for whom there are many payoffs, both immediately, in the sense of parental and teachers' approval, and eventually, in the form of better jobs, a better life, and so forth. Education is not a reinforcer unless, like other reinforcers, it is made potent. Nor is the child in surroundings which make education potent, but who does not learn to read, necessarily traumatized or pathological. The concern which his illiteracy produces in such circumstances can make consequences other than education highly potent. He may be very sensitively attuned to the *individual* contingencies governing his *individual* behavior. Operant analysis is of individuals in their own individual ecologies.

THE PREMACK PRINCIPLE

Some behaviors occur more frequently than others. Premack found that high-probability behavior may be used to reinforce and increase the frequency of occurrence of lower probability behaviors. This is known as the *Premack principle* (Premack, 1965).

The Premack principle states, quite simply, that behavior that has a high probability of occurring may be made contingent upon behavior that has a low probability of occurring, and, thereby, the latter behavior is increased. A mother may say, "When you eat your spinach, you may have your dessert." Eating dessert is a behavior with a high probability of occurring, and eating spinach, for many children, is a behavior with a low probability of occurring. Eating dessert can be used as a reinforcer for eating spinach, and thus can be utilized in any program of providing a balanced diet for a youngster whose mother things he needs spinach.

The Premack principle is important for both the analysis and the modification of behavior. It can be a useful procedure for the clinician. Take the example of a highly active child. A program might be devised to develop (shape) incompatible, more appropriate responses. For example, a child plays baseball with a higher frequency than he reads. If reading is the desired goal, baseball can be made contingent upon his reading, that is, might be allowed only after a certain amount of time is spent in reading.

The Premack principle is of theoretical value since it states that behaviors can be used as reinforcing stimuli. It is of practical value since it provides a clue to the possible reinforcers which may be found in a person's ecology. In this case, the ecology is the person's own behaviors.

STIMULUS PROPS

There is a set of events which are present during both the increase of certain behaviors and the decrease of others. They are present during delivery and nondelivery of consequences. They seem to be the givens, the constants which are a backdrop when learning occurs. They are ignored. However, if they are changed suddenly, the behaviors may be disrupted. Such stimuli are called constant or stimulus props (Goldiamond and Dyrud, 1967b; Goldiamond and Thompson, 1966).

Any change in a client's behavior, especially a sudden change, should be examined for changes in the stimulus or ecological props. An example is a twenty-seven-year-old Puerto Rican man who was arrested for exhibitionism. He had recently arrived from Puerto Rico, where he had been functioning quite well. However, the change from a warm, friendly island, where he knew many people, to the cold city of Chicago, where people were more distant and the language was strange, proved to be a severe disruption to heterosexual activities which had been previously reinforced. Upon his return to Puerto Rico, the exhibitionism stopped, and he once again resumed heterosexual relationships. A change in ecological props or a disruption of the ecology under which sexual behavior had been learned and had been reinforced seems to have produced this behavior.

Stimulus or ecological change will maintain new behavior if the prop performs discriminative, potentiating, or consequential functions. In the exhibitionism case, the behavior that resulted as a product of the drastic stimulus change may very well have been an example of operant behavior. It may have provided consequences (attention, and a return to Puerto Rico) important to the individual. In such a case, exhibitionism would be not the result of stimulus change, but rather effective operant behavior to attain reinforcing consequences that he had obtained through other means in Puerto Rico.

TOPOGRAPHICAL AND FUNCTIONAL DEFINITIONS OF BEHAVIOR IN THE OPERANT ORIENTATION

Another important concept, central to the idea of operant or consequential behavior, is the difference between topographic and functional definitions of behavior. Topographic behaviors are behaviors that are defined by their effects on some recording system, be it a machine, a gauge, or a human observer (Skinner, 1953). When behaviors are defined functionally, or consequentially, they are defined by the consequences which govern their continuance (Skinner, 1953).

Another way to express the difference is that, functionally, a stimulus or response is defined by its role in the A-B-C sequence. Thus, the topographically different behaviors of foot-braking, hand-braking, or deceleration are *functionally* similar behaviors because they are maintained by the same consequence, namely, stopping the car. The red light, stop sign, and policeman's whistle are *topographically different,* but are functionally similar to the extent that they all "cause" a car to be stopped (Goldiamond, 1966).

If a person runs his eyes over some black and white symbols (letters) on a page, he can be seen by an observer to be engaging in one kind of behavior. If he runs his fingers over some raised Braille dots on a page, the same observer would say he is engaging in another kind of behavior or in the same kind of behavior, depending on whether the observer is classifying the behavior topographically or functionally. Topographically, the muscles governing the eyes and the hand would, to a mechanical recording system, "register" as quite different, and they *are* different: they are topographically different. However, both these activities are functionally similar. They are governed by the same consequences, namely, "finding out" what happens next. At "dull" points, both will slow down, and at "exciting" points, both will speed up. Both are given the same functional label: both are called reading (Goldiamond and Dyrud, 1967*a*).

A child may throw a temper tantrum, he may cling to his mother's skirt, he may not eat, he may overeat, he may whine, he may hold his breath until he gets purple; all these behaviors are topographically different. They are different behaviors, topographically, for if one had a kind of measuring instrument, or if these actions were noticed by an observer, they would measure differently. However, each of these topographically different behaviors might have the same consequence—they get and possibly hold his mother's attention.

One individual may be observed doing many topographically different things, such as the child above. Different people in our culture and throughout the world may be observed doing topographically different things. If the consequences are the same in these cases, the behaviors are in the same functional class. Stated otherwise, *they are similar operants.*

In many cases seen in the clinic, clients display different behaviors. However, many "symptoms" in what is called "mental illness" are functionally equivalent. The question to ask is: What are the *consequences* of these behaviors? It may be that the girl who overeats and the girl who undereats, while engaging in topographically different behavior, are engaging in functionally similar behavior. Hence, much of the persistence of what we call "symptoms" is due to the consequences and not to the severity of the symptom per se.

If behaviors which are topographically different can be functionally similar, then behaviors which are topographically similar can be functionally different. Topographically, a scream is the same whether it is a scream for help, a scream at the children, or a scream for joy. However, all these screams are different. They have different meanings (Skinner, 1957). Functional or operant behavior is meaningful behavior. It is purposeful, has goals, and is motivated.

For professional helpers, the consideration of classes of functional, or consequential, behaviors not only facilitates the task of analysis, and thus simplifies the task of intervention, but also comes close to what is called the "true meaning" of the behaviors to the individuals, as well as to the significant others in his environment. Thus, since it considers the functional rather than the topographical, the operant analysis of behavior is a dynamic analysis.

THE PROGRAM

Another critical variable is the program itself. A program is a defined set of procedures by which behavior, behavior-contingencies relations, and the contingencies themselves are changed. There are different ways to program. One way is through trial and error. However, in this kind of learning the individual makes many errors and can suffer in the process of learning. He can also learn through a trial-and-success program. This is designed in steps which are attuned to, and built upon, his progress. In the course of this kind of learning he will not make mistakes. Both methods of learning may produce the same pattern, but, although the outcomes of learning are the same, there may be important differences in other areas. For example, the child who is taught to swim by being thrown into water over his head may eventually swim as well as the child who is gradually introduced to water. However, the first child, once he is away from his watching parents, may shun water. One can say that they have had different histories or experiences, or one may state that each has been involved in a different program (Goldiamond and Thompson, 1966).

In behavior analysis, the program steps are made explicit, and programs are developed which produce the kind of outcome that the client, in consultation with the therapist, wants.

THE OPERANT PARADIGM

The variables and sets of variables which are called "contingencies" provide a framework for the analysis of problematic situations. This operant orientation can provide leads, techniques, and avenues for intervention that are observable and measurable. The variables that have been discussed are the following: the events that follow behavior (consequences); the events that precede behavior (discriminative and instructional-abstractional variables); the procedures that precede it (potentiating variables); events that prop behavior (ecological or stimulus props); and the procedures that provide change (programs). When put together, these are called the "operant paradigm" (Goldiamond, 1962, 1969). This conceptualization is obviously more involved than a simple stimulus-response relationship.

TRANSLATION OF THE OPERANT MODEL INTO TECHNIQUES OF BEHAVIORAL CHANGE

The view of behavior as summarized by the operant paradigm has generated a whole armamentarium of behavior change techniques. Furthermore, additional procedures and techniques are constantly being developed, tested, and revised. In this section, we shall describe some applications for effecting change. Respondent techniques, techniques of modeling and imitation, and further implications of the operant model will be discussed in Chapter 6.

Most of the procedures in this book are related to the consequences, although some are concerned with the antecedent factors and some are concerned with changing the behavior itself. Just as problem classification and diagnosis, in the traditional sense, are topographical rather than functional, so is the listing of techniques (as an end in themselves) concerned with the topographic rather than the functional classification. These techniques should be used as a continuing part of a functional approach, an analysis of each case within the ecology of the individual-contingency relation. Procedures should never be applied routinely.

Thomas, one of the first and most influential of the behaviorist writers in social work, states that one criterion for the choice of intervention procedures is the objective toward which the intervention is directed. Thomas suggests that the therapist utilize techniques from *all* behaviorist orientations, and he classifies techniques in terms of whether the task is to help to establish, strengthen, weaken, or eliminate behavior (Thomas, 1970). For example, he states that if the therapist wishes to help the client to acquire a behavior, he may use "response shaping, classical conditioning . . . to cue prosocial reflex behavior, behavioral rehearsal, rule-making, model presentation, stimulus shaping, and verbal instruction."

If the therapist wishes to help strengthen behavior that is already in the repertoire but is either weak or does not occur frequently enough, then the techniques to be used may be "positive reinforcements, classical conditioning, behavioral rehearsal, rule-making, model presentation, stimulus shaping . . . verbal instruction . . . and systematic desensitization and differential reinforcement . . . which often have behavior strengthening as an important secondary objective."

If the purpose is to help a client reduce or weaken behavior, Thomas suggests the use of "extinction, punishment, classical conditioning employed as aversive conditioning, systematic desensitization, flooding, satiation, and negative practice; . . . rule-making, model presentation, stimulus shaping and verbal instructions may also be used . . . [as well as] differential reinforcement . . . and behavioral rehearsal . . . to reduce problematic behavior as well as to establish behavior" (Thomas, 1970, pp. 214–15).[2]

By "verbal instruction" Thomas means "directions and advice . . . that serve as discriminative stimuli . . . and compliance may . . . be positively reinforced" (Thomas, 1971, p. 1222). This is a technique to establish stimulus control over behavior. Similarly, what Thomas called "rule-making" is setting a rule to "govern behavior and establish the reinforced contingencies" (ibid.). This corresponds to our discussion of discriminative stimuli, that is, "rules for reinforcement." What Thomas calls "response shaping," we call "shaping," a complex process that includes the "method of successive approximations" and encompasses several techniques, such as behavior rehearsal (role-playing), behavior assignments, and others.

[2] There are, of course, many classification schemes possible. Bandura divides operant techniques into the categories of positive control, aversive control, and extinction (Bandura, 1969). Jehu has divided the techniques into those of stimulus control (the antecedent factors) and those of outcome control (consequential factors). He states that the consequential procedures most likely to be used are positive reinforcement, negative punishment, and extinction (Jehu et al., 1972).

SHAPING: THE METHOD OF SUCCESSIVE APPROXIMATIONS

The procedure of shaping, also identified as "successive approximations" (White, 1971), is a major contribution of operant conditioning. In this process, a final behavior is specified. The therapist builds upon behavior that is already in the client's repertoire by selectively reinforcing those behaviors that more and more resemble the final behavior and by not reinforcing— indirectly extinguishing—behaviors that do *not* do so. The individual takes steps toward achieving or performing that behavior. The steps should be small enough to avert setbacks or failures that might discourage him. Each step he takes more and more resembles the final behavior; therefore, it more and more approaches or "approximates" the final behavior.

An example that will clarify this is the case of a young man who expressed a desire to "be independent." In behavioral terms this meant, among other specifications, that he wanted to travel as he wished in his free time and that he would live away from home. One intermediary subgoal in achieving independence was for him to obtain his driver's license. A final objective was to own and drive his own automobile. He could not drive.

The initial behavior that was in his repertoire, that we could build upon, was his ability to speak English! Because he could speak and read English, he was able to complete the application for a learner's permit, which was the first step toward the final goal. The next step was to read the manual, then take a written test, then to take one short driving lesson a week, then two, then to drive the car under varying circumstances that more and more approximated the intermediate goal of buying and driving his own car, which was a subgoal of the final goal (behaviorally defined) of "independence." Thus, through steps that were small, and achievable, he more and more approximated his final goal of "independence."

In the process of shaping, a therapist engages in a process of deliberately reinforcing some behaviors and deliberately not reinforcing other behaviors. This kind of positive reinforcement of desired behaviors is called "differential reinforcement." Much behavior is shaped, from early infancy on, by sources in the environment that differentially reinforce some behaviors under some conditions and do not reinforce others. For example, the human infant is born with the capacity to make any of the almost infinite number of sounds that constitute the many languages known on earth. In the United States he speaks English because those sounds which approximate English words are systematically reinforced by people in his environment, while those that do not are ignored, or technically extinguished. Thus the infant says "w-w," then "wa," then "wa-wa," then "water." Each of these sounds is generally greeted with approval; a mother in China would not react with approval.

Differential reinforcement as part of a shaping process is also used in a slightly different, although related, sense. People can respond in several ways; the social environment may selectively reinforce one response and shape it further. Of course, the environment may use aversive techniques against the others, such as time-out and punishments. This choice also extends to intervention procedures. A therapist may use aversive procedures to eliminate behaviors the client would rather be without. However, rather than trying to eliminate such behaviors as overeating, or eating the "wrong" foods, the therapist can work with the individual toward eating the "right" foods, toward eating sensibly. This is the preferred approach. If a client's problem is lateness, the therapist may concentrate on ways to help him get somewhere on time (he cannot simultaneously be late and on time). In practice, of course, the social environment often uses the techniques simultaneously.

Although the principles are used also in the reduction of behavioral excess, shaping is particularly useful in establishing new behaviors and in the elimination of undesired behaviors by reinforcing competing, incompatible behaviors.

Sometimes it is not the behavior which is at issue but the relation of behavior to the antecedent stimuli. For example, a person may speak very well before a small group, but he may break down completely before a larger audience. He may then experience intense anxiety. One treatment approach is to try to eliminate the anxiety in a direct way, through procedures such as systematic desensitization (discussed in Chapter 6). Another way might be to start out with small audiences, where the speaker feels at home and comfortable, and add one or two people at a time. Notice that the approximations are not being applied to his speaking behavior, since he already speaks well. The approximations are being applied to the *stimuli* which precede speech (the audience, which of course also applies consequences). This procedure is called "fading." Stimuli can be *faded in,* as in this case, or *faded out.* This latter holds true for intervention, where we try to pass program control from the therapist to the client as quickly as possible. The therapist may provide less and less of the program stimuli, and the natural ecology may take over more and more. The therapist gradually "fades" from the picture. This is also a goal of the traditionally oriented therapists, and it is also a prime goal of the behaviorally oriented therapist.

EXTINCTION COMPARED TO DIFFERENTIAL REINFORCEMENT

The process of differential reinforcement involves the selective reinforcement (heightening) of some behaviors and the nonreinforcement of others. Extinction is a procedure in which consequences that have previously reinforced or punished behavior no longer occur. The behavior is now neither reinforced nor punished; it no longer has any consequences.

Extinction may have two effects. If behavior has previously been reinforced, the rate may ultimately go down; if behavior has previously been punished (treated aversively), the rate may ultimately rise. Theoretically, one would imagine that extinction would be a technique of choice for lowering or eliminating rates of undesirable behavior or for raising or maintaining a rate of desirable behavior. However, this is not the case, for extinction is a complicated technique and one of the most misunderstood means of behavior change. It is also easily misapplied if all of the complexities are not understood.

An early example of the effective use of extinction was reported by Williams (1959). The subject was a little boy, twenty-one-months old, who had been ill for a good part of his life. He demanded much parental attention and displayed tantrums at bedtime, insisting that his parents could not leave the room until he had fallen asleep, which took from thirty minutes to two hours. When he was fully recovered, and there was no danger in the procedure, the child was put to bed in a leisurely fashion; then the parent left the bedroom, closed the door, and did not reenter. The child screamed for forty-five minutes the first night, less the second, ten the third, and progressively less until screaming was extinguished by the eighth night. A week later, screaming returned when he was put to bed by an aunt, who reinforced the screaming by returning to the bedroom, so a second extinction trial was made. This time he cried for over fifty minutes the first night, twelve the second night, four the third, and then over twenty minutes the fifth, but again the crying was extinguished by the eighth night. Follow-up at age three years and nine months indicated no recurrence of the behavior and no aftereffects or symptom substitution.

This example is a rather straightforward illustration of extinction. Extinction was successful here, however, because there were no competing positive reinforcements. On the one occasion that an aunt reinforced, the behavior, being intermittently reinforced, returned stronger than ever. Extinction has a high response cost and is painful for the extinguisher as well as for the subject, for it must have been quite a trial for the parents. Many parents could not have gone through this immediate discomfort for the ultimate good.

Extinction, in treatment, should be used only with great caution. If it is used, it should be combined with a program of positive reinforcement for more desirable behaviors. Extinction often results in an increase in the behavior to which it is applied (at least, in the short run). The baby, for example, may increase crying as an immediate reaction to extinction. When

extinction is not consistently followed, the schedule can become one of intermittent reinforcement (variable ratio), and, as
described in the experimental literature, behavior that is reinforced on an intermittent basis is extremely resistant to extinction. Further, the undesired pattern may escalate into an even
more undesirable one (Goldiamond, 1974).

FURTHER REINFORCEMENT TECHNIQUES

Early studies and some contemporary ones have utilized reinforcers, such as food. Fuller (1949) shaped arm movements in a
"vegetative idiot" by utilizing a warm, sweetened milk solution
as a reinforcer. Much early work was with seriously deteriorated clients, not because the operant conditioners were particularly masochistic and chose the hardest cases, but because
for a long time these seriously deteriorated clients were the
only clients they could get. No one else wanted to bother with
them, and they obviously were not amenable to dynamically
oriented psychological "talk therapies."

One case that illustrates the use of such reinforcers is the
case history reported by Kassorla (1969). Kassorla treated a
man "believed to be the 'sickest man in a British mental institution' as judged by a group of medical consultants" (*ibid.,* p. 71).
Hospitalized at age twenty-one, he became extremely depressed, his speech was "garbled and confused," he received
shock and drug therapy, and thirty years later was found by
Kassorla to be extremely deteriorated, mute, and catatonic. Before intervention he remained absolutely silent for 89 percent
of the time, and 11 percent of the time made only noises. Kassorla used food as a reinforcer to shape speech. At first, *any*
movement of the lips whatsoever that approximated speech
was met with verbal praise, but by the fifth day the patient had
to imitate a word, and by the fourteenth day the patient's imitation had reached the 92 percent level of appropriate imitative
behavior. For the first time in thirty years, as the author excit-
edly reported, "we had control of his verbal behavior."

In the next phase, the patient was shown a picture (visual

stimulus) of a dog and then had to imitate the word "dog." He reached 90 percent correct imitation by the ninth day.

In phase three the question was asked, "What is this?" of the picture of the dog. He first commented, "I don't know" (negativistic, but a three-word sentence after thirty years of near silence and mutism). This continued for seven days. "Punishment" (actually a "time-out"), consisting of the experimenter turning her head away for ten seconds, was ineffective, so a more drastic "punishment" was tried. They removed the patient from the room (another time-out procedure) when he said, "I don't know," and after repeating this procedure for four days he said, "dog," and the time-out stopped. The response requirement grew more difficult as part of the "shaping by successive approximation" procedure. By the thirty-first day of the study he successfully labeled all the objects (furniture, experimental equipment) in the room without a single instance of negativism. The study continued for 134 days; the patient asked questions, made demands, and took more control. By the end of the study, his original symptoms had disappeared; he was speaking, taking part in hospital activities, and, of course, no longer needed the food reinforcement but would work for social reinforcement, such as talk, praise, and so forth. He was still in the institution after thirty years; there was no place he could go, and he was still "sick," according to the author, but he had come a long way from being the "sickest man in a British mental institution."

Although much of the work with retarded, autistic, and schizophrenic children initially used unconditioned reinforcers, such as food, these reinforcers were quickly combined with social ("conditioned") reinforcers as soon as possible, and the food reinforcers were phased out as soon as possible. For example, Milby (1970), working with two seriously disturbed psychotic patients, made social reinforcement (talk, praise, and so forth) contingent upon social interaction with other patients or with staff. The level of social interaction of each patient was increased, and there was generalization to other behaviors and aspects of the patients' life.

We shall illustrate the use of conditioned reinforcers

throughout the next chapter and with two illustrative cases in Chapters 4 and 5. The use of reinforcement contingencies, which is central to the operant procedures, has been described at great detail elsewhere (Ullmann and Krasner, 1965; Bandura, 1969; Kanfer and Phillips, 1970; among others). However, there is a limit to the use of positive reinforcers for desired acts, whether they are unconditioned reinforcers, such as food, or conditioned reinforcers, such as praise, social recognition, and the like. First of all, reinforcement, to be effective, should be immediate. If there is a delay between behavior and its consequence, the reinforcement might come after an intervening behavior, and thus the "wrong" behavior might be reinforced. Second, reinforcers work only as long as they are potentiated. One way to make a reinforcer potent is to deprive the individual of it. This raises an immediate ethical question about the desirability of depriving a person of a reinforcer, especially if it is a necessity, such as food or a bed. Third, if the reinforcer is made contingent on a behavior, and the procedure is successful in increasing the rate of behavior, this will produce an increase in the consequence, which lessens deprivation, hence lessens the potency of the reinforcer. This loss is called "satiation." Fourth, it might be inconvenient to reinforce after each occurrence; the act might be part of a chain, and so forth.

One way around these and similar dilemmas is to develop conditioned reinforcers. Certain stimuli can be paired with different events which are already potent reinforcers. The same reinforcer may be potentiated for *many* behaviors. This is then called a "generalized reinforcer." Money is an example of a generalized reinforcer. Money is reinforcing because it can, at some point, be exchanged for goods, services, and other things people desire. These items are called *"back-up reinforcers."* Money by itself is meaningless; it is valuable only in so far as it can be exchanged for back-up reinforcers.

Many of the behavioral advances in recent years have been made possible through the development of generalized reinforcers, which can be given in a number of situations for a number of behaviors. The most famous of these is the "token economy," and it is through the token economies that many of the nonoperant therapists have become aware of the wider applications of operant principles.

The Token Economy. Tokens are generalized reinforcers. According to Kazdin and Bootzin (1972), tokens as generalized reinforcers have a number of advantages: (1) They "bridge the delay" between target response and back-up reinforcer. (2) They permit the reinforcement of a response at any time. (3) They may be used to maintain performance over extended periods of time when the back-up reinforcer cannot be parceled out. (4) They allow sequences of responses to be reinforced without interruption. (5) They maintain their reinforcing properties because of their relative independence of deprivation states. (6) They are less subject to satiation effects. (7) They provide the same reinforcement for individuals who have different preferences in back-up reinforcers. (8) They may take on greater incentive value than a single primary reinforcer, since "the effects resulting from association with each primary reinforcer may summate" (Kazdin and Bootzin, 1972, p. 343).

Tokens have further advantages: (1) The number of tokens can bear a simple quantitative relation to the amount of reinforcement. (2) They are portable, and can be carried away from the situation in which they are earned, thus facilitating generalization. (3) If it is considered desirable, there can be no maximum number earned. (This is often not desirable, for hoarding tokens can present obvious problems and may be an indication that the program is not working adequately.) (4) If desired, tokens make possible a system of automatic-machine delivery of reinforcers. (5) Tokens are durable, can be standardized, will not deteriorate, and can be made unique and therefore contingent upon the desired behavior (Ayllon and Azrin, 1968, as summarized in Kazdin and Bootzin, 1972).

Among the first of the token economies was the pioneering work of Ayllon and Azrin (1965, 1968), who dealt with long-term, regressed, and deteriorated female schizophrenic patients at Anna State Hospital (in Illinois) and radically improved their functioning in a number of areas. One overt message of the token economy, incidentally, is the notion that the behavior that is being reinforced is "desirable" behavior. The attendant or nurse (the token dispenser) is forced to pay attention to what he desires of the patient rather than to what he does *not* desire. He is forced to concentrate on repertoires he can build up rather than on those he wishes to eliminate. The norm becomes "health," and it is "health" that gets the token. Previously, the patient performing ordinary (normal) behavior was often ignored, while the patient who was screaming, hallucinating, and so on received the reinforcement of staff attention.

Although they have been outlined elsewhere, we present a brief summary of the procedures for establishing a token economy, for which we have drawn heavily from Kazdin and Bootzin (1972). The target behaviors (those to be altered) must be identified in specific terms. Then the present and potential reinforcers in the environment must be evaluated and counted. (The Premack principle, discussed earlier, is an excellent basis for potentiating some reinforcers.) Back-up reinforcers also may include nonmaterial items, such as going on walks (for psychiatric patients). The tokens must be established as conditioned reinforcers, and there are a number of procedures in the literature for doing so.

There are problems to be overcome when applying a token economy. The conditions for earning, dispensing, and redeeming tokens must be established and must be clearly understandable. One important aspect of any token economy is that *the staff that is to administer the economy must be trained.* This is crucial; it presents some of the greatest problems and promises and challenges of any token program. To repeat, the norm is health. Healthy behavior is to be reinforced, and the conditions that promote this behavior are identified and built up. This message is given both to patients and to staff.

There is often staff resistance to the token economy since, initially at least, it often means more work for staff to deal with an active, groping client group than with a passive and dependent client group. The ultimate payoff for all, of course, is greater, and it is a task for the behavior therapist to get this fact across to the staff. This is as important a part of any token economy as the advantages. The reader is referred to Kazdin and Bootzin (1972) for a review of the literature on staff training for token economies.

There is often resistance to the token economy on the part of the subjects or residents (this may be only resistance to *any* change). This resistance may often take the form of trying to circumvent the system to obtain the reinforcers by other means, and it may lead to disruptive behavior, and so on. Some clients are nonresponsive to the token system; in this event, careful examination should be made to see if the back-up reinforcers are truly potentiated, as well as to see if the response requirements are realistic and whether there is undetected and subtle (or not so subtle) sabotage of the program by staff.

Token economies have been applied to a large number of client categories, have been used with individuals and with groups, and have been applied by a number of different kinds of professionals. We have mentioned the pioneering work of Ayllon and Azrin in the psychiatric hospital. Token economies are in widespread use throughout the Veterans Administration, in at least two dozen hospitals, and have been used with many hundreds of patients (Upper and Goodenough, 1971). Dependent variables have been self-care behaviors, such as grooming, continence, and personal appearance, among others; out-of-hospital behaviors, such as vocational adjustment; and social responsiveness behavior, such as visiting, conversation, decreases in assaultive behaviors, and the like.

Token reinforcers have been used with the mentally retarded (Watson, 1967); in public school settings (O'Leary and Becker, 1967); with juvenile delinquents (Cohen and Filipczak, 1971; Rose *et al.,* 1970); with autistic children (Ferster and De-Myer, 1962); with retarded adolescent boys (Burchard, 1967); with adolescent girls (Lent *et al.,* 1970); with preschool children in a Head Start program (Miller and Schneider, 1970); with "discipline-problem" soldiers in a psychiatric ward (Boren and Colman, 1970); with a chronic psychotic patient who had been hospitalized twenty-six years (Patterson and Teigen, 1973); with chronic paranoid schizophrenics (Wincze, Leitenberg, and Agras, 1972); and with a depressed patient (Reisinger, 1972).

The token economies are kinds of societies in miniature,

and they have behavioral implications for the larger society. Kagel and Winkler (1972) have used a behavioral approach in the study of economics. In *Walden Two* "continued presence in the economy" was contingent upon the performance of certain chores, for which credits were earned (Skinner, 1948).

The success of the token economies has encouraged many people to apply them willy-nilly, without a comprehensive knowledge of the operant principles underlying the logic of their application. For example, many workers have set too high a behavioral requirement for tokens to be earned; clients have given up. In operant terms, the clients were on a fixed ratio schedule with too high a response cost, and they exhibited ratio strain. Similarly, when the responses are too easily achieved, the tokens soon lose their effectiveness, since the back-up reinforcers lose their potency. In operant work, as in all work, a little knowledge can be more than dangerous. Inadequate knowledge of the procedures and principles not only can hurt the people we are supposed to be helping, it can prematurely doom what is, in our opinion, a promising approach. This is one of the dangers inherent in the almost faddist-like growth in popularity in the use, and misuse, of the token economy.

One of the questions frequently asked about the token economy is, "Does behavior, changed in the institution, remain changed outside the institution?"—that is, once the individual has left the controlled environment and is again exposed to many differing kinds of competing stimuli. The answers to this question vary, but the development of procedures for carry-over into the natural environment is an area of highest priority for future research. Fairweather, for example, used a token economy to establish behaviors during institutional stay that *would be reinforced* by the ecology outside. There was far more carry-over in the token group than in a control group. However, stabilization of behavior (even stabilization within the walls of the institution or the classroom, and even when it is directed only to specific target behaviors) often has a beneficial effect on clients that spreads to other areas. This stability often gives the therapist a base upon which he can build, and it is also important for effective program evaluation.

In short, the token economy is an application of positive reinforcement, in tangible form, using generalized reinforcers. Sometimes these token economies are used in conjunction with a system of moderate (sometimes, unfortunately, not so moderate) punishment in the form of penalties. We believe that the results of the applications of these systems of positive reinforcements, despite the problems associated with them and the misuse that comes from a faddist popularity, indicate that they show promise in providing an entry into locked systems, such as a parent and child who cannot relate to each other, or a teacher with a recalcitrant class. They force the system to make public and explicit what it desires.

Contingency Contracting. The token system makes behavioral requirements quite clear. It eliminates confusion, and it is easily taught to parents and other nonprofessionals to be used in shaping desirable behaviors. These requirements are often expressed in mutual agreements between, say, a parent and child, in which their mutual expectations and consequences are verbalized. These agreements are called "behavioral contracts."

Cantrell, Cantrell, Huddleston, and Woolridge (1969) devised contingency contracting procedures in which written contracts were prepared, specifying desired changes and the reinforcers to be delivered upon approximation to these behaviors. Parents and teachers kept daily records, and results were encouraging enough to warrant further investigation of contingency contracting as a clinical method.

Later, Christopherson, Arnold, Hill, and Quilitich (1972) devised a token economy system to be administered by two sets of parents with a total of five children between five and ten years old. Parents specified desired behaviors and recorded and distributed reinforcers. The systems were successful, with Family No. 1 modifying fifteen behaviors and Family No. 2 modifying six behaviors, or twenty-one in all. Homme (1969) devised what he called "contingency contracting" whereby students, after completing previously agreed-upon chores, could spend time either in a reinforcement area in the classroom or at their desks in activities that they had chosen from a "reinforcement menu." For example, after working for, say, fifteen minutes (or thirty minutes, depending upon age and so on) the child could spend five or ten minutes in the reinforcement area playing with a puzzle, or listening to a record, or talking with a friend. Homme's work has been replicated in many, many schools.

The use of contingency management evolved from having the therapist set the terms of the agreement to having the client himself set the terms, with the therapist as a consultant. One example is the work done in Lawrence, Kansas, at Achievement Place, a facility for "predelinquent" boys. In one of the first published reports, Phillips (1968) describes a token economy used in this community-based, home-style (small, with resident "foster" parents) institution. The tokens were awarded by houseparents upon completion of "specified appropriate behaviors," and there was a system of fines. Points could be cashed in for privileges such as visiting home, riding bikes, and so forth. The author reports that aggression decreased, while tidiness and homework (among other behaviors) increased. The author concluded that the token system was an effective part of the rehabilitation program.

In a later study (Phillips *et al.,* 1971), several experimental conditions were run, but the token economy was still managed by the houseparents and controlled by these houseparents. By 1973, however, the emphasis had switched to a "semi-self-government" system (Fixen, Phillips, and Wolf, 1973). The boys set many of their own rules and monitored their peers' behaviors and their own. The results were more favorable, and the participation of the boys was much higher.

Tharp and Wetzel (1969), utilizing "behavior analysts" (paraprofessionals without formal academic training but trained by the authors in a short course), intervened in difficult parent-child cases. The behavior analyst mediated contracts between the parent(s) and the child. These contracts stated the mutual behavioral expectations and their consequences. For example, if a young man fed the dog before the evening meal, he was to receive ten cents. If he observed curfews when using his car, he was paid forty cents per night, but failure meant loss of specified times of using the car.

Contract management, with its inherent emphasis on self control, has potential for the field of criminal justice and rehabilitation. In a discussion of methods of sentencing lawbreakers, Rest (1973) suggests that the prisoner himself might be the one to determine when he had been "rehabilitated." She suggests that the prisoner set up a "series of behavior criteria" for himself which might include learning occupational skills, earning a high school or college diploma, and so forth, stating that most prisoners do not have the knowledge to "negotiate the system" and that life in an institution does not prepare one adequately enough for an eventual return to society. Several examples are included, such as the work of Brierton (1969) at Vally View, a correctional school in Illinois, and the work of Gadbois at the St. Cloud State Prison, in Minnesota (Gadbois, 1972). At St. Cloud, the prisoners are engaged in "contract performing," in which "behavior changes are translated into performance objectives," such as learning skills, and these goals are to be accomplished before their release from prison. The system, which is still in the experimental phase, should be watched closely, for it offers a great deal to the admittedly frustrating and somewhat conceptually sterile field of corrections. An earlier effort, incorporating some earlier versions of performance contracting, showed, among other positive results, that the recidivism rate, as one indicator, had been cut from 70 percent to 30 percent (Clements and McKee, 1968).

TECHNIQUES BASED ON PUNISHMENT AND AVERSIVE CONSEQUENCES

We are philosophically committed to the use of procedures based on the principles of positive reinforcement. The research on token economies clearly points out the importance of positive reinforcement procedures. However, there may be extremely serious situations, in which a short and controlled application of an aversive stimulus will put an immediate end to even more severe self-destructive behaviors which otherwise would result in serious harm or even death to the individual. These behaviors often make it impossible to formulate a positive program for the client. As we shall elaborate in Chapter 6, these situations involve the making of serious ethical choices on the part of the therapist.

In this section, we discuss punishment and negative reinforcement, approaches which we classify as "aversive." These approaches should not be confused with the general body of techniques called "aversion therapy," which will be discussed in Chapter 6. Here we are considering a class of punishment and aversive techniques that differ from aversion therapy, although there can be, of course, overlapping between the two models. Here we are considering punishment as a consequence, a response that makes the rate of behavior drop. Similarly, extinction can also decrease the rate of behavior. However, the difference is that, in extinction, the environment simply does not respond to behavior previously reinforced, while in punishment the environment does respond. In punishment, the environment can either present an aversive stimulus or remove a positive one; in either case, the rate of behavior will drop. (Once again, punishment should not be confused with negative reinforcement, which is a procedure that *maintains* behavior by removing an aversive stimulus when the behavior is produced. People will work to get rid of, or avoid, the aversive stimulus; thus negative reinforcement is a reinforcement, and not a punishment, procedure.)

We can illustrate the various usages of punishment in the following example. A small boy constantly sticks his hand into the cookie jar and steals a cookie. If his mother discovers the child sticking his hand into the jar, she might slap his hand. This is a *punishment* procedure if the rate of cookie-taking drops. (She has presented an aversive stimulus.) She may forbid him to play baseball that afternoon, or on any afternoon as long as he continues to take cookies. This is also a punishment procedure: she has removed a pleasant event from the boy as a consequence of his taking the cookie.

She might also take the cookies out of the jar, so that when he reaches into it he does not get anything. This is an *extinction* procedure, and eventually the child will stop reaching into the jar, will stop "testing the situation."

She might leave the cookies in the jar and forbid him to enter the kitchen for a certain length of time. This is a *time-out* procedure, for he has been deprived of the opportunity to engage in a desired activity. (Another form of time-out would be for the mother to put the cookie jar on a high shelf for the rest of the day, stating that she will return it and that she hopes she will not have to remove it again. This is also a "time-out" procedure, although it involves a certain inconvenience for the mother in putting the jar up high.)

The reader can probably think of other and better ways this mother might handle the situation, but these procedures are cited simply to illustrate the differences between the procedures of punishment (extinction and time-out).

A comparison between the effectiveness of punishment and that of reinforcement procedures is difficult, for many reasons. Often the same behavior might produce punishment or reinforcement, either of a positive or a negative kind. In fact, if we examine the world around us, it is very difficult to think of situations in which punishment is delivered that are not also, under some other conditions, reinforced. Speeding in an automobile, for example, is punished if we are caught by a state trooper but reinforced, if we are not caught, by getting there earlier, among other things. On the other hand, one can think of situations in which reinforcement alone is delivered.

An excellent summary of the laboratory research on punishment may be found in the discussion by Azrin and Holz (1966). They conclude that the effectiveness of punishment is related to the *conditions* under which it is used. This also is true, of course, for positive reinforcement, even though the former procedure lowers the rate of behavior and the latter increases the rate of behavior. Accordingly, preference of techniques is usually based on considerations other than the effects on the behaviors which are the target of the intervention. These include the emotional and social effects of the procedures on the person being punished or reinforced. They also include the person who defines the contingencies and the social system of which they are both a part.

Ethical considerations, of course, are a primary issue. *Should* one use punishment? The issue is too complex for a full discussion here. Despite the fact that aversive techniques can be used (and, indeed, find widespread social use) in the form of punishment to decrease or eliminate behavior, and in the form of negative reinforcement to increase and maintain behavior, the procedures have found very little use or advocacy by practitioners in the operant brands of behavior modification.[3]

Punishment is certainly a controversial method of effecting behavior change, and it is susceptible to abuse (Chaiklin, 1973). In fact, a number of very inhumane programs have attempted to justify their existence through the use of punitive methods under the guise of "behavior modification" (Goldiamond, 1974).

Lovaas and his colleagues, who are associated with the dramatic use of aversive procedures, also use positive reinforcement techniques to reduce undesirable behavior. They state that self-destructive behavior can be suppressed by building incompatible behaviors and perhaps this would be the most humane and effective procedure (Bucher and Lovaas, 1968). This is the procedure generally used in most behavior modification in the operant tradition.

Lovaas and his associates have used aversive techniques in situations that could be described as "desperate." Among other cases, they cite the instance of a seven-year-old boy with an IQ of 25, who engaged in a series of self-destructive behaviors, such as head-banging that was so severe that his head was covered with scar tissue. Treatment was twenty-four-hours-a-day restraint, with the boy being tied down physically

---

[3] Early writers, such as Keller and Schoenfeld (1950), state that one reason punishment is used is that it produces an immediate result—at least temporarily—and thus our use of punishment is positively reinforced. Skinner's concern with the development of social systems which eschew punishment and use positive reinforcement is well-known (Skinner, 1971).

and drugged heavily. The ward staff, overworked and un-
trained, were not able to reinforce competing behaviors; the attention understandably given these bizarre behaviors probably
increased their frequency and made the situation worse. The
institutional characteristics, and the severity of the behaviors, ruled out the use of extinction and the establishment of
competing behaviors; the danger of permanent damage was
too real and too immediate.

Aversive stimulation seemed the quickest, the most effective, the most humane, and the immediate choice of intervention procedures. They applied a one-second delivery of electric
shock every time the boy banged his head, accompanied by the
verbal "NO!" Only twelve shocks were needed in three widely
spaced sessions, plus several boosters during a fourth session,
and the results were dramatic. The boy stopped the behavior
and was released from restraints. This permitted the establishment of a program by which he would be able to receive positive reinforcement from his therapeutic environment.

The problem of this boy was acute. While other children
learn desirable repertoires, children such as this one, who suffer long periods of institutionalization, learn those repertoires
relevant to isolation in a hospital. However, in cases in which
punishment or aversive techniques are used—even in cases
this severe—they are usually simultaneously combined with
programs that provide positive reinforcement for desirable behaviors.

Time-out. Time-out procedures have been used extensively in
so-called "controlled" environments, such as schools, institutions for delinquents, and so on. They were not invented by
behaviorists. In the school, a child may be placed out of the
classroom, or in a corner, and so denied the opportunity to
engage in reinforced behavior. These procedures have been
used in the same way to treat antisocial behavior in a children's
institution. They are often used by themselves, in combination
with each other, or in combination with methods of positive reinforcement. They are generally applied for a short and limited
time, and are applied immediately upon the occurrence of

specified behaviors. These procedures, as reported in the behavior modification literature, are used sparingly, and they are discontinued as soon as possible.

For example, Pendergrass (1972) found that brief isolation from a group situation suppressed high-rate antisocial responses in two extremely withdrawn retarded children. Time-out was administered with no accompanying reinforcement of competing responses or other techniques.

Wahler (1969) showed that highly oppositional behavior of two negativistic children dropped with use of time-out. Treatment also made parents more aware of the effects of positive reinforcement, for reinforcement of competing behaviors was higher during treatment than before intervention. White, Nielsen, and Johnson (1972), working with retarded children, found that aggression, tantrums, and self-destruction were reduced significantly by use of time-out procedures.

Time-out has been used by a variety of people in a variety of settings with a variety of children. Rose (1973) uses the technique with both nonproblematic and delinquent juveniles as part of group treatment. Rose finds this "time out from positive reinforcement" a most effective and short (thirty seconds to five minutes) way of eliminating disruptive behavior and repotentiating the positive reinforcement aspects of the group treatment situation. Sulzer and Mayer (1972) recommend the selective use of time-out in the classroom situation to maintain discipline in classes of nonproblematic children.

Time-out is, as we have stated, an aversive technique that works best when used in combination with techniques of positive reinforcement.

This brief survey of techniques has focused on changing behavior by manipulation of consequences (the C in the A-B-C formulation). It is also possible to change behavior by attention to the antecedent factors.

Changing antecedent factors may often eliminate the necessity of using aversive procedures. In an institution for emotionally disturbed children, a ten-year-old boy awoke regularly at 7:00, one hour ahead of official waking time, and awakened everyone else. The staff had tried reasoning, reprimands, threats (later, withdrawal of privileges), and bribes (promises of privileges later), to no avail. They then decided to try time-out: an isolation room to which he was to be dragged if he persisted. The boy made such a racket when they tried this that he awakened all the other wards. Goldiamond advised the counselor to sit at the child's side at 6:30 and, when he awoke, to whisper quietly: "If you tiptoe to the bookcase and get a book, I will read to you. But let's be quiet about it, because if the others wake up I won't be able to, because I'll have to take care of them all." The child tiptoed quietly as suggested, and the others awoke at 8:00. The next day, he awoke at 7:30, and the same procedure was followed. Soon he was tiptoeing to the desk when the counselor was filling out forms. Some complex pop-up and do-it-yourself books were purchased, and the child was told that he could either read these special books to himself or ask the counselor to read him something else. The problem was solved by changing the conditions so as to make more likely, behavior that would compete with the undesired behavior—and then reinforcing it as soon as it occurred (Goldiamond, 1970).

Also involved in setting up this program was an analysis of the consequences assumed to be maintaining the child's disturbing behavior in the morning. These consequences were the individualized attention paid by the counselors. Through the program they tried to provide these consequences, contingent on behavior more desirable to the counselor. The disturbing behavior can be described as "learned, operant, or instrumental social behavior." Waking up the ward may not be as dramatic as head-banging, but their analysis as operants suggests procedures for elimination. In the head-banging case, aversive consequences were used. In the early-waking case, variables affecting the setting, or antecedents, were changed.

STIMULUS CONTROL

When a behavior occurs under one set of antecedent conditions and not under another that behavior is said to be under *stimulus control.* Both the antecedent stimulus and the behavior (the A and the B) are functionally defined by the consequences (the C). The term "stimulus control" refers to the effect that these discriminative stimuli have on behavior. For example, singing is reinforced by the teacher in a music period but not in a mathematics classroom. School behavior would be considered as under the different stimulus control of each of the two classes, and it would be said that discrimination had been established. In the case of the student whose behavior was not different in the two classes, a program might be developed that produced such differences. This might involve analysis of the classroom settings and work with the staff, or work directly with the student. The latter would exemplify *discrimination training.* Although the student is probably aware of the upset he produces, he may not realize all the other consequences contingent upon his behavior. He may not care. He may actually be discriminating between courses which are important to him and those which are not. In all events, discrimination training involves attention not only to the rules or the conditions of reinforcement but also to the recognition of the linkage of those rules (controlling conditions) to the consequences, and attention to the potentiating variables.

There are a number of technical ways to establish appropriate stimulus control. Appropriate behaviors may be in the repertoire but not under the stimulus control required. It may not be necessary to "shape" them—they may already be there, but in the wrong time and in the wrong place.

In a university setting many individuals have trouble studying. Examination of the behavior of these students often shows that they spend a lot of time in the school library but get very little done. Examining their behavior in the library shows that much of this time is spent in talking with friends, going in and out of the snack bar, and so forth. In this instance, the library does not provide the stimulus control the student desires. He both studies and socializes in the library. Goldiamond has labeled this the "scrambled eggs" effect; it is a condition encountered in many cases (see Chapter 4, the case of John Smith). In order to increase studying behavior, the control the stimulus (or preceding conditions) has on behavior must be delineated. If possible, students should study in the library for a fixed period and socialize in the lobby or student lounge for another period of time.

One student set aside a table in his home which was to be used only for studying. The light was to be turned on only when he studied. (If such a table has to be in the bedroom, it should not face the bed, for studying while lying down on a bed is a discriminative stimuli for escape behavior—sleep.) The student was to spend a short time at this table, engaged only in studying. The time was to be gradually increased until some criterion level had been achieved. If he felt sleepy, or began to daydream, he was to turn off the light and leave the table. Other times could be scheduled to make up the time lost. In a very short time, that table and that light assumed stimulus control over that student's studying behavior. Operant discrimination had taken place. When he had to use the library, the library was to be used either for short intensive periods of reference or he was to require himself to put in certain amounts of time before taking a break (the Premack principle). If he felt that he wanted to socialize with someone, then he certainly could, but not in the library; he was to invite that person out for coffee. These procedures replicated a technique originally used by Goldiamond (1965c).

Beneke and Harris (1972) found that they could teach study techniques to students, combining stimulus control with self-reinforcement of "high-probability behavior, money, food, and other reinforcements" and a mild punishment in the form of fines for not following procedures. The students utilizing these techniques scored impressive gains in academic averages; no difference was found in grade point averages between students who underwent training in groups or as individuals.

Goldiamond, treating an overweight young man, assisted him in bringing his eating under stimulus control. He was instructed "to eat to his heart's content and not to repress the desire . . . [but] to treat food with the dignity it deserved" (Goldiamond, 1965c, p. 855). He was to eat in one place only, to do nothing but eat at that place, and to concentrate upon and enjoy the food and not "contaminate" food with such distracting activities as watching television. This was to break the relation of television as a conditioned reinforcer for food, and vice versa.

The effort to place behavior under stimulus control was one of the earlier efforts in transferring control from the therapist to the client himself. It is the basis for the model of this book. In the problem mentioned above, the principle was to teach the student to place the control of his studying under the control of his table, thus equipping the student with the techniques that he could use to maximize his studying behaviors. The student had ultimate control over whether or not to put these procedures into effect. These techniques are also transferable to other situations and other behaviors.

The principle of changing antecedent conditions also has been utilized in child-parent interaction problems. In an early work, Smith and Smith (1966) speak of the need and the importance for parents to specify the instructional discriminative stimuli for children's behavior. In other words, parents should make clear and manifest the "rules" (Smith and Smith's term) for required behavior, which is the guideline for which behavior is desired and will be reinforced, and make clear which behaviors will not be reinforced.

Most interveners use a combination of techniques focused on antecedents, such as some form of discrimination training along with reinforcement techniques. In a sense, differential reinforcement is a discrimination training technique, for the differential reinforcing of some behaviors and the nonreinforcement or extinction of others may lead to a discrimination process (decision) on the part of the client. The whole process of shaping and successive approximations, although discussed here under "consequential" techniques, is (from another viewpoint) a process of discrimination training—discrimination sharpening.

Risley and Wolf (1967), working with autistic children, utilized not only techniques related to the *consequences* (extinction, time-out, and differential reinforcement), but also the fading in of new stimuli and the fading out of verbal prompts first to establish imitation and later to transfer speech from imitative control to control by appropriate stimulus conditions. The effects transferred to other behaviors.

Azrin and Foxx (1974) developed a program to enable parents to toilet train their children in less than a day (actually, an average; some will take more time, some will take less time). In the program, the parent increases the child's fluid intake (his favorite drink), thus increasing frequency of urination. The child then "trains" his doll, being reinforced by pretending that the doll is urinating on the toilet, and then being reinforced for his own urination on the toilet. The program is aimed toward stimulus control of internal stimuli that signal bladder distension and impending sphincter change, and these are brought under the stimulus control of the toileting procedures. No aversive controls are used. The packaging of the procedures into a "do-it-yourself" book for parents is also a complex antecedent event. The reinforcements for following the directions are, of course, obvious for the parents and also for the child, in the approval for dryness and the changed behaviors of the child which, among other things, make for a sense of mutual accomplishment for both parent and child.

The procedures that Azrin and Foxx followed stem from the model of programmed instruction. Indeed, Goldiamond (1974) argues that the appropriate model for operant behavior modification is not the operant laboratory but programmed instruction derived from the operant laboratory. The approach is to teach the student new concepts, new insights, and new ways to analyze the material. The outcome is in terms of increasing a person's options, increasing his competence in terms of what additional skills he should obtain, what has to be *constructed,* rather than in terms of deficits to be overcome or patterns to be eliminated. This approach is called by Goldiamond a "constructional" approach (Goldiamond, 1974). This approach is differentiated from a "pathological" approach, which focuses on deficits, patterns to eliminate, the history of the patterns, and so forth.

ORIENTATIONS TO BEHAVIORAL TREATMENT

Jehu *et al.* (1972, p. 16) state that there are several orientations to behavioral treatment. The first is to change the client's behaviors and responses without necessarily changing the environment. The second approach is to change the client's environment without changing (primarily) the client's behavior. The client's behavior is expected to change as a result of the environmental change.

A third approach, which overlaps the second and does not necessarily ignore the first, is to teach the client to be his own behavior analyst and then to program his own procedures for change. This process aims toward equipping the client with an orientation, a method of analysis, and with the techniques that should carry over outside the therapeutic situation and sustain him at other times throughout his life. This procedure of enabling the client to be his own behavior analyst and therapist is often referred to as "self control," in the sense of assisting the client to independence. There is a poster which bears the caption: "Beat the System! Program Your Own Life!" This poster reflects the essence of this third approach, one that has been pioneered by Goldiamond and is the orientation of the self control model of casework and social work intervention presented in this book.

three

A CONSTRUCTIONAL APPROACH TO SELF CONTROL

ISRAEL GOLDIAMOND *

A married woman applies for psychotherapy in an obviously agitated state. She reports a crippling fear of cockroaches and other household vermin. She is immobilized and stiffens uncontrollably for no apparent reason. Her husband, who comes with her, confirms these complaints in every detail. They cannot understand her stiffness, and they both consider her fears to be unreasonable, since they live in a new and clean high-rise apartment building that has no vermin. Nevertheless, the fears and immobility are there. Both husband and wife are distressed over the problem and the effect this is having on their lives.

Although problems differ from one person to another, people come to one of the helping professions, as did this couple, because of the distress or suffering produced by the presence or absence of certain repertoires. The current prevalent approach to treatment focuses on eliminating, alleviating, or otherwise overcoming the distress. An approach so directed can be designated as a *pathological* approach (from the Greek *pathos,* suffering). It considers the problem in terms of a manifest or underlying pathology which, however it was established or developed, is to be eliminated or overcome.

Elimination of problems may be achieved through a variety of means, including psychotherapy, counseling, behavior ther-

* This chapter and Chapter 4 were written under a grant from the state of Illinois, Department of Mental Health, entitled "Self Control Procedures in Psychiatric Problems." Some of the material and all logs and forms appeared in Goldiamond (1974) and are reproduced with permission of the publishers of *Behaviorism.*

apy, or chemotherapy (or combinations). However, presented with the same problem, the helping professional can focus on the production of desirables through procedures which extend repertoires or develop additional ones. Approaches so directed can be designated as *constructional.* To clarify the distinction between the two orientations, the types of intervention that might be used to deal with the problem of the couple cited will be compared.

PATHOLOGICAL APPROACHES

These approaches can be applied by professionals with behavioral or dynamic orientations, among others. For example, a behavior therapist *might* apply desensitization (see Chapter 6) to the vermin phobia. He might get the wife to relax while she is thinking of some insects she can tolerate, and then gradually to go through a hierarchy of vermin gradually resembling those she fears.

If the therapist's orientation is operant, he *might* instruct the husband to apply differential reinforcement by being inattentive or casual when the wife is immobile or phobic (extinction), and to pour on attention, praise, and delight when she is mobile (reinforcement).

In a psychodynamic orientation, the problem *might* be defined in terms of an underlying conflict in which the symptoms serve as defense mechanisms. The therapist might try to gain insight into the conflict, examine its history, and so on.

Pharmacological intervention *might* be the prescription of tranquilizers or relaxants to alleviate the distress.

Other behavioral, dynamic, or chemotherapeutic procedures could be applied, of course, as well as other psychological and organic procedures. The kind of information sought would also differ.

CONSTRUCTIONAL APPROACHES

An alternate approach is to view the repertoires (or symptoms) which cause the distress and are interpreted as a pathology to be eliminated (or as indicative of one) as patterns which successfully produce desirable and even logical consequences, but at a distressful cost. That they persist despite the distress suggests that they might be the alternatives of choice, so to speak, given the social history and behavioral ecology of the person involved. The therapeutic task in this approach is to help construct new ways of producing these critical consequences by means which are accompanied by satisfaction rather than distress.

As applied to the couple cited, the interviewer might ask what happens as a result of the wife's patterns (symptoms) that might not happen without them. He might learn that, as a result of her fears and immobility, her husband must wake up ahead of her every morning, sweep the floors to make sure they are clear of vermin, and prepare breakfast and bring it to her bedside, where they both eat together, she in bed and he at her side. This support is a necessity for her to be able to get out of bed at all. Otherwise, she cannot make it through the day. When he leaves for work, he again makes sure that the "coast is clear," and telephones her regularly every two hours. Both are distressed by this state of affairs. Her suffering and distress are genuine. She *is* afraid; she *is* immobilized; she *genuinely* wants not to be such a burden on him. He is also distressed and depressed. Both want help.

Her patterns may be considered to be operants, maintained by the tremendous involvement by her husband. The fact that the patterns pay off does not make them any less genuine, since an operant is defined by its relation to its consequences, not by whether it is voluntary or involuntary, or both, or whether the person is aware or not aware of the relation. A dynamic analyst might agree completely with this formulation, except that he would say that the symptoms (patterns) provide secondary gain (reinforcement). Secondary gain is defined by its relation to such consequences, and not by whether or not the distress is genuine, or whether the contingency relation is or is not available to the conscious mind. The dynamic therapist would add that the primary gain derives from the role of the symptoms in defending against anxiety. He might ultimately concentrate on the primary gain and on eliminating the conflict in accord with a pathological orientation.

In effect, the dynamic analyst goes beyond the ecology of the symptoms and their secondary gain and delves into individual history for a fuller picture. A behavior analyst would also go beyond the ecology of the patterns and their maintenance by marital consequences and delve into individual social history for a fuller picture. Perhaps her husband's intense involvement has become so potent a reinforcer because she went through a protracted period when he almost completely ignored her. Stated otherwise, prolonged deprivation is involved.

Now, however, the tables have been turned: he is totally attentive to her. Indeed, if she starts to improve, he immediately slackens his intense concern. The operant appears to be the only possible way for her to get his attention. It is dramatic, and she is suffering acute distress, but this kind of "heroism" (Goldiamond, 1975) seems to be her only possible resort, given her circumstances and social history. Atypical contingencies have shaped atypical patterns. The constructional approach to be used will not be devoted to eliminating this pattern—it is highly useful. Instead, effort will be devoted to working with her to produce repertoires which will provide the marital involvement which is legitimately hers by means which also will permit her to return to the professional work she enjoys, permit them both to have a social life, and permit her to go out by herself as she did before, and so on. The strategy suggests working with her husband to produce repertoires whereby he learns to "read" his wife's patterns (see Goldiamond and Dyrud, 1967b). The normal contingencies of everyday life may then govern their communication.

Needless to say, more could be stated about each of the participants in this scene. But this could be done from a constructional orientation as well as a pathological one. It must be reiterated that constructional is not being equated with behavioral, nor pathological with dynamic. Behavioral approaches can be pathological in orientation, and dynamic approaches can be constructional in orientation. Indeed, a dynamic therapist might aim toward many of the goals just ascribed to an operant contingency orientation. He might simply use a different language (secondary gain, supportive therapy) to describe what is going on. Ultimately, however, the formulation of the cases will differ, as will their dispositions. Anyone who examines case descriptions in what is at present the prevailing formulation will note that they are long on pathology, on describing how things are wrong and how they went wrong. Indeed, the classifications themselves are pathologically based. They are short on strengths, the history of strengths, what and how to *construct.* (For a more extended discussion, see Goldiamond, 1974.)

This chapter will present a delivery system for intervention and research which is constructional. It has been developed and assayed with a wide variety of clients and problems in a clinic run by the Department of Psychiatry of the University of Chicago. A major aim of the approach is successful intervention. However, this is done within the context of continuing research.

Any constructional program can be analyzed in terms of the four elements common to programmed instruction. These are:

1. *Target, or outcome.* This is stated in terms of what will be established or constructed. It must be stated explicitly, that is, in observables, so that its attainment can be assessed.

2. *Entering repertoire.* This is the extant repertoire which is relevant to such construction. Since this repertoire will serve as a starting point to build on, it is stated in terms of repertoires available.

3. *Change procedures.* These are procedures designed to alter the repertoires from those presently available to produce those desired. The effort is directed toward producing such changes by means of programming built on continual success.

4. *Maintaining variables.* Typically, progression through

the program is maintained by the consequence of delivery of the next steps in the program. This consequence reinforces appropriate behavior and facilitates attaining the target specified by the program. Of course, the target itself has to be important to the client. This implies that if (a) attaining the outcome produced by the program is critical to the person, and (b) progression through the program brings the person closer and closer to his desired goal, then (c) no extrinsic reinforcement, such as tokens or candy, need be used. Presentation of the next step contingent upon mastery of the preceding step will be the consequence which maintains continued progression.

What keeps the client going through the program is getting what he came for. Accordingly, the approach is highly individualized. The outcome is set through negotiation between client and therapist; both must agree. The current repertoires relevant to the outcome will, of course, differ from one client to another, even when the outcomes desired seem to be identical. Clients with the same problems have different social histories which will be used differently to help attain these outcomes. The starting points will also be mutually established. They will be aimed toward the next subgoal to produce the changes desired. If the program is skillfully handled, the cient's repertoires or ecology, or both, will increasingly approach his desired ends. The critical consequences which maintain this progression are to be found in the ecology outside. However, while the therapist may help the client change his behavior to meet the needs set by the ecology, the preferable solution may be to change that ecology, or perhaps do both.

In all events, the therapist helps the client clarify what he is after and the means of obtaining it, if this is what both agree to. The complexity of the situation will be evident if one considers the couple discussed above. At the present moment they are in an interlocking control system. He maintains her dependent behaviors by the differential reinforcement he dispenses. He is attentive and concerned when she is infirm, and neglectful when she is well. It might be said that he is producing and maintaining the infirmity. However, he is behaving in this manner because if he is inattentive when she is even slightly infirm, her infirmities escalate. Accordingly, it might be said that she is requiring and maintaining his patterns, through the differential negative reinforcement she dispenses (that is, his concern is under avoidance control). They are both paying a high cost for this mutual control.

Each partner must learn to analyze his (her) own contingencies, and to change these by changing his (her) own behavior first. Effective behavior change will then serve to maintain and extend the partner's changed behaviors. As stated elsewhere (Goldiamond, 1969, p. 225):

To establish and maintain . . . control over his own behavior requires *insight* by the patient into the contingencies and consequences governing his own behavior, as well as his ability to control and manipulate these variables. Such self control over complex behavior requires the patient to observe and relate his behavior to other events, and to bring to bear upon such relations a body of effective procedures which change them. He is to *discover* which variables are relevant to his own behavior by recording and analyzing the data he has collected; he *changes* his behavior by developing and applying appropriate programming procedures."

As Skinner noted earlier, when a person takes an action, such as planning a course of action, he is controlling himself "precisely as he would control the behavior of anyone else through the manipulation of variables of which behavior is a function" (Skinner, 1953, p. 228). These statements are paralleled, among others, by Kanfer and Phillips (1970), who speak of "self regulation," and by Watson and Tharp (1972), who speak of "self modification." Further readings are to be found in the collection by Goldfried and Merbaum (1973) and in a recent overview and analysis by Thoresen and Mahoney (1974).

The task of casework in this orientation is to help the client develop procedures useful in specifying the changes *he* wants, in analyzing *his* current life situation (his person-contingency ecology and as much history as needed), and in developing procedures which produce these changes. The therapist functions as consultant who helps the client design *his own* program of intervention to produce the changes *he* desires. In the course of this analysis the client makes explicit those variables

controlling his behavior and sets up a plan, a program, to mod-
ify his behavior. Consultation is gradually phased out. Thus
more of the client's life comes under his own control, hence
the title "self control" and the rationale of the approach.

AN OVERVIEW

The major instruments developed by the author for this purpose, and utilized in the program, include: (1) the Self Control
Questionnaire, used initially to help assess the four program elements as they apply to the client; (2) the contract; (3) different
logs and record-keeping procedures; (4) program work sheets
used weekly to evaluate outcomes; and (5) client work sheets
and other supporting data.

These instruments can be classified, more conventionally,
as they relate to: (1) intake and assessment; (2) the actual interchanges involved in intervention, here designated as programming; and (3) the termination and follow-up phases. Before discussing the instruments in detail, it may be worthwhile
to present an overview of these three phases, as the setting in
which the instruments are applied.

THE BEGINNING PHASE: INTAKE AND ASSESSMENT

Although study and assessment go on throughout the contacts,
the process is emphasized during the first phase. After a period
of study and assessment, which may take place during the first
interview or after a few interviews, client and consultant jointly
determine the goals of the interventions, the terminal repertoire. This is what the client would like to see happen when the
therapy is successful. It is also what the consultant can work
toward. He may be instrumental in helping to sort out realistic
from unrealistic goals. However, the formulation of final goals

is a joint process, and it is always formalized in a written contract. The purpose of the contract is to make explicit the outcomes toward which the program is directed, and what is required on both sides to attain these outcomes. Such attainment will signify to the client the termination of the program or therapy sessions. If the outcome is produced, the client has attained what he came for. For the consultant-caseworker, such attainment suggests that procedures appropriate to attainment were utilized.

If these are to occur, it is necessary that outcomes be expressed in objective, identifiable, and observable terms. Directness and forthrightness can be *very* reassuring, especially to those clients who are anxious or who may have an unclear idea of what is involved in a therapeutic relationship. Much research has shown that most individuals do *not* have a clear idea of what is involved, what will be asked of them, what they will be expected to "do," and what the intervener is going to do. "Magical" changes are often expected. This manifest structuring of the therapeutic process is sometimes initially disconcerting to those clients who have had previous therapy, especially of the types in which expectations and roles are not clearly defined. However, these clients "catch on" quickly.

As with any contract, it is signed by each party. The contract may be changed or renegotiated at any time only by joint agreement of the client and the caseworker. The client's right to self-determination is respected.

If the client has rights in the situation, so too does the caseworker, since he must assent to the contract. He need not accept terms which in his judgment are unethical, illegal, contratherapeutic, or otherwise objectionable. The contract is between two consenting adults, both of whom will benefit by its fulfillment.

Some clients often have "hidden agendas." They might complain of phobias, obesity, frigidity, and some behavioral deficit, conditions widely known to be treated by behavior therapists. These are occasionally used by anxious clients as "admission tickets" to behavioral clinics. The task is to find out what is the desired outcome, what is the real problem.

Signing of the contract follows an assessment period. This includes an initial interview in which a structured questionnaire is used. The questionnaire is designed not only to obtain information on the four elements of the program, but for the client to learn what the examiner considers important, how he will go about it, and so on. Accordingly, not only does the worker learn about the client, but the client learns about clinic procedures, and these are made explicit to the client.

The interview is followed by an assessment in which the caseworker tries to make "sense" of the interview, that is, to obtain a coherent picture of the client. The client is viewed as a person who has developed behavioral styles which have been highly functional for him and have obtained his desired outcomes, given his resources, social history, and ecology. The very success of these patterns may underlie his present difficulties. While these operants are still reinforced (typically on an intermittent schedule), they are exceedingly costly, either through aversive control applied by others, or because their high response cost keeps him from attaining other goals which are also important, or for other reasons which jeopardize him. A tentative program is devised, and the rationale for it is given.

The assessment is time-consuming, since it requires planning in advance the outcomes to work toward, the procedures to be harnessed, and the support to be mustered, but the effect is to assure the client that his problems are being given serious attention. The contract can provide this assurance to the client.

THE MIDDLE PHASE: PROGRAMMING AND EVALUATION

The purpose, or function, of the program is to enable the client to use his strengths (utilize his current relevant repertoire) to attain his goals (attain his terminal repertoire). The criterion for success of intervention is quite clear. Was the terminal repertoire reached, or was it not? If it was reached, the intervention was successful. If it was not, it was not. If the repertoire was partially reached, the intervention was partially successful and the contract should be renegotiated. The process is clear, overt, and there is full accountability.

Evaluation goes hand in hand with programming. A number of written report forms (called "logs") supplement the client's verbal reports and the worker's (and client's) observations. One virtue of written reports and graphs is that both worker and client chart where the client is when he begins and follow progress thereafter. These verbal reports and the various logs and records kept by both client and worker provide a continuing monitoring of the process. Through the records client and worker can gauge, appraise, and assess the client's progress, from the gathering of data for use as a baseline to their use in charting and gauging progress.

THE END PHASE: TERMINATION AND FOLLOW-UP

The final phase consists of termination and follow-up. Followup is an essential part of the casework process as well as being necessary for research and evaluation purposes. Concern for the welfare of the client does not end at the end of programming, but involves follow-up and maintenance of therapeutic gains in the referent behavioral ecology.

Termination is a complex matter. It occurs when the objectives (the terminal repertoire) have been reached and/or the contract has been filled to the mutual satisfaction of client and worker. (Unplanned termination, however, is a different matter.)

There is another criterion central to the model. The client should learn to analyze his own contingency relations and to formulate intervention plans to attain his goals. This knowledge may equip the client with a set of analytic tools, or tools for "insight" into the relation of his behavior to that of others, for future use. For example, parents whose program has been centered on changing their own repertoires in order to bring about improvement in the behavior of a problem child, often transfer the analysis to their relations with other members of the family, to gain a more pleasant home atmosphere all around. Relations with other members may not have been a part of the original program. Where the client is to learn these skills by the time he terminates, self-programming becomes part of the terminal repertoires of intervention.

THE INITIAL INTERVIEW AND QUESTIONNAIRE

An interview in which a questionnaire is used does more than simply obtain information. It conveys to the subject messages concerning the approach, attitudes, and expectations of the interviewer. This is especially critical when the interview is a prelude to a relationship as important as extended psychotherapy. Modeling, imitation, instruction, affect—all the terms that can be applied to a relationship [1] between two people—enter, of course, into psychotherapy and counseling, and this access begins during the initial interview. This is when intervention starts.

The approach presented stresses explicit recording and observation of events, to facilitate the analysis of contingency relations. The language (categories) which directs what will be observed and recorded has developed out of a laboratory tradition whose investigators have operated within a scientific context of public agreement, replication, and verification.

One of the aims of the interviewer is to give the client confidence that he can assume control over the solution to his own problems. What the client may interpret as failure and deficit on his part the therapist may actually interpret as signs of success and strength. For example, a nagging mother may consider herself ineffective in changing the behavior at issue. However, she may thereby be successfully reinforcing noncompliance, which she discovers when she devotes this amount of attention to behavior she desires. Therapists who employ transactional analysis have noted how difficult it often is to get patients to indicate their strengths, or what is good about them. This difficulty is not necessarily a sign of malfunction. Rather, it suggests that the patient is in tune with a culture

[1] For a further discussion of relationship see Chapter 7.

that is heavily oriented pathologically and has applied this orientation to himself (Goldiamond, 1974).

The initial interview is centered on the structured questionnaire which follows. The questionnaire, which takes about one and one-half hours to administer, will be discussed section by section.[2] Sentences and phrases which are in parentheses are intended as notes to the interviewer.

The items are designed to obtain information, *not* merely to be read word by word. The wording is suggestive; any other wording or ordering which produces the same consequences may be substituted. The questionnaire is in seven sections, plus an introduction. Each series of questions is introduced by a brief statement about the purpose of the questions.

CONSTRUCTIONAL QUESTIONNAIRE

(The purpose of these questions is to obtain information; hence their wording is to be tailored to the occasion.)

INTRODUCTION

I am going to ask some questions to help us both understand what it is that we should work toward.

The questions have three purposes:

First, we'll need information to help acquaint us with you.

Second, from the questions people ask, you can learn things about them, so this should help you learn about our approach.

Third, to see how we're progressing, we need records, and befores and afters. This is a kind of "before" on how you see things now, and what aims you want now, so please speak up.

QUESTION 1. OUTCOMES

I am going to ask you a group of questions about our goals. You are here because you want certain changes to occur, or want something else.

a) *Presented outcome:* The first of these is: Assuming we were successful, what would the outcome be for you?

---

[2] The questionnaire form discussed here is the author's revision (dated March, 1974) of an earlier version, dated February, 1970. The earlier version was the one used in the Smith case in Chapter 4 and in the Johnson case in Chapter 5. The chief difference is in the added section spelling out the precise nature of the reinforcers in the client's ecology. The illustration of the Martians is optional, as noted. As also noted, the specific phrasing of all the questions is optional. The interviewer should use the phrasing most natural to him.

b) *Observable outcome:* What would others observe when the successful outcome was obtained?

Alternate or added form: Now, this may sound silly, but suppose one of these flying saucers is for real. It lands, and 2,000 little Martians pour out. One of them is assigned to observe you—your name was chosen by their computer on some random basis. He lands some time after L-Day—Liberation Day from your problems—and follows you around invisibly. He records his observations, and these are put on IBM (Interplanetary Business of Mars) cards. Their computer will decide on the basis of the sample of 2,000 Earthlings they have, what their disposition toward Earth should be. What does he observe?

c) *Present state:* How does this differ from the present state of affairs?

d) *Example:* Can you give me an example?

QUESTION 2. AREAS CHANGED, UNCHANGED

The next group concerns things in your life which are going well, and things which are not.

a) *Areas unchanged:* What's going well for you now, and what areas of your life would not be affected by our program?

b) *By-products:* What areas other than those we'd directly work on would change?

QUESTION 3. CHANGE HISTORY

This next series concerns your efforts to change things.

a) *Present attempt:* Why start now? How come?

b) *First attempt:* When did it first occur to you to try to change? What was going on? What did you do? How did it come out?

c) *Intervening attempts:* What did you do then? What was going on? How did it come out? [Series continues until present.]

QUESTION 4. ASSETS

The next series is concerned with the strengths and skills you have that we can build on. No one starts out from scratch.

a) *Related skills:* What skills or strengths do you have which are related to what you'd like to program?

b) *Other skills:* What others do you have?

c) *Stimulus control:* Are there conditions when the present problem is not a problem?

d) *Relevant problem-solving repertoire:* In the past, what related problems did you tackle successfully? What related programs did you succeed in? How?

e) *Other problems solved:* What other problems did you tackle successfully? How?

f) *Past control:* Did you once have mastery of the present problem area? If so, when, and under what circumstances? Any idea of how?

QUESTION 5. CONSEQUENCES

I am going to ask some questions about effects produced, and effects you'd like to produce.

a) *Symptom reinforcer—positive:* You've heard of the proverb, "It is an ill-wind that blows no good." With regard to some advantages that might have "blown your way," has your problem ever produced any special advantages or considerations for you? Please give specific examples (in school, job, at home).

b) *Symptom reinforcer—negative:* As a result of your problem, have you been excused for things—or from things—that you might not be otherwise?

c) *Symptom cost:* How is your present problem a drag, or how does it jeopardize you? [Note: Omit if answered in 3a. Why start now?]

d) *Possible behavioral reinforcers:* What do you really like to do, or would like to do? Is there anything that really sends you?

e) *High-probability behaviors:* What do you find yourself doing instead (or getting instead)?

f) *Social reinforcers:* Who else is interested in the changes you're after?

g) *Past social reinforcers:* What people have been helpful in the past? How did they go about it? How did you obtain this from them?

QUESTION 6. COMPLETION

Is there anything we left out or didn't get enough about? Was there something we overlooked—or made too much of? Are there any impressions you'd like to correct?

QUESTION 7. TURNABOUT

We have asked you a lot of questions. Are there any questions you'd like to ask of us? Any comments? Anything you'd like to know about our goals, or approach?

INITIAL INTERVIEW: SERIES 1. OUTCOMES

As is evident from the introductory statement, the aim here is to ascertain possible terminal repertoires or targets in terms of a program. This is the first requirement.

Question 1a: Presented outcome. The current repertoire with which clients present themselves for treatment is seldom a positive one. Clients are usually prepared to describe how "sick" they are *now* and how difficult their problems are *now*. They have often experienced failure.

Some clients may respond with positive outcomes, but these are stated in terms which make it difficult to visualize what is required. Everyone knows what it is like to be "happier," to have "a stronger ego," a "happier marriage," a "happier child," to "be doing better at work," but what contingencies specify this is difficult to ascertain. For example, for Mr. Miller, a "happier marriage" means going out with his wife five times a month in mutually satisfying activities, and "healthier children" means spending at least thirty minutes each day with his child in similarly satisfying activities. For Mr. West, a "happier marriage" might mean agreeing on religious differences, and "healthier children" might mean children who do not demand attention.

If, on the other hand, the client pours out problems to be eliminated rather than outcomes to be gained, then this is respected and accepted as his current presenting repertoire, or "starting where the client is."

Question 1b: Observable outcome. This question is intended to produce outcomes which can be constructed, targets to be established rather than eliminated, which are explicitly stated. Either the first or second form may be used. In either form, this question often turns out to be very difficult for clients to answer. The interviewer must often prompt and encourage the client to make this translation from eliminative globals to positive specifics.

One example of an individual's goal might be, "I would be good on my job." This is difficult to ascertain. If phrased in terms of "others observing," though, he might say, "Others would see me get to my job at nine in the morning and leave at five; they might see me doing *x* or *y* or *z* during the course of the day. They would see me getting raises and promotions and so forth."

If a client says, "I would be happy," this is difficult to pinpoint. The Martian is handy here. One client, when asked to elaborate in terms of what an observer would see, said that it was self-evident. However, the (ignorant) Martian saw him walking down the street and heard him singing. He saw him with a grin on his face doing this or that activity.

The client might say, "I'd be better," or use some other

comparative form. However, the newly arrived Martian "didn't see you before. What does he observe that you define as 'better'?"

Question 1c: Present state. Since the question is closely related to the repertoires typically associated with treatment, it often opens floodgates. For example, one drug addict answered: "My sisters and I get into arguments over children and other things. . . . I'm drinking heavy, two or three pints of wine, shacking up. I get depressed. I'm on methadone, but I'm not clean. I take nerve pills. . . . Librium when I'm not drinking." Her answer to the "Presented outcome" (1a) had produced a typical response: "I'd stop taking drugs and I'd be clean off methadone." Her answer to question 1b had produced observables: "I'd be a housewife, in my own home. I'd be working, too, in beauty culture. I'd find a nice husband—a different one." Her answer to question 1c gave a clearer picture of the current problematic state of affairs.

Question 1d: Example. This question is a probe, designed to facilitate answers to the previous question; it may not be necessary for the interviewer to ask this question if he receives an adequate answer to the previous question. (Probes, encouragement, reflections—the standard interview techniques—are used whenever necessary to further the process of the interview.)

   If the client indicates a range of goals, the interviewer may ask him to specify present states and examples for each.

INITIAL INTERVIEW: SERIES 2.
AREAS CHANGED, UNCHANGED

The second series of questions contributes to the current state of affairs, the "current relevant repertoire." These questions help differentiate the areas in which the client is experiencing difficulties from the areas in which he is *not* experiencing difficulties.

Question 2a: Areas unchanged. Question 2a was answered as follows by a young man who had serious problems with girls: "I'd still be a student. I'd maintain my interests in music, art, and literature, but there would be more time available for them." He answered question 2b (areas changed) as follows: "I might be more aware of what I'm doing. I'd be more stable emotionally. I'd waste less time on girls. I never realized that it was this bad until I got my failing grades. Chasing girls never used to affect my grades in college [as an undergraduate], but now it's in the way scholastically."

Many clients are so deeply troubled that they tend to overlook the fact that there *are* areas that are going successfully. This is especially true of parents with "problem" children. Some clients are quick to grasp this; others need a great deal of encouragement and support from the therapist in order to state their strengths. It is interesting that in American culture many people think it is "bad form" to talk about one's strengths. They fear that it may be mistaken as boasting. When discussion of strengths is placed in the proper context of assessing strengths as assets which can be used in a program, the client often relaxes and is able to speak about them.

The question may serve yet another purpose. It may indicate to the therapist what areas he should stay out of. One man who came for help to quit smoking indicated that he did not want to discuss his relations with his wife, although he felt that she was implicated. This was respected.

Question 2b: By-products. The answers here often suggest hidden agenda or other areas, including reinforcers, which might be considered. With regard to hidden agenda, a female college student who came for treatment of a phobia answered that she'd be "going out with boys and getting along with girls my own age." An additional reinforcer was suggested by a diet case who reported he would be able to play basketball again.

INITIAL INTERVIEW: SERIES 3.
CHANGE HISTORY

The purpose of the third series of questions is to obtain a history of attempts to solve the problem. This history of interventions should be differentiated from the history of problems, although the history of problems is often given and it may be solicited in addition to the intervention history. What are the circumstances surrounding his seeking help now, and why is he seeking help from this particular approach?

It is common for many clients to have made previous and obviously unsuccessful attempts to change certain behaviors and problematic situations. These attempts are regarded as strengths; the clients are informed that they had perceived a problem which was beyond their scope, and had tried to get help to solve it.

The questions related to circumstances are designed to help visualize the patterns as operants which function to produce consequences. As Azrin notes, instead of asking, "Why is the man an alcoholic?" one might ask, "Why isn't everyone an alcoholic?" The difference may be in the conditions under which drunkenness and sobriety are reinforced. Instead of "curing" the alcoholic a worker might try to replicate the situations in which people are not alcoholics (Hunt and Azrin, 1973).

The therapist, of course, is interested in the more traditional questions, too. Is this particular kind of treatment the most appropriate for this person? Perhaps another kind of therapeutic intervention is indicated. Are there physical complications? To what extent are medical personnel and medical procedures to be used? Are there indications that a physical examination is needed? Access to medical consultation and continuing medical supervision of cases in which there are complicating organic factors is a necessity. Similar precautions are indicated whenever any of the tranquilizing drugs are used. Expressions of depression accompanied by suicidal impulses immediately suggest intervention under controlled situations where constant observation is possible, such as a hospital ward.

INITIAL INTERVIEW: SERIES 4. ASSETS

The fourth series of questions is designed to obtain the current relevant repertoires expressed in terms of available strengths and skills. The client is often "thrown" by the question and prompts have to be given. People are often so overburdened by problems that their vision, understandably, is blocked by the overwhelming presence of the problems. Further, this line of questioning conflicts with role expectations of illness.

This series of questions supplies answers useful in assessing current relevant repertoires. For example, in response to question 4a, related skills, one young man who was shy with girls stated that he could carry on a conversation "once the ice was broken." The problem became redefined immediately from one of lacking conversational skills with girls to one of possessing skills once the conversation was initiated. The programming task here was the development of initiative repertoires. Other examples are sense of humor, ability to think abstractly, complete competence with the technical aspect of computer programming (this for a young man who was having difficulties with career stagnation as a programmer), presentable dress and appearance.

In answer to repertoire question 4b, other skills, a stutterer answered, "I enjoy sports, play balalaika, can carry a tune, played drums in a soul band back at school." The relevance of these repertoires to a constructional program is evident.

The repertoire question 4c, stimulus control, asks, in essence, if the problematic behavior is at any time under stimulus control. The young man who was shy with girls said that conversation with girls was no problem when he was in a group. The computer programmer said that he had many fewer problems on the night shift when there were fewer people there.

INITIAL INTERVIEW: SERIES 5. CONSEQUENCES

The intent here is to ascertain reinforcers, positive and negative, which maintain the present patterns, and the costs of these patterns. Either question 5a, symptom reinforcer—positive or 5b, symptom reinforcer—negative may yield a prompt answer. A woman with dizzy spells reported that her husband was especially solicitous when she had such spells. A stutterer reported that stuttering often got him "off the hook, and people generally stop nagging me to answer when I stutter."

Question 5c, symptom cost, occasionally yields totally new information. A patient hospitalized for continual vomiting and anorexia reported that she loved to ski, and this led to a hitherto unnoticed area. She had won a women's championship.

This series of questions was not in use when the clients reported in Chapters 4 and 5 were interviewed.

INITIAL INTERVIEW: SERIES 6 AND 7. COMPLETION AND TURNABOUT

The last two groups of questions are designed to terminate the formal fact-gathering section of the initial interview and to begin discussion of the approach and the terms of the contract, to begin the process of programming, most generally with the gathering of formal baseline data. The programming aspect of the process will be elaborated later in this chapter.

Question 6, completion, serves as a further probe, as a "catch-all" question to fill in the gaps. The manifest content of the question is quite apparent. Follow-up interviews with clients, after intake interviews in agencies, have revealed that many people "forget" important matters that they remember after they have left the interview, or did not come out with because of some inhibition. All of us have had the experience of visiting a physician and remembering later that we forgot to ask some question. It may be that what is "forgotten" may be as important as what is said. It is best to start the process with maximum information. Both client and consultant are free to probe, and the client is free to "correct" any matter he has not stressed sufficiently or that he believes has been overstressed.

The questions in group 6 lead to those in group 7, in which the client is encouraged to seek information from the worker about clinic procedures. Usually the responses to question 7, turnabout, are: "What happens now?" "How does it work?" "How long does it take?"

Many clients, especially those who have had no previous psychotherapeutic experience, do not have a clear idea of what actually goes on during a "therapeutic interview." Some clients expect the therapist to start giving advice immediately. Some clients believe that the interview will be less than thirty minutes long, and many clients believe that the course of therapy will take not longer than five sessions (Garfield and Wolpin, 1963).

An orientation period is a good idea in *any* kind of therapy. Research has shown that those who *do* receive some orientation, whether in groups or through role-induction interviews, tend to stay in therapy longer and, on a number of indices, to profit more from being in therapy (Goldstein, 1973). An orientation to operant therapy is often a necessity because of the vast amount of misinformation and misconception that exists in both professional and lay communities on the nature of applied behavior analysis.

Other illustrations of the use of the questionnaire are provided in the initial report (Goldiamond, 1974).

PROGRAM DECISIONS AND ANALYSIS

The contract will specify the goals of therapy and the expectations of both parties in the transaction. Defining the goals is, of course, the outcome of a decision process. Decisions require information, and it is the purpose of the initial interview to provide that information. While the initial interview may suffice for most cases, it may sometimes take several sessions before the worker can feel safe in suggesting goals. The amount of information required or provided will, of course, depend on the client, the caseworker, the ecology of the client's behavior, the instruments used, among other factors. For example, a particular outcome may be highly desirable, but the ecological resources and the client's repertoires may suggest that, within the time available, more modest outcomes should be chosen. In all events, sooner or later, a decision must be made.

Typically, a caseworker puts together the information collected and tries to draw a coherent picture of the client's current situation, how things got that way, a diagnosis of the patient, and suggestions for disposition. Such descriptions are often long on pathology, but extremely short on treatment. A constructional presentation may also be used to draw a coherent picture of the client's current situation, and how things got that way. However, it is extremely long on treatment and short on pathology. This does not mean that history or diagnosis is minimized, but the history is instead a history of the client's strengths. What is conventionally regarded as pathology may often be interpreted as successful coping—albeit at a price. The diagnosis is in terms of the class of programs (rather than class of pathologies) that is required for achieving therapeutic goals.

An outline useful in making a constructional presentation explicit is presented below.

CASE PRESENTATION GUIDE

A. Introduction
  1. Identifying information
     Include a brief description of the client and a few qualifying statements which are relevant to what follows.
  2. Background for the program
     Use A3 as the resolution toward which this presentation is directed. Weave in various items from questionnaire and other sources to present a coherent picture of a person functioning highly competently, given his circumstances and implicit or explicit goals, and personal and social history. Infer how symptom may have been shaped and its functional history.
  3. Symptom as costly operant
     Infer how, as a result of A2, the patterns shaped and reinforced up to now are now too costly or otherwise jeopardizing the client. Infer what reinforcers are presently maintaining patterns, sources, and type of jeopardy and its source. This should be brief and simply stated as the logical outgrowth from A2, which presented in somewhat more detail what led up to this.
B. Tentative program directions
  1. Outcomes which seem reasonable as targets
  2. Evidence for each of these
     a) Relation to reinforcers maintaining symptom

              b) Likelihood of producing additional reinforcers
              c) Feasibility of substitution for jeopardizing symptom
              d) Relation to present repertoires
                  (1) Personal
                  (2) Environmental and available
       3. Feasibility (cost, resources)

C. Current relevant repertoires

      1. General, for program-recording requirements:
          a) Analytical; types of relations explained
          b) Recording repertoires
      2. For each of targets recommended:
          a) Previous programs
          b) Current relevant repertoires: assay of current resources
          c) Social repertoires
          d) Environmental assets
          e) Maintaining and available consequences; accessibility. Symptom as reinforcement indicator

D. Change procedures: programming guides

      1. For program-recording and analysis of each target
          a) Analytic procedures to be used (texts, manual, discussions)
          b) Records to be kept; graphs
      2. For target areas
          a) Programs and repertoires in past to be transferred or modeled—how?
          b) Shaping, modeling, or transfer procedures for changing present repertoires
          c) Getting and shaping program cooperation from others; reinforcing such cooperation
          d) Ways current environmental resources might be used; facilities; possible social models
          e) Social and other possible support; analysis of symptom as successful operant

E. Maintenance guides

      1. Through program
          a) Records, graphs, other assignments
          b) Other possibilities
          c) Reliability checks
          d) Extraneous consequences
      2. Thereafter

F. Specific programs

      1. Available specific programs
      2. Staffing
      3. Other suggestions

CASE PRESENTATION GUIDE

A. INTRODUCTION

As noted, the symptom is considered as an operant which has become too costly or otherwise jeopardizes the patient. With regard to the couple concerned about the wife's phobias and immobility, paragraphs 1, 2, and 3 might indicate that the wife is a highly intelligent, resourceful, and well-trained woman with a keen interest in people and sensitivity to their behavior (she was effective in her personnel job) who is so competent that her husband had increasingly delegated more and more responsibility to her while he concentrated on managing his firm. He is a thoughtful person and is attentive to illness, and so on. A separate presentation might be made for her husband. His willingness to participate in family sessions indicates that he is concerned—the immobility might not have developed if he had not been. The costs to each are quite obvious.

B. TENTATIVE PROGRAM DIRECTIONS

The terminal outcomes are depicted as "tentative." Every effort is made to state the targets constructionally (but see Goldiamond, 1974).

   In the case of the couple, the major outcomes would be establishment of the communicative patterns already discussed. The reader can fill in much of A2 (evidence) from what has been presented.

C. CURRENT RELEVANT REPERTOIRES

Part 1 deals with the repertoires necessary to go through the program. Both husband and wife realize the importance of records. They are also aware of some of the causal factors. Indeed, they have quarreled over who was to blame, or who was the *cause.* (*She:* "It was your neglect." *He:* "But you enjoyed taking over.") Needless to say, this is not particularly helpful in straightening things out, but it often involves less response cost than finding out what *should* be done. This may hold for psychotherapeutic transactions as well as marital ones.

Part 2 discusses the current repertoires relevant to each of the particular goals presented in Section B. Note that paragraph 2*e* lists the symptom as a guide for isolating an important and usable reinforcer. In the case of the couple, the reinforcers are demonstrations of concern for each other.

D. CHANGE PROCEDURES

These are keyed to the current repertoires presented in Section C. They answer the "from here" part of "Where do we go from here?"

Part 1 specifies the types of records that might be used, as well as source material for a contingency analysis.

Part 2 would provide detailed means of successful change, including social supports.

E. MAINTENANCE GUIDES

Part 1 delineates the reinforcers which might be used to maintain the effort necessary for program advancement. Paragraph 1*a* deals with the intrinsic reinforcement of demonstration of progress—what is called "feedback." Paragraph 1*b* concerns reinforcing changes outside, as recorded in 1*a.* Since the record forms are filled out by the client, the necessity for paragraph 1*c* is evident. Finally, some consequences extraneous to the program might be harnessed.

Part 2 deals with carry-over and follow-up reinforcers. If the program has established the repertoires necessary in the patient's behavioral ecology, the program outcomes will be maintained. So far as possible, these should be planned in advance.

F. SPECIFIC PROGRAMS

Part 1 deals with other available programs and therefore need not be developed anew. The laboratory has developed special programs and instruments for establishing speech fluency (stuttering cases) and new eating patterns (obesity cases), to cite two. A Masters and Johnson program for sexual dysfunctioning cases is available elsewhere in the outpatient clinic. Of course, all programs are tailored to meet individual needs or requirements.

Part 2 makes explicit who will be involved, and Part 3 covers areas possibly neglected.

SUMMARY

Following this outline is quite time-consuming; it takes between three and six hours. One alternative is not to prepare such a report, but to improvise as one goes along. Although comparative studies have not yet been made, the time involved, both in working out the details and in the duration of treatment, may be far longer when one has only a vague therapeutic plan and improvises as one goes along.

THE CONTRACT

By this time, the contract is almost self-evident. The worker can state explicitly what the targets should be and what means might be used to attain them. These include the resources already available to the client. For the client, the contract is a different affair. The fact that the caseworker has done his "homework" in thinking through the case and its requirements may suggest that the client has chosen a competent professional. This is encouraging. Further, the discussion of goals and the procedures for their attainment often suggest the possibility of hope to the patient. Some patients, however, have had their hopes shattered in the past, and conclude that hope is lost (even though they have applied for treatment). In attempting to increase the patient's hopefulness, the beginning therapist is cautioned against overselling the approach and making it appear too simple. This may not only lead to false expectations (which may realistically be based on the caseworker's overzealous "sales pitch"), but may make progress more difficult, since the client may then expect an easy and rapid solution, and the work requirements necessary for advancement may undergo extinction. The fact that the task may not be easy, that it will require considerable effort and attention, should be made explicit in advance. Also, whatever progress is made may also be accompanied by reverses. However, a purpose of the recording system is to make explicit the conditions under which progress is made and the conditions under which reversals occur. Accordingly, to the extent that these conditions may be understood and changed, the outlook is cheerful, *provided records are kept.* "Rather than concentrating on what can go wrong, let's see how we can get things to go right. They may be little things, but we shall then be ahead of the game."

The contract is a voluntary agreement between at least two consenting adults (a child may sometimes be considered an adult for this purpose). The term "contract" is perhaps unfortunate, because one thinks of lawyers, legal documents, and other more impersonal transactions. The contract is not to be viewed in stilted legalistic terms, but as a *process.* The contract serves as a mutual clarification and specification of goals and expectations, a dynamic process that may undergo change as the therapy progresses.

Contracts are often renegotiated, for example, when a set of preliminary goals has been met and/or when there are new or other problematic areas in the life picture of the individual. With increased competence, the client often decides to "take on" problems that he was previously reluctant to take on. The therapeutic relationship established, the specification and concrete nature of the intervention mean that the goals of the process, as well as the process itself, are constantly being reexamined. The contract makes these goals overt. Objectives are stated explicitly.

The use of the contract as a therapeutic device has long been a part of the operant approach, and references to its use can be found throughout the operant literature. Sulzer, in an early article (1962, p. 271), states that "unless clearly explicated otherwise, the therapist is the agent of the patient and undertakes to teach only what is specifically determined jointly by the patient and the therapist." He adds: "Fulfillment of the psychotherapeutic contract is the sole criterion of success, and since each contract is unique, success may be determined only by study of the individual case" (p. 272).

There are a number of contract forms in use. The form developed for this program follows. Each agency and therapist may wish to experiment and devise their own to suit the needs of the particular practice situation.

CONTRACT

PART I

For the agreed-upon outcomes to be obtained, cooperation is required. The signatures below indicate that:

On your part, you agree   *On our part, we agree*

1. Appointments

Attend sessions we set up. If you find it impossible to attend, please notify us at least 24 hours in advance.

Keep appointments we set up. If we cannot meet them, we shall try to notify you the preceding week, barring emergencies.

2. Records *

You will be assigned a record book in which you will make regular entries.

We shall explain purpose of entries, analyze them regularly, and provide feedback.

3. Program requirements

You will try to fulfill various other specified assignments, as made.

We shall similarly explain purpose of assignments, analyze them, and provide feedback.

4. Research, training, and confidentiality

Data from your records can be useful for consultation with other staff members, training of staff, and research

We shall preserve the confidentiality of your records and take every precaution to insure that any data dis-

publications which help other professionals and thereby other clients. You consent to the use of such data for these purposes, with restrictions noted in Part II.

seminated are not identified with you, in accord with prevailing practice with medical and psychiatric records and research. Any other type of dissemination is specified in Part II.

5. Carry-over

Attainment of the desired outcome need not end our relation. Your cooperation in follow-up and its analysis is necessary.

We shall explain the type of follow-up required, your role, and provide feedback.

6. Regular Fees

Regular fees are required.

Conditions and personnel for our sessions and their analysis will be provided.

7. Additional charges

Additional charges for supplies, etc. may be made.

Supplies and other items will be provided as indicated by additional charges.

* Please note: Item 2, Records, is indispensable for attaining our objectives.

Renegotiation Clause: The requirements and goals are open for renegotiation at any time upon the request of either party, at which time any changes which are agreed upon will be entered into a new written contract, or written amendment.

Signed _____ Client   Signed _____ Consultant
                                   _____ Consultant

PART II

Current contingency requirements   *Goals: Terminal repertoires*

1. Appointments
    Time:
    Place:
    Telephone:
    Consultant:
    Monitor:
    Others:
2. Materials to be brought regularly
    Work sheets:
    Log, up-to-date:
    Graphs, from log:
    Objective outcome:
    Summary:
3. Other assignments
4. Types of dissemination agreed upon
5. Type of carry-over procedure

6. Fees
7. Additional charges
8. Other understandings

Agreed on:_____Date
_____Client
_____Consultant

    Part I of the contract lists the current contingency requirements, which state the commitments on the part of the therapist and the commitments on the part of the client. The reader should note that for every client requirement listed, there is a corresponding requirement for the social worker (consultant). The commitments on the part of the consultant, which are fairly self-explanatory, will be developed further in the course of this chapter. On his part, the client agrees to keep appointments, to keep records, to fulfill the program requirements, to cooperate in follow-up, and, if indicated, to pay fees and additional charges. He also explicitly consents to use of the material obtained.[3] The exact use is negotiated and specified in Part II.

    There is a renegotiation clause which stresses that the contract can be renegotiated at the request of either party, but that any changes must be mutually agreed upon.

    Part II is a statement of time of appointment, required materials, carry-over procedures, fees, and so forth. On the right side is the section for terminal repertoires. Space is provided for other assignments, type of carry-over, and other understandings (a time limitation might be noted here). The use to which the data are put (paragraph 4) must also be agreed upon, especially if they are to be disseminated beyond the clinic.

PRIORITIES IN THE PROGRAMMING PROCESS

With regard to the outcome itself, the presenting problem may not be the problem of most concern to the client; it may not even be the problem of immediate or highest priority. As part of

[3] The material is sometimes disguised and used for demonstration, training, and for research purposes.

the process of negotiating a contract, the client and the therapist establish a priority of goals toward which they will work. Of course, an individual may work on one or more goals simultaneously. However, the process of assessment and contract-signing entails the establishment of a twofold system of priorities. The first set of priorities is centered on urgency of solution. If there is a series of problems and one is life-threatening, then obviously this problem must be worked on first. One example was a woman who was referred by an internist for the treatment of emphysema. She was given six months to live if she did not stop smoking. There were other problems in the client picture which, of course, played into, and were connected with, the excessive smoking that caused the emphysema. However, reducing or eliminating smoking obviously took first priority.

The second set of priorities is defined by likelihood of attainment, from "easiest" to "most difficult." To continue with the example of a smoking problem, it is often easy to substitute other patterns for certain smoking patterns. For example, a man who smoked when he found meetings dull was able to substitute note-taking. Over the course of the week's cumulative curves, this substitution represented a perceptible drop of a hundred cigarettes a week. Reinforcement for program participation was thereby made immediate. More difficult tasks can be undertaken later, such as elimination of the cigarette with after-dinner coffee. Indeed, what often happens is that by the time such incidents are approached, they either cease being problems, or become paper tigers—that is, goals which are easy to accomplish.

WHO CONTRACTS WITH WHOM?

As a rule of thumb, the contract which is negotiated should be between those affected by its terms who were also involved in the negotiating process. Parents have at times requested treatment of their child. Unless the child is a party to the negotiation for something *he* desires, such "third-party" treatment is generally declined. Rather, the offer is made to train the parents so that *their* repertoires change. They become the clients for such change. If they behave differently, the child may react to them differently, and possibly in the direction they desire if the contingencies are such that they "earn" this.

Ethical problems are minimized by this approach. However, the prescription exemplified by a "shotgun" contract, in which two parties consent that something will be done with an unconsenting third, does raise ethical problems. These are especially relevant to institutions. A mental hospital, for example, may contract with a caseworker regarding treatment of patients. A school may contract to treat unruly children. However, in some cases these are unavoidable ethical questions. For example, one might be asked to do something *to* someone who is doing irreparable damage to himself. He may be thankful later that he was stopped. The fact that he is not a consenting party to a contract concerning himself, and which may use coercive means, raises ethical questions. However, if knowledge and means are available which will prevent irreparable damage, is it ethical not to apply them?

These ethical conflicts are not confined to the helping professions; they characterize many areas of life. The least that the therapist can do is to state the conflict explicitly and to provide the explicit information necessary for ethical decisions. Increasing ability to provide such explicit information is one of the major contributions of applied behavior analysis. It *can* contribute significantly to ethical intervention decisions and practices (Goldiamond, 1974 [4]).

INTERVENTION:
CHANGE PROCEDURES, AN OVERVIEW

The four major elements of a program are: (*a*) target, or outcome; (*b*) current relevant repertoire; (*c*) change procedures; and (*d*) maintaining variables. In a constructional program the

---

[4] See the discussion under "Self-determination" in Chapter 7.

target is a repertoire to be established, in contrast to a pathological program, in which it is a repertoire to be eliminated. Target outcomes are explicitly and objectively defined. The worker tries to ascertain what the client wants to change, and in what order, and specifically how he wants to change it. These questions are all related, ultimately, to the achievement of the terminal repertoire as mutually agreed upon in the contract.

A principal task of intervention is *to teach the client the logic of the approach and to teach him to be his own behavior analyst.* As the client learns the logic by analyzing his behavior, he may increasingly become more and more skilled in devising his own programs. The consultant and the client are engaged, not in the process of behavior change per se, but in the analysis of the behavior within the context of contingency relationships.

The point of intervention might be any problematic aspects of the individual's life situation as viewed within a behavior-contingency framework. While often intervention may be restricted to one point, at one time, interventions on several points simultaneously are possible and frequently occur.

When the client first comes to the office he wants help with some aspects of his social functioning, usually expressed in terms of alleviation of distress. By the end of the therapy he may have changed the behaviors and ecologies of his contingencies so that new contingencies are constructed, in line with the terminal repertoire specified in the contract, accompanied by the feelings related to such success. The time and effort needed to attain the terminal repertoire, or desired end state, depend, of course, on a number of factors, such as the nature of the terminal repertoire, the current relevant repertoire, the nature of the ecology of contingency relationships at the beginning of the therapy, the amenability to change of these ecological factors, and, of course, the adequacy and effectiveness of the program.

A number of therapeutic stratagems may be included in the program.

The choice of intervention stratagems is dictated by a

number of considerations: the initial interview provides a beginning lead into information that will point to areas which can be programmed and also to areas in which further information is needed. Ascertainment of the current relevant repertoire of the client enables the worker to assess the client's potential for change, his assets, his strengths (not emphasizing the deficits), upon which the client may be brought to the attainment of the terminal repertoire. Equally important, the initial interview provides information about those areas which are not programmed, those areas which are "left alone."

INTERVIEWS

The interview is a major tool of intervention. Discussions between caseworker and client also include analysis of the logs. Warmth, tact, understanding, support—all the attributes assigned such interviews—are necessary here as well. However, the therapeutic interview is not assigned the burden of therapeutic change. Rather, the caseworker is a consultant whose main effort is to interpret the data explicitly presented about events in the natural ecology. He is an active consultant whose recommendations may help the client obtain the reinforcers he considers necessary, and to expand other repertoires as well.

These instruments (logs, work sheets, and interviews) will be discussed below, as well as in the next two chapters, in which two case illustrations are presented. Currently, most interviews are held in the caseworker's office, although an increasing number of interventions are taking place in the natural setting—home, school, job, and other "real-life" settings. Consultation *in situ,* that is, within the natural environment, is one direction of this model, and increasingly the trend is for interventions to take place outside the conventional agency and office settings.

Tape-recording. Interviews are generally tape-recorded (sometimes videotaped) for a number of reasons. The first is for consultation with other staff. A second is that tape-recording the interviews provides a good training technique for a beginning therapist, since the tape is available for playback and for supervision. Moreover, experimentation has begun with the client's use of these tape recordings between sessions, and with videotape recording for use in modeling.

While tape recording has research possibilities, it poses some of the same problems for research as are posed by direct observation of interviews themselves. During the past six years of the clinic's existence, only one of over 140 clients has refused permission to allow tape recording.

The Monitor. An innovation that was initially intended to help with the tabulation and research aspects of intervention, but soon had a payoff for the intervention process itself, is use of the "monitor," a third person who sits in during the interview. Thus the usual intervention relationship is based on a triad. This is increasingly becoming less rare with the development of dual therapy (Flescher, 1970) and group and family methods of intervention (Liberman, 1970).

Traditionally, the presence of a monitor in the interview situation is unusual in social work. The primary objection has been that a monitor will inhibit the client and, furthermore, will violate the confidentiality of the relationship. However, such objections have simply not been borne out. The third person is introduced at the beginning of the program and his function and utility are fully explained. The monitor is introduced to the client as someone who is there to help with both the research and the therapeutic aspects of the case. Confidentiality is not violated if the usual safeguards of records and information are taken. Very few clients have objected to a third person in the interview. Those who have objected have, without exception, been individuals who have had long periods of prior treatment, generally psychoanalytic in orientation.

The chief function of the monitor is to help with the research aspects of the case. In general, he keeps a record of the interactions, according to whatever research plan is decided beforehand. Although he is involved in the process, the monitor is able to observe both the consultant and the client, and he often raises questions about the direction of the program and the procedures used which may not have been evident to the consultant.

Another important function of monitoring is its use in training therapists. The experienced therapist serves as a model for the inexperienced monitor, and, through postsession discussion and critique, the consultant's approach serves a didactic purpose. Needless to say, the "errors" or missed opportunities are also invaluable learning opportunities for the less experienced therapist. On occasion, this procedure has been reversed: the less experienced person serves as the therapist and the more experienced person as the monitor. The model, of course, is supervision of a teacher-to-be by an experienced schoolteacher. In the casework situation, presence of the supervisor right in the room need not occasion anxiety for the student, especially when an explicit contract between the student and the supervisor is made stating that the supervisor is there to assist the student attain his explicit outcome of developing specified program skills. Indeed, the supervisor can intervene and "bail out" the student, especially in the beginning. It is at this beginning stage of the process that pertinent, on-the-spot observations, suggestions, and clarifications from a more experienced therapist are most helpful.

In cases where such training is involved, the client is so informed. Any objections he might have to being assigned to a trainee rather than the professional are usually forestalled by noting that he is getting both the professional and a possibly fresh viewpoint.

Baselines. In order to trace change and to begin the process of analysis, the consultant needs to know how often something has been occurring, and under what conditions, *before* any intervention procedures are begun. The rate of behavior before intervention is called a *baseline.* Obtaining baseline information is a procedure associated with applied behavior analysis. The prescribed period in the program under discussion is a two-week period, although in pressing cases a shorter time may be used. In a few rare cases in which the situation seems complicated and there is no immediate threat to health, the baseline period may involve a longer period.

The necessity for baseline procedures is explained to clients as "our need for a record of the way things are so that we can evaluate what we do. The physician requires heart rate, blood pressure, and other readings before he starts, and so do we." This request is accepted by most patients, with no more fuss and bother than characterizes such record-keeping for physical purposes.

The length of baseline periods can be negotiated.

THE USE OF WRITTEN LOGS

Intervention revolves around written records of "outside-of-the-office" events, called "logs." The use of the logs has been generally accepted by clients, even those with minimal education and literacy. Their utility in the therapeutic process is explained to the client. The medical analogy is reiterated: the doctor keeps regular records, such as fever charts and so forth. Written logs, even if they only mention an incident, also serve as the trigger to set off a string of associations. The logs are the data for the interview, supplemented by what the client says.

The nature and variety of the logs are limited only by the needs of the situation, the reasonableness of the request (they should not take an excessive amount of client time, impose too great a response cost), and the imagination of the programmer and the client.

The logs may be either specific to a particular topography or they may be general. Which log is used depends, of course, on the nature of the program and its stage. Early in the sessions, the log requirement may be simple, but later it may become more complex.

Unless a continual recording is kept of a person's activities, any logs about him are necessarily samples of his life, his daily routines. The sample may be a time sample or an event sample or a combination of the two.

Some events are not comparable. One full-blown paranoid

episode may upset a family for a week, whereas ten minor incidents of an individual expressing suspicion, for example, may
have only transient effects. In such cases, comparisons in
terms of frequency counts would give a misleading picture.
Thus the client is asked to record those incidents *he* considers
as relevant in addition to fulfilling the therapist's requirements.
Sometimes, to facilitate the process and to help pinpoint the
problem, a kind of sampling procedure is instituted, such as
limiting observations to an arbitrary time period, such as the
last ten minutes of each day, or to a specific period, such as
dinnertime, or interactions at one place, such as work, or in the
bedroom of feuding marital partners.

The logs can be used to indicate program progression.
Clients are encouraged to compare recent logs with earlier
ones, either through direct examination of their file, or indirectly through graphs. Their importance for treatment is indicated by the fact that keeping logs is one of the conditions in
the contract. Sometimes a simple log is the first requirement,
and the use of a more complex log may be one of the subgoals
of the program. Clients have been generally cooperative in the
matter of keeping records. Interestingly, most of the resistance
to record-keeping has been on the part of therapists, especially
therapists trained in other methods of intervention. Detailed
comments on the logs are intended as one source of consultant reinforcement; preliminary research suggests that such
comment can serve this purpose. The literary ability of the
client is seldom an issue. Tape recorders have been used in
cases of near illiteracy.

The continual monitoring provided by the logs offers the
opportunity for an ongoing "fine-grain" analysis and evaluation
of the process. It also facilitates outcome evaluation. If a procedure has been prescribed, and it does not "work," this is important to know. Indeed, the very name of the approach, the
"applied behavior analysis or the experimental analysis of behavior," points to the close interweaving of the therapeutic interventions and constant evaluation.[5]

[5] Furthermore, the overt nature of the process and the ease of evaluation lend
themselves to accountability procedures, such as cost-benefit analyses. This

Initially, the worker may have to shape the logs and possibly model appropriate log-keeping until logs are produced that are of value to him. Of course, the utility of the logs depends to a great extent upon the guidelines, the amount of structure that is given in the instructions about the purpose of the logs. There have been some initial difficulties in a few cases in persuading frustrated authors that these were clinical logs and not Joycean autobiographies. Interestingly enough, very "disturbed" clients, who seemingly are clinically "out of contact," can keep useful records if attention to the entries is properly and quickly given, and if they are related to progression toward the terminal repertoire. Occasionally, monetary reinforcement has been necessary. Ideally, the major reinforcement would be the utility of the logs in the therapeutic process, as evidence to the client that he is continually changing.

The specific kind of log required will vary from case to case and often from time to time within cases, the nature of the log being changed to fulfill the requirements of the therapeutic information and of research. Many clients have record-keeping in their current repertoire, either as part of their jobs or as part of their lives. Many keep records, such as checkbooks, homework assignments (a dormant repertoire), and the like.

Space precludes extended discussion of the various logs used (see Goldiamond, 1974), and since they will be considered in greater detail in the two case presentations of the following two chapters, the present discussion will be limited to a few general characteristics.

Logs can be classified as exploratory logs, target behavior logs, and interaction logs. At times, more than one log is used simultaneously.

The *exploratory log* is just what the name implies. It is used in situations in which the problem needs further clarification and definition or when more detailed data on the frequency and rate of behavior are needed for diagnostic and remedial purposes. While client problems are sometimes specific, they

---

will be discussed in the final chapter. For a discussion of accountability in social work, see Schwartz (1970).

are at times worded in very general terms, and information is needed to supplement and clarify the information gained from the initial interview. In an exploratory log, the client might specify his activities hour by hour (or at more frequent or less frequent time intervals) and also specify conditions, who was there, and so forth. The exploratory log is a beginning log, a descriptive log which may be changed later to gain other specific information as soon as the therapist and the client get a closer idea of what is actually happening in the case, in terms of behaviors and/or controlling contingencies. Both problematic and nonproblematic situations are listed. The reader may see such a log in the case of Mr. Smith (Chapter 4).

The *target behavior log* is used initially when the target behaviors for intervention are clearly different from the nontarget behaviors. It is often used following a period of exploration utilizing exploratory logs. The target behaviors are defined, and if the controlling conditions are not clearly defined, this type of log is also useful in "zeroing in" on the controlling conditions.

The main purpose of this type of log is to determine the rate or frequency of the conditions of occurrence of the target behavior. Among the conditions under which the behaviors occur are those which are concurrent with the behavior, those which precede the behaviors at issue (the antecedent, or discriminative stimulus events), and those which follow the behaviors (possible consequences).

In situations in which the target behaviors (the problems) are fairly specific, the therapeutic intervention is often in the form of stimulus control over the behavior and/or some sort of change of consequences. With some problems (such as smoking, scratching, tics, overeating), the therapeutic strategy might be the installation and differential reinforcement of competing behaviors. For example, when the worker knows the length of time that elapses between emissions (occurrences) of the behavior (in technical terms, the interresponse time), the therapeutic strategy may be to lengthen the interresponse time by reinforcing competing behaviors or by changing the controlling conditions. In antismoking programs, for example, the amount of time between cigarettes may be increased, as one strategy. The intervention, of course, is not this simple. It is based on data from target behavior logs in which the client records, for example, the time when he smoked, where, who was there, the concurrent behaviors, the antecedents, the consequences, and so forth. The form would be changed for eating, although there would be some similarities.

The *interaction log* is used when the problems are basically problems of interpersonal relations. In these kinds of situations it is essential to obtain information on the actions of "significant others" in the client's social field (home, job). These data result in the "analysis of social transactions." Examples are marital conflict, interpersonal interactions on the job, social inadequacies, and stuttering logs (which will give information needed to compare situations in which the individual speaks fluently with those in which he stutters).

In some cases, problematic behaviors are behaviors which are being reinforced by significant others. These behaviors can be considered as operants, with the consequences of these behaviors (no matter how pathological) considered as meaningful to both the individual and these significant others.

A typical log for a marital or social interaction would have the first column state the time; the second, the setting; then "What I wanted," "What I did," "What he (she) did"; "What I then did"; then a column each for client comments and for consultant comments. This type of log was also used in the Smith case (Chapter 4).

In a typical interview, a client brings his records to the office and, after the usual greetings, the worker generally reads them aloud and analyzes them. The records are read aloud for several reasons, one being to reduce misunderstanding since not everyone's handwriting is legible. During the reading, the client may also fill in additional details of some of the contingencies surrounding an incident that is being analyzed, or the consultant may ask for amplification. Clues and ideas for further programming may also arise. Depending upon the kind of log used and upon the stage of therapy, the consultant and client may work their way through the entire log or, on certain occasions when a record is especially "rich," may spend the entire hour or a good portion of it in a depth analysis of only one or two incidents.

As the process goes on, the client does more and more of the analysis. The *client* reads the record, with the therapist holding a Xeroxed copy or listening and making notes. The therapist may analyze the incidents as they relate to the operant paradigm. For example, he may try to ascertain what factors, variables, contingencies are reinforcing a pattern of behavior which may be desired or undesired by the client. He may analyze the record to determine the antecedent conditions or the stimulus conditions that control the behavior. Furthermore, he may look for information about what is potentiating certain consequences.

The reading aloud is also part of a process whereby the worker overtly shapes both the keeping and the form of the records. Clients are also encouraged to bring a list of things they want to talk about.

Of course, the content or process of an actual session depends upon the client. The therapy sessions do not follow any rigid schedule or routine. A client may bring in problems that are not covered in the records; certain events may have been too upsetting for him to be put down on paper or may have been very recent; or he may not have completed the logs that week. However, most of the time the client brings in logs that are more than adequate for both intervention and research purposes. (This is always surprising to the new operant therapist.) The actual process of the interview, however, is directly and ultimately determined by the needs of the client, not the needs of the researcher or the intervener. It is hoped, of course, that the two will coincide.

Validity and Reliability of Logs. Some issues can be raised about keeping logs. These involve sampling bias, validity, and reliability. How do we know that the client is not simply shifting his selection of which transactions he reports? How do we know that he is not lying? How do we know that he is not distorting? Is the client merely reporting the same kinds of events differently and in accord with the demand characteristics of the consultant?

Verbal reports of behavior and consequences are as amenable to such determinants as are the more classic verbal reports of dream content, early childhood experiences, perceptions, and feelings. Both classes of reports can be influenced by the procedures of the therapist, whatever his persuasion. This means that the therapist can shape events (even if he is "passive"), and can get out what he puts in. Accordingly, construct validity based upon such reports will also depend on the shaping skill of the therapist-consultant, whether implicit or explicit. What is the difference between the two types of reports?

Reports of behavior, reactions by others, and conditions, although subject to the same invalidating control as reports of dreams, childhood experience, and past history, are subject, in principle at least, to validation. The consultant can institute "spot checks," phone calls, or other procedures (the principle having been agreed upon in advance) to validate the verbal reports sampled. Nonbehavioral reports of the type cited can not be so validated.

Determination of validity, sampling bias, and reliability is aided by some form of independent observation. This can be done by sending trained observers to the locale (home visits by the social worker), making telephone calls, interviewing significant others, comparing the independently prepared logs of two partners, and requiring a log of the programming session itself or of similarly monitored events. (The last-named procedure can also be deployed for reliability training.) Independent observation may enter into concurrent and predictive validity, but it is not required for construct validity. If a student actually put in the hours of studying that he reported during the semester, has his grade average at the end of the semester changed? It is helpful to stipulate, in advance, the appropriate logs, graphs, and other measures that would help in making internal validity and consistency checks.

It can be argued, of course, that sampling and validity do not matter; it is *what* the client chooses to report and *how* he reports it that are relevant. If, for example, the client's verbal behavior during sessions changes over treatment from deprecatory and depressing statements to nondeprecatory and optimistic statements, this may be significant, whether or not the referents for these statements have changed. Further, it can be argued that, if the determinants for such changes over time include the reinforcements, shaping procedures, response requirements, and other variables related to the explicit or implicit demand characteristics of the therapeutic setting, these are highly important. It may be important that the client is "trying to please" the therapist.

The fact that the referents in nonbehavioral reports cannot (at least, at present) be checked, thereby making the reports incapable of validation *in principle* does not imply that such reports should be dismissed from consideration. They can, like the contingency reports, be regarded as instances of verbal behavior, subject to control by all the variables governing verbal behavior. The procedures described can be used to record such reports and relate them to other events, including those that are amenable to explicit validation. Our procedures do not conflict with psychoanalytic and other "classical" approaches, nor were they intended to serve this purpose. They are research tools developed in accord with the requirements for explicitness of behavior analysis, and they may be useful for research relevant to other forms of analysis, since behavioral change and a change agent are common to them all.

Certainly the kinds of therapeutic encounter that depend upon the client's weekly recall of events that may have occurred as much as seven days earlier are notoriously inaccurate, for they are distorted, of course, by the passage of time. There is sufficient evidence that shows that retrospective data (data based on recall) are notoriously unreliable (Yarrow et al., 1964). Retrospective accounts are obviously biased by preconceptions and distortions, and such distortion generally increases directly in proportion to the time that has elapsed between the occurrence of an incident and its reporting during a therapy hour. This problem is not fully overcome by our procedures, but the requirement of daily recording cuts down the effects described. The requirements of specific categories often "refresh" the client's memory, as does the interview itself.

GRAPHS

Graphs are often helpful; their nature depends on the problem. In an eating problem, clients are asked to keep a weekly cumulative record of calories ingested. If the client sets 1,200 calories a day as his goal, a red line is drawn from 0–8,400 for the beginning and end of the week. If he ingests 1,400, 1,100, and 1,300 for the first three days, this is cumulated as 1,400, 2,500, 3,800, and so on. If his cumulative line goes above the red line he has not met his own goal; if it goes below, he has done better. Clients will often "save" calories right before an anticipated "binge." This is often done without benefit of behavioral advice, but the program makes this explicit.

Every effort is made to convert graphic recordings to constructional behaviors (the graph cited, rather than one of cumulative weight loss).

A CONTINGENCY ANALYSIS OF EMOTIONS

Many theories have been formulated to account for emotion, and to relate it to behavior. Some approach emotion from an evolutionary, developmental point of view, citing its functions in the survival of the organism. Others take a physiological point of view, focusing on the role of the autonomic and central nervous systems. Emotions have been considered to be a complex set of autonomic and skeletal responses, from which the practitioner makes inferences, and it has been argued that the emotional experiences of the client himself derive from such responses. This, in essence, is the James-Lange theory of emotions. It states that emotions are the experiential concomitants of such responses which, in turn, are the feedback from the behavior itself. This is reflected in the statement, "He threatens me; I hit him; therefore [the feedback from hitting], I am furious." This statement is in opposition to the more classic formulation, "He threatens me; I am furious; therefore, I hit him." Experimental distinction between the two formulations has been inconclusive, and other theories have been proposed, including physiological theories.

The position to be taken here is a contingency analysis. The formulation for the foregoing events might be that (1) a certain class of conditions (for example, being threatened by certain people), (2) had been successfully altered in the past (the people withdraw or shut up), by (3) aggressive behavior. Stated otherwise, when certain environmental contingencies occurred, then aggressive behavior was an operant which succeeded in altering these contingencies (operated on the environment). The person might then also have felt furious. For example, an attack may have been appropriate to eliminate a punitive childhood bully. It may not be appropriate to eliminate a punitive bureaucratic bully. The successful resolution by attack in the former case may also lead to anger in the second, since the contingency seems similar. However, lashing out at one's supervisor may not be advisable. Acting on one's emotions can become a poor guide, unless the *action involves a fine-grain analysis of the contingency conditions.* This is no news to the psychoanalytic practitioner who may ask for detailed answers to, "What made you angry?" or may ask, "What were you afraid of?" when the patient reports anger. Nor is the contingency analysis in conflict with psychoanalytic theory when it discusses the importance of impulse control. Viewed in terms of contingencies, the client is now in distress because his aggressive operant is now punished severely by others. The reason he behaves aggressively is because this behavior has been highly reinforced in the past. Indeed, it may even now be reinforced on an intermittent schedule. Stated otherwise, it is a successful operant which now jeopardizes him. The therapeutic task is to teach him to be sensitive to the emotion and when it occurs, to "stop, look, and listen" for the contingencies involved. These are limited to certain classes, which can be identified and taught. The client is to identify these and to engage in behavior appropriate to the change of these contingencies (if undesirable) or to their maintenance (if desirable). Emotions and feelings are not ignored. They may point to significant contingencies which the client may have overlooked or misstated. They are to be recorded in the "comments" column in every log.

It is not difficult to find evidence for a contingency analysis in the animal experimental literature. For example, it has been noted that when a specified area of a baboon's brain is electrically stimulated, he will attack another nearby baboon. The area has accordingly been labeled an "aggression area," and it has been assumed that such physiological stimulation *causes* aggression. However, the same baboon, stimulated the same way, will not attack when the baboon close by is the dominant male who heads the colony. He fawns on him instead. Obviously, the head has attained and keeps his lead by the "law of fang and claw," and the stimulated animal reacts in accord with the consequences of his behavior.

In intervention, the explicit statement of affect can lead to a number of questions for the client to consider. Among these are: What are the conditions under which the troublesome emotions he experienced are expressed? That is, what are the antecedent and consequent events? What contingencies do the stated feelings describe? What concomitant behaviors may be observed? What are the consequences of the behaviors? If these questions are asked and answered, then feelings and emotions can and do serve to produce a finer diagnostic or assessment picture and more leverage for intervention activities—either by client or by therapist.

Laboratory investigations, which cannot be discussed here, suggest that a variety of contingency relations—for example, extinction, punishment, increase in response cost—can be described by the same pattern of behavior (and presumably internally on the same affect), depending on the animal's past history in governing his environment thereby. Further, different patterns of behavior (and different affect), such as escape, aggression, sexual mounting can be elements in the same contingency. Accordingly, a one-to-one relation between affect and behavior ("I attack when I am angry") can be a road to disaster. The contingencies involved must be carefully analyzed.

An advertising executive who was a client of the author smoked when he was tense. His records showed an almost clockwork pattern of lighting a cigarette every fifteen minutes when a "sales pitch" was being made to a client or to media representatives on the opening of a campaign. "I become very tense on these occasions," he said, "and I smoke and relieve the tension." He agreed that the tension was related to the importance of the occasions, which were highly consequential. With regard to his interpretation that alleviation of tension maintained smoking, the consultant raised another possibility, namely, that the transactions or sales pitch frequently reached a point at which it might rupture relations or otherwise endanger success (a consequence). Apparently, fifteen minutes was the maximum nondisruptive period, given his style under these conditions. The cigarette seemed to serve to limit his "pitch time" to fifteen minutes, or before trouble occurred. The consultant recommended closer attention to the contingencies related to the rising tension, and that termination of these contingencies be fulfilled by more honest means, such as saying, "Whew, it's getting hot. Let's cool it." His secretary would then bring in soft drinks, sandwiches, and coffee. When this plan was put into effect, the cigarette smoking and allegedly causative tension disappeared during conferences. Thereafter, *on his own initiative,* the client began analyzing and using other affective states as guides to changing the environmental contingencies which controlled smoking.

A behavior-contingency approach enhances sensitivity to affective states. The analogy is to a sensitive room thermometer whose readings are to be used as signals to change conditions. The thermometer is not to be ignored. A rise may be the signal to open a window, check on the air-conditioning, examine the furnace, or possibly see if a fire has started. The client is to become sensitive to the slightest rise, and to correct the condition, if need be. Further, if such rises are a frequent occurrence, he might install a new furnace and prevent such rises in the future. That is to say, he might start examining his pleasant affects in terms of their contingencies and try to establish, maintain, and enhance these.

The logs play a crucial role in this process, since they enable the therapist to point out the relations clearly. Statement of affect is also critical to log-keeping. If, for example, the client records joy and delight for transactions that would suggest otherwise, something needs mending. Either the affect reported should be reconsidered, or the transactions, or something should be added to make a more comprehensible picture. Here, the therapist would express puzzlement and try to get the necessary change.

It should be noted that the logs are not used to record "inners," but the emotions are used as guides to contingencies that the worker or the client might have otherwise overlooked. If the analysis is correct, and the relevant contingencies are changed, change in affect would be expected.

WEEKLY WORKSHEETS

The mini-program, or unit step in the program, is presented to the client each week in the form of a weekly program worksheet. This provides space for explicit specification of the four elements: the subgoals to be met for the coming week; the entering repertoires on which they can be based; and programming guides, which include change procedures and possible added consequences. This worksheet, which follows, is a subprogram, and since it sets targets it can also be considered a subcontract. It is set every week with all the considerations for mutual consent and priorities noted in the discussion of the larger program and contract.

At the beginning of intervention, the terminal repertoire is often beyond the capability of a client. The troubled individual has come for help because he has difficulty in performing the behaviors and activities that are part of the final repertoire.

The main task in the programming is for the client to move

gradually through a series of steps from the behaviors in his current relevant repertoire to his goals, the terminal repertoire. The client sets up contingencies (with the aid of the worker) through steps that more and more resemble the final desired state of affairs as specified in the terminal repertoire. The burden of the program is to *specify* these steps. Such progression is called the "method of successive approximations."

Each week a set of subgoals is established which, if the program is going well, may change each week. Furthermore, as

PROGRAM WORKSHEET

Date:

Current Relevant Repertoire	*Subgoal: Subterminal Repertoire*

Program Notes

these subgoals are attained they become part of the client's current relevant repertoire, and they provide the base on which the client can take the next step. Weekly auditing provides feedback (and reinforcement) to client and worker on the efficacy of the program, as well as data for research purposes.

Assessment of a client's weekly progress is not left to chance. The program worksheet is used by client and therapist to chart this progress. At the top is a space for the client's name and the date of the session. On the right side is the place where the therapist and the client, at the end of a therapeutic session, list the subgoals to be achieved by the next week. These "behavioral assignments" are the steps in the shaping process toward achievement of the client's terminal repertoire.

They are also those aspects of the terminal repertoire that the client is *now* capable of achieving.

On the left side is the heading "Current Relevant Repertoire." These are the behaviors, abilities, assets, that the client now has. For each subgoal listed on the right side, there should be an item in the client's current relevant repertoire. In other words, the subgoal represents one step further toward the terminal repertoire on that particular aspect of the program than the corresponding item in the left column under current relevant repertoire. For example, the client might be a man who had a fear of going up high in tall buildings. His subgoal for the next week might be to go up in the elevator to the sixteenth floor. On the left, as part of his current relevant repertoire, would be the comment, "He is now able to go to the fifteenth floor." If he achieved the behavioral step, and actually went as high as the sixteenth floor, then the next time he came in, "able to go to the sixteenth floor" would be part of his current relevant repertoire and a step further in the shaping process toward the final goal (which might be "to go to the ninety-fifth floor observation deck"). The subgoal for the next week might be, "go to the seventeenth floor." Naturally, this illustration is deliberately oversimplified for purposes of clarification. The program, in actuality, might involve far more factors than just the simple "floor a week" in this sample.

At the bottom of the page are "Program Notes." These are generally comments on the relationship of the left column, the current relevant repertoire, to the right column, the subgoals. There may be references about the specifics of the logs to be kept; there may be a theoretical note to the client, or a functional analysis, of the relationship of the two. For example, in the case of the young man with the height phobia, the worker may suggest that, if he feels a high level of anxiety, he step out of the elevator or go back to the floor below or to one where he felt comfortable, and start the program again. If these approaches do not work, he is to discontinue the program for the day and start afresh the next day. These program notes are to assist the client in taking the step from current behavior to new behavior.

The ever-expanding current relevant repertoire can function to reinforce taking further and further steps in the program. Of course, if the subgoals are not achieved, they do not become part of the current repertoire. This indicates that something is wrong with the program, for it is not working. Further "work" is then necessary for the therapist and the client.

The current relevant repertoire should represent a cluster of behaviors larger than the subgoals. In the initial interview, the worker and client review those aspects of the client's life that were "going all right" (the nontarget behaviors) and those that were "not going all right" (the target behaviors). Those abilities, behaviors, and strengths that the client already has in his repertoire can be used; he can draw upon them in order to advance further. *The continual enlargement of the current relevant repertoire means the further progression of the weekly subgoals.* As the current relevant repertoire is increased, the possibility of attainment of the terminal repertoire is increased.

The current relevant repertoire should increasingly approximate the terminal repertoire. For each subgoal there should *always* be something in the current relevant repertoire. If the worker is programming subgoals without accompanying "strengths," or items in the current relevant repertoire, he is probably programming "too fast"; that is, the steps are too large for the client to attain, and therefore the program may not work. *It is always better to err on the side of conservatism and make the subgoal steps too small.* Steps that are too small, that are too easily achievable, have the potential danger of boring the client and lowering his "motivation," but experience has shown that the program, at least in the beginning, should consist of steps that are *achievable.* The steps can always be made larger as the process goes on and therapist and client gain an increasingly realistic view of what the client is capable of doing. The client himself will eventually set the pace of the programming as he becomes increasingly skilled in the functional analysis of his own behavior.

The following is a weekly program worksheet taken from the fourteenth interview (the middle phase, in this case) of the treatment of Robert Jones (a psuedonym). Robert was an artistically gifted university student who wished to pursue a career in painting. However, at the age of twenty-five he was still living at home, desperately wishing to be independent of his parents, who were quite willing to let him go. He was also shy with girls, so the program included work in three areas: independence, career choice, and relations with girls.

In reference to independence, he decided that he should learn to drive and then buy a used car, so that at least he would have the mobility to leave home and return, even for short periods of time (he lived in the suburbs, and public transportation to the city was infrequent and mitigated against his staying late in the city, or in the university area, for special events). The "independence" program thus had a subgoal of learning to drive, which in turn was broken down into a number of weekly subgoals, two of which can be seen on the following worksheet. The one he accomplished was to take the written driver's test; upon passing the test, the next step was to pay the tuition at the driving school he had contacted and to take his first lesson.

PROGRAM WORKSHEET: ROBERT JONES, JUNE 28

Current Relevant Repertoire	*Subgoal: Subterminal Repertoire*
1. Passed written test for driver's license.	1. Pay tuition at auto school. Take at least *one* lesson.
2. Received catalogues from art school.	2. Discuss with Profs. X. and Y. re next steps.
3. Spent last Sunday in Loop.	3. Plan and carry out activity for Saturday and Sunday in downtown Chicago (or Hyde Park).
4. Had coffee with Jean two times.	4. Ask Jean to lunch.

Program Notes

1. A great step forward toward eventual "independence."
2. Career choice.
3. Break the weekend "depression," also tied to No. 1 "independence."
4. The next time you have coffee with Jean you might suggest that you have lunch together.

The second step was concerned with career choice. He was finishing his degree at the universiy, and he decided to go to New York for a trial period to test his future in painting. Savings and a contribution from a bachelor uncle, plus some part-time work, were to finance him. He had received encouraging letters from one of the New York schools, and he was to discuss this with his favorite professors, who were encouraging him.

The third goal was related both to independence and to a feeling of weekend depression. The weekend depression was actually the result of a kind of behavioral deficit, an extinction trial that could be averted if he planned his activities. Hence, he was to plan activities out of his home, back in the city.

The last goal was related to his loneliness, his shyness with girls. Jean was a fellow student who had been friendly; in fact, many girls had eagerly approached him with a request for information about library hours or some other academic ruse by which girls meet boys, and vice versa. A previous step had been preceded by behavioral rehearsal (role-playing) with both the consultant and a female volunteer on how to approach and ask a girl to have coffee with him. He had achieved this step. The next step was to ask Jean to lunch. Actually, the step proved to be too large, and the program had to be slowed down. Two more "coffees" and a walk preceded the lunch invitation, which occurred successfully three weeks later.

Another example of the use of the program worksheets is presented below. The records are for three middle weeks and the last week of a weight program run by the author. The client was a young, overweight chemistry student.

PROGRAM WORKSHEET: LARRY JAMES, FEBRUARY 13

Current Relevant Repertoire	*Subgoal: Subterminal Repertoire*
1. Almost exactly 1,100 calories a day.	1. New graph is set at 1,100 a day. Keep there.
2. Resisting (albeit with difficulty) but resisting under conditions of previous eating, e.g., lunch seminars; free food; food break, drank Fresca instead.	2. Doing superbly. When in condition that you wanted to eat, and didn't, note this in book. Also, that this equals a weight loss.
3. Measuring gaps on pants. Initially, 5½", 5", 4½". Now 3.2". (8 cm. up; 13.6 cm. up).	3. Continue pants-gap measure, records, stimulus control.

Program Notes

1. Has stocked up on fish, likes fish; can thereby maintain lower intake.
2. Intake record (from graphs): to maintain weight currently need 1,800 calories a day. 700 @ 7 = 4,900, 1.4 lbs. a week.
3. Soon you may be able to wear them.

The program worksheet is almost self-explanatory. Subgoal No. 1 was based on behavior No. 1, which was already in the repertoire. Subgoal No. 2 was intended to reinforce the procedures of his own that the client was developing. The gap measure, current No. 3, was converted to centimeters and to the constructive record of how far the zipper went up, rather than the decreasing gap. The caloric requirements listed under program notes were derived from assessment of intake for several weeks and of weight losses. Such requirements, of course, shift as weight changes. The program worksheets for ensuing weeks were as follows:

PROGRAM WORKSHEET: LARRY JAMES, FEBRUARY 20

Current Relevant Repertoire

1. Almost continuously under 1,100 calories a day.
2. Control over eating when at mother's and lasagna served! When heavy lunch, compensated by low dinner. Stimulus control at home.
3. Zipper at 14 cm. (from 13.6 last week). Superb!
4. Has book (*Royal Canadian Air Force Exercise Book*).

Subgoal: Subterminal Repertoire

1. Continue as before; try to keep below 1,100.
2. Continue stimulus control. Continue compensatory eating.

3. Continue pants-gap measure.

4. Read RCAF book; bring it to session.

Program Notes

Continue as you're doing. Report "no bad hunger pangs." When any occur, say: "This is a condition for eating." Eat. Calories per lb.: 13. (The calories expended per pound were calculated from new information.)

PROGRAM WORKSHEET: LARRY JAMES, FEBRUARY 27

Current Relevant Repertoire

1. Almost continually less than 1,100.
2. Stimulus control: Eats at given places. When eating, engages in no other activities.
3. Zipper at 15½ cm. (up from 14 cm. last week). Gap is 4 cm. Could zip up if sucked in stomach.
4. Brought RCAF book.

Subgoal: Subterminal Repertoire

1. Continue as before.
2. Continue.

3. Continue.

4. Do chart 1, page 68. 2 or 3 days at each level. Do not exceed.

Program Notes

1. Extend controls to RCAF exercises. Try not to miss a day. Important for circulation, etc., and appearance (eliminate saggy-baggy skin).

PROGRAM WORKSHEET: LARRY JAMES, APRIL 2

Current Relevant Repertoire	*Subgoal: Subterminal Repertoire*
1. RCAF to Exercise C, highest attained before.	1. Continue to age level. Continue RCAF.
2. Tested jeans, size 32; wore them to session.	2. Continue to wear size 32.
3. Eating at specified time and places.	3. Continue to eat at specified time and places.
4. Eating honey, wines, butter, living it up at exotic restaurants, makes it up within the next few days.	4. Enjoy this.

Program Notes

1. You have the repertoire to control eating patterns, so that when intake is in excess at exotic restaurant, or with mother, or at some particular time, can decrease intake in enjoyable manner at some later date.

THE PROGRAM WORKSHEET AS AN ASSESSMENT DEVICE

The effectiveness of intervention can be measured at the finish of therapy by an analysis of outcome. Were the contracted goals met? The therapy can also be monitored weekly through use of the weekly worksheet simply by asking if the weekly contracted goals were met and, if not, why not. If the program is well-planned, the subgoals of any one week should be in the current repertoire of the next week. If the subgoals were not met, then the task is to analyze what went wrong and what corrective procedures should be used. The successive steps and subgoals should more and more approximate the final desired behavior or relevant final repertoire, which is the goal of the therapeutic intervention. The written logs, plus the interviews and other sources of information, guide the establishment of the weekly subgoals. During the interview the therapist and the client analyze the data and look for consistent patterns. The data are constantly analyzed for the controlling conditions, and the program steps are derived directly from this analysis.

As soon as possible in the therapy, the client begins to write his own weekly program worksheet, setting his own subgoals, first in consultation with the therapist and gradually increasingly on his own. Thus the control shifts from joint control to client control. One device that has been used to facilitate this transfer of control is a form and set of instructions called the "in-between-session worksheet" (IBSW) or the "client worksheet" (the two terms are used interchangeably).

The In-Between-Session Worksheet (*IBSW*). The purpose of this worksheet is to facilitate the development of the client's skill in self- and situational analysis and in program-planning. It also is intended to facilitate the comparison, on an overt level, of the client's and consultant's views (agreements and differences) about the direction and pace of the program. Use of both viewpoints may make it easier to pinpoint where the program is going "right" or the apparent reasons why the program is not proceeding smoothly. The worksheet, as it is currently being used, includes six areas:

1. Statement of subgoals
2. Statement of relationship of subgoals to goals of terminal repertoire
3. Understanding of programming variables
4. Client comments on subgoals/programs (cols. 1–3)
5a. Next steps in program
5b. Justification
6. Tentative agenda for coming sessions.

The form appears on page 125.

Both the client and the consultant are asked to complete this form. Each, of course, has access to the other's worksheet, and often, if there is a "problem"—perhaps the program is not "working" as well as it "should"—the two are compared for discrepancies, programming ideas, and so forth.

The instructions for use of this form vary slightly; the client is asked to make entries on the worksheet as ideas occur during the week and to complete the form before the next session. The consultant fills out another form after the session and reviews it before the next session.

For those clients for whom the form is appropriate, it is intended to start them on the road to being their own program-

IBSW

1. Statement of Subgoals	2. Your Understanding of How Stated Subgoals Relate to Contracted Goals	3. Programming variables: Manner and Extent to Which Subgoals Were Reached; Controlling Variables	4. Comments about Subgoals/Program
5a. Tentative Next Step for Program: Your Suggestions	5b. Justification: Relation to Contracted Goals	6. Tentative Agenda for Coming Session: Your Suggestions	

mers, their own behavioral analysts, as soon as possible. Depending upon a number of circumstances (and there are some clients for whom the worksheet would not be appropriate), the client should complete the form as soon as possible in the process, as soon as he has learned some of the elements of the approach.

The client is phased into the use of the form by being asked to fill in parts of the form until he gradually gathers expertise to complete and utilize the entire form. If "control" is narrowly defined as the proportion that each party contributes to the process of programming, then measurement of a client's increase in knowledge is the degree to which he takes the initiative in the programming or, in other words, the increasing degree to which the program and the discussion of it are transferred from the hands of the consultant into the hands of the client.

The client is first encouraged to fill in column 2 (the way in which the subgoals relate to the contracted terminal goals). On occasion, this has led to restatement of goals and even necessitated renegotiation of the contract. Columns 1 and 2, which are an indication of agreement/disagreement on goals, provide a good way of clearing up any misunderstandings over goals, process, and so on. The restatement of the weekly goals and their achievement, if the program is going well, is a constant reinforcement, a feedback to the client of the efficacy of the program, and it should heighten the client's confidence in his ability to program, handle the contingencies, or, in other words, to "solve the problems."

Column 6, the tentative agenda, is also completed by the client as soon as possible, to hasten transfer of the control of the agenda from consultant to client. Step 6 is designed to incorporate suggestions by the client. If something has happened during the week, which is not part of the program, but whose discussion is essential, for example, being descended on by in-laws, this is the place to note it. Here the consultant can advise and help the client to formulate smaller program steps that are achievable. As previously cautioned, it is better to program in too small steps, at the risk of producing boredom and impatience, than in steps that are too large, producing extinction and, possibly, discontinuance of the program.

It is generally advisable for the client to have mastery of steps 1, 2, and 6 before he begins the other parts of the form, although, of course, there is nothing mandatory about this order. The order makes logical sense which is not always the same as clinical sense.

Column 3, the programming variables, is intended to facilitate functional analysis of behavior. The therapist may provide a model for such analysis, ask the client questions, and so on, within the context of the operant paradigm. The therapist is instructed to gradually "fade" himself out as he turns more of the responsibility over to the client.

The foregoing process, especially column 3, is based on the assumption that the client is the individual who knows his own situation best. If the client uses procedures other than those specified, and is successful, he is congratulated, for he has indicated that he has taken the initiative. Further, the therapist may learn something new. If the procedure does not work, he still is encouraged to engage in the analysis and is helped to formulate procedures that will attain the goals.

The particulars vary from case to case. If the client goes into extinction and analyzes the reasons why, and possibly takes steps (even though smaller than specified), he is to be congratulated for realistic and effective programming. From the consultant's point of view, this is heartening evidence that the "control" is indeed passing to the client and he is becoming more facile in the analysis of his own behavior-contingency relations.

The form, as well as all these procedures, should be a *guide,* a help to programming, and a facilitator, not a strait jacket, in the therapeutic process. In this kind of intervention, as well as with all other kinds, there are emergencies, sudden happenings, emotional upsets, and so on, that might take precedence over previously programmed topics *if it is the desire of the client.* Of course, the consultant should always be alert to the possibility that new or extraneous matters are sometimes brought in because of failure to complete the program due to reluctance to go further (deeper) with some problems; in other words, what is called, in dynamic psychology, "resistance."

THE MONITOR AS PROGRAM CHECK

Another check on what is going on is provided by the monitor, whose presence was noted earlier. In general, he is instructed to raise the following questions in extratherapy sessions with the consulant:

1. Is the current relevant repertoire stated explicitly and understood by the client?
2. How does the therapist abstract this from the logs?
3. Has he overlooked anything?
4. To what extent are subgoals reasonable and understood by the client?
5. Are the subgoals evident in the next week's logs?
6. Are the program notes explicit?
7. Are the procedures programmed?

These questions are more directly related to the operation and direction of the program than to the research. It is difficult, and not necessarily desirable, to separate the questions related to the process from the questions related to the research, as the intervention and the research are so cosely interwoven in this approach. As a research function, however, the monitor often keeps interaction records on the relevant variables. The monitor can, on occasion, intervene at a "sticky" point, when client and consulant may either be bogged down in irrelevancies or sidetracked into a nonproductive way station. As is known to all therapists, not all of a therapeutic hour is spent "on the point," and the third person in the situation can serve as a guide to keep the session on the track and running smoothly.

TERMINATION AND CARRY-OVER

Intervention ends when the client and the worker agree that the terms or the goals of the terminal repertoire have been reached. Another way to put it is that treatment ends when the contracted terminal repertoire is actually the current relevant repertoire of the client, when the two are identical. Still another way to phrase this is to ask, "Did the client get what he came for?"

The contract, of course, often is renegotiated so that some items stated as the terminal repertoire when the sessions began, are no longer so considered. Either they have been achieved and thus have become part of the client's relevant repertoire or, perhaps, have been superseded or considered irrelevant to the terminal repertoire by other, perhaps more pressing matters in the hierarchy of "problems." This can be monitored and verified constantly during the course of the intervention by examination of the weekly worksheets.

Another criterion for the termination decision is evaluation of the extent to which the consultant has been successful in teaching the client to become his own behavior analyst and in equipping him with a set of analytic skills and procedures so that he should be able to handle similar, and other, problematic situations throughout his life.

Evaluating success by attainment of the goal can be complicated; the client, upon approaching the goal, may become satisfied with what he has done and decide that enough has been accomplished. A rather simple example is the case of a dieting client who contracted for a weight of 120 pounts (representing a 50-pound loss), and who decided, once she had reached 135 pounds, that she was satisfied. Since the contract can be renegotiated at any time, the changing of terminal goals and the imminent possibility of terminating or shortening therapy are certainly within the power of any client. Here the consultant and the client must discuss fully just what is involved; the "flight into health" so often discussed in the dynamic literature is often seen here, too. The "flight into health," of course, may function as a kind of avoidance behavior, in which the client is resisting the undertaking of either further steps in the program or the programming of another aspect of the agreed-upon terminal repertoire. The client may also balk at continuing on to other goals in his priority (see Hersen, 1971).

Another sign that termination may be indicated is seen in changing patterns of keeping logs. Often the client has been keeping good and full logs and then seems to become more sporadic in this activity, or in appointment-keeping, and so forth. He may be showing, essentially, that the logs no longer have the payoff for him that they once had. Why keep records when they are no longer needed?

CARRY-OVER

"Carry-over" refers to that stage in intervention when the target repertoires specified in the contract have been established, and the contract now calls for maintenance of the repertoires in their natural ecology. In essence, the client attempts to alter the contingencies to maintain the new pattern, as opposed to altering them to establish the pattern. Follow-up records serve for such analysis. The intervals between considerations of such records may be included in the original contract, or may be negotiated as a new contract. The interval is progressively increased over time. The records are sometimes mailed to the laboratory and commented upon by return mail, or they may involve face-to-face contact. (Speech clients sometimes mail samples on cassette tapes to the clinic.)

Procedures involving analysis of the conditions that are likely to lead to success or to failure facilitate making the relevant variables explicit, testable, and communicable. Keeping explicit analytic records during establishment of the targeted repertoire may help to set up a pattern that will carry over into maintenance periods.

It should be noted that if the therapist becomes a therapeutic ally of the client, the client becomes a research ally of the therapist. The research-application dichotomy is minimized here as it is in operant research in general. One can ascertain the functional relations which govern behavior either by changing the conditions to see what happens to the behavior (the laboratory), or by changing the conditions in an effort to get behavior to happen a certain way (the clinic). The fact that certain problems are so prevalent that institutions are set up to treat them suggests that these are not trivial or relatively infrequent phenomena. To perform research on functional relationships requires explicit attention to the fine grain of the environment as well as of behavior (Goldiamond, Dyrud, and Miller, 1965). The model supplied by the experimental analysis of behavior developed around the long-term study and change of individuals can serve as a useful guide for intervention, as it does for research.

four

THE SMITH CASE

ISRAEL GOLDIAMOND
AND ARTHUR SCHWARTZ *

In Chapters 4 and 5, two cases are presented to illustrate how cases are conducted within the framework of a self control behavioral casework model. Both cases involve marital problems and work problems; the second case also includes financial problems. These are typical problems seen in behaviorally oriented agencies. Although marital crises were present in both cases, the program in the first case dealt with the husband alone; in the second case, with both partners. Since the purposes and mechanics of the forms used in the two cases are similar (for example, the questions appearing in the self control form are almost identical), they will be considered in detail only in the first case, that of Mr. Smith. Dialogue between Worker and Client is interspersed with comments by the authors.

Mr. Smith is a middle-aged (forty-four years old) white lawyer who works in a distinguished law firm. He is in charge of the section on securities and exchange law. This section, though small and not considered as exciting as others in the firm, is central to the firm's business. Mr. Smith also serves as consultant on such problems for clients handled by other lawyers in the firm. He is financially successful and, seemingly to the casual observer, personally fulfilled. However, he reported little personal, marital, or job satisfaction. His marriage was crumbling. He took work home with him, and his family saw little of him. His wife had recently "kicked him out," precipitating the crisis which brought him into therapy.

* The initial interview was conducted by Israel Goldiamond, the case was carried by Arthur Schwartz, planning and analysis of the case were a joint effort.

Mr. Smith's presenting complaint was of a severe and prolonged depression, which was crippling him in his work and marriage. He was able to work, but only at a tremendous cost and without any joy in the work. His appearance reflected his complaint. He spoke in a low voice, with frequent pauses and downcast gazes. The interviewers were shocked to learn his age: he appeared to be in his early sixties. A physical examination revealed that he had no medical problems.

INTAKE AND INITIAL INTERVIEW: THE SELF CONTROL QUESTIONNAIRE

The self control questionnaire was administered as the initial interview [1] in the program. Its purpose was to obtain information relevant to: (a) terminal repertoire to be established; (b) the current relevant repertoire which could be used to start; (c) programming procedures that were necessary and current programs that were available in the client's repertoire; and (d) natural reinforcers which would maintain progress in programs and their possible sources. An additional purpose of the questionnaire was to communicate to the client both the rationale and the procedures.

1. *Worker: The questions I am going to ask can be grouped into clusters. Before asking you to answer individual questions, let me present the first group, and then we'll go over them one by one. These questions are about why you are coming here. You're coming here because you want certain things to change, you want certain things to be different. Assuming we are successful, the questions are: (a) What would the outcome be like? (b) How would others recognize it? (c) How would it be different from the current state of affairs? (d) Can you give an example? Let's take these one by one. The first question is: If we were successful, what would the outcome be for you?*

2. Client (*Slowly, drawn out, voice almost inaudible, manner depressed*): Well, I would not be such a mass of tension and such a

---

[1] The interview has been edited, disguised, and shortened for purposes of presentation.

complete wreck and so scared of people. I would be able to handle the many aspects of things that need handling . . . (pause) considerably better and, uh, my, uh, wife and everybody in my family would be happier and I'd sleep a great deal better, which is a problem. I would just be an altogether relaxed, effective individual.

> (Comment: As is common, client starts with a recitation of what he would not be. He'd be less "pathological." He speaks in very general terms and refers to unobservables both here and when he switches to what he'd like to be. His opening statements are often characterized by reported "inadequacies," since this is typically the "ticket" for admission to psychotherapy. Worker goes on to the second question to get specifics, to start working with the client toward observable problematic and nonproblematic behaviors.)

3. *Worker: A more relaxed, effective individual?*

> (Comment: Worker is responding to one element in the response just given. He is asking for elaboration which can be used to establish positive outcomes.)

4. Client: Yes. More relaxed, more in tune with others.

5. *Worker: (Question 1b) You'd be more relaxed, effective. How would others observe this? What would others see when they looked at you? When they saw you?*

> (Comment: Worker attempts to translate the unobservables given by the client into observable terms, observable by others and to which they respond.)

6. Client: More relaxed in company.

> (Comment: Client has narrowed down what "others" means, but his statement still does not refer to observables. Worker tries to prompt observables.)

7. *Worker: It's kind of difficult to seem "more relaxed in company," in tune, and so forth. What would someone who didn't know you see? What would he observe? How could he tell?*

8. Client: Well, uh, I don't know. If he saw me he wouldn't see anybody who would stand out because of his tenseness.

> (Comment: Again, a definition in terms of negatives and unobservables. Worker is "pushing" the client here.)

9. *Worker: What would he see?*

10. Client: Uh, it's, uh, it's uh very hard, very hard for me to grasp it, to say it . . .

11. *Worker: Yes, it is often very difficult. (Silence)*

12. Client: He'd see an individual going along, doing his job.

    (*Comment: The response is being shaped.*)

13. *Worker: What would he see at work?*

    (*Comment: The worker moves to an area in which the client will be more likely to be specific and positive.*)

14. Client: He'd see a very busy fellow.

15. *Worker: What would he see at home?*

16. Client: He'd see an individual, if we were successful, who, well, who went out more with everybody and took out his wife more . . . (*long pause*). He would see a man who enjoys his family.

    (*Comment: The juxtaposition of enjoyment of family and taking out wife more often suggests possible target area.*)

17. *Worker: You mentioned going out with your wife. How often would you be going out with her?*

18. Client: More frequently.

    (*Comment: "More" is unobservable.*)

19. *Worker: How often?*

20. Client: Two or three times a week.

21. *Worker: How often do you go out with her now?*

    (*Comment: This information anticipates the next question but is relevant here.*)

22. Client: Not too often. Every several weeks or so. Maybe three times a month. Maybe twice. Certainly no more frequently.

23. *Worker: Is that what your wife would like? Two or three times a week?*

24. Client: Yes. I think she'd like that very much.

25. *Worker: What would you be doing?*

    (*Comment: Defines the subrepertoires subsumed by "going out."*)

26. Client: Well, going to parties, meeting friends, doing some sports, perhaps golfing—we sometimes used to do that together—swim in the summer. I'd also sleep better.

    (*Comment: Sleep better? What does this mean exactly?*)

27. *Worker: Sleep better?*

    (*Comment: Worker would like this targeted, but he has stated his question too vaguely.*)

28. Client: I don't sleep well.

   (*Comment: Worker got just what he asked for!*)

29. Worker: How much do you sleep now?

   (*Comment: The question is restated in numerical terms.*)

30. Client: Well, actually, I suppose I'd sleep less. What I mean is, I'd stay up later, but get more sleep.

   (*Comment: The intent is obvious: sleep would be sounder. However, the program is directed toward making the client's analyses clearer, not those of the worker.*)

31. Worker: I don't understand. How late would you stay up?

32. Client: Well, I'd stay up until midnight, but when I went to bed I'd sleep soundly, wouldn't toss, turn, dream so much, be more restful in sleep.

33. Worker: You'd sleep soundly. What time would you get up?

34. Client: Oh, about 7:00.

   (*Comment: Day-to-day behavioral routine is very important for programming purposes.*)

35. Worker: You say you'd be more relaxed and more effective? What do you mean by that?

36. Client: Well, you would be seeing a man puttering in his garage and with his books at his desk and talking with his children and taking them out and swimming with them and staying around, spending more time with them.

   (*Comment: Client has caught on! Excellent.*)

37. Worker: And . . . ?

   (*Comment: Worker reinforces the client's statement by saying "and" which indicates he wants to hear more—a major way of reinforcing speech.*)

38. Client: And in more company with others, he is like them, more normal, less hassled, less harried, less of a goddamned feeling that he is on a treadmill, working his ass off and not having a thing to show for it . . . (*long pause*) . . . someone who's organized.

   (*Comment: The request for "more" turns to the negatives, which are stronger in his repertoire than the positives.*)

39. Worker: Organized?

   (*Comment: Positive area to be established.*)

40. Client: Organized, more efficient, knowing what he'll do and what he wants.

41. *Worker: Organized at work? And at home?*

42. Client: At home. More relaxed at home. More efficient at work.

43. *Worker: You mean when he's at work, he's at work, and efficient. And when he is at home, he is relaxed?*

   (*Comment: The attempt is now made to define the repertoire involved.*)

44. Client: Yeah, that's it. That's it in a nutshell.

45. *Worker: Let's see if I get the picture. A successful outcome would be somebody at work who is a busy person, efficient at his job. At home he is with his family and enjoying it. Taking them out, doing things, spending time with them. He'd go out with his wife two or three times a week. He would stay up till midnight, doing things, then go to sleep, sleep soundly until 7:00, then go to work. After work or on weekends, he'd be puttering in his garage, or with his car, basically an organized person.*

   (*Comment: Worker summarizes goals [terminal repertoire]. Some of the client's responses are beginning to define outcomes in observable terms. Emotions, as one can see, are not ignored but viewed as guides to underlying contingencies and not as causes of behavior.*)

46. Client: Yes, that sounds like it.

47. *Worker: When he is at work, he is at work. But when he is at home, he is at home.*

48. Client: Yes, that sums it up.

   (*Comment: The inference is that when the client is at work, he does not do his job, hence it is carried home. Working at home results in a lack of reinforcement, which adds to the loss of reinforcement on the job. Obviously, to obtain the reinforcements available in each environment, different repertoires are required at work and at home.*)

49. *Worker: (Question 1c): How does that differ from the current state of affairs?*

50. Client: Well, I'm very busy at work. (*Long pause*) . . . . I work with inefficiency.

   (*Comment: The inference was reasonable, but now requires detailed specification.*)

51. *Worker: You're busy at work but inefficient. Tell me about it.*

52. Client: I am tense, disorganized. I just don't seem to have any definite purpose. I don't seem to have any concrete objectives, just disorganization. I am marginal at work.

53. *Worker: What kind of law do you practice?*

54. Client: Security and exchange law. I'm a security and exchange specialist.

55. *Worker: How are you at it?*

56. Client: Well, you may find this hard to believe, looking at this caricature of a human being, but I am one of the top ten experts in the country in this particular area. It's specialized, maybe that's another way of saying that it is dull. It's goddamned dull. Maybe that is why someone like me, without imagination, could go into it and do well, at least financially.

57. *Worker: Do you enjoy any of it?*

58. Client: No. There are no kicks at work. Only pressures.

59. *Worker: You say you don't enjoy it, yet your face lit up. You might even say that you said it with pride. You said you are one of the top ten in the country.*

60. Client: Well, I do all right, that is, as far as meeting my commitments; it just takes a hell of a lot of work and time.

   (*Comment: It always did, but something is now different.*)

61. *Worker: More time than you feel you should spend to get the work done?*

62. Client: Hell, yes. When things are going well, I spend a lot of time, but then it isn't the pain it is now.

63. *Worker: What things aren't going well that make work such a pain?*

64. Client: Things at home.

65. *Worker: Then the problem is not work, but home?*

66. Client: Yes and no. There is a problem at work, organization and mess sort of thing has always been a problem at work, but (*pause*) recently much worse.

67. *Worker: Is the "recently much worse" due to things at home rather than things at work?*

68. Client: Yes.

69. *Worker: Can you tell me about them?*

70. Client: (*Long pause, sigh.*) Well (*pause*) the story is, well, really, that my wife, my wife kicked me out of the house a couple of weeks ago and put a suit for divorce against me, and I took the children, but I had to put them back after a couple of days, I couldn't take care of them, and uh, she let me back in the house after a few days (*pause*).

71. *Worker: She let you back?*

72. Client: She let me back with the stipulation that, uh, I do this, which uh, is all right because, uh, it's her own good idea, and I, uh, should have done it, oh, a long time ago.

> *(Comment: The fact that his wife let him back into the house suggests that the suit for divorce was a drastic operant on her part to force change.)*

73. *Worker: She took you back on the condition that you get therapy?*

74. Client: Uh-huh.

75. *Worker: What about the divorce suit?*

76. Client: She dropped it.

77. *Worker: I see. Then the therapy is your wife's idea, not yours?*

> *(Comment: This is an attempt to assess the extent to which therapeutic change is more critical to the wife than to the client. If this is the case, a different program and client may be indicated.)*

78. Client: No. Not really. I just wouldn't have done it on my own. I wouldn't have had the courage, but now that she sort of forced me—yes, you could say that, she forced me into it—I think it is a good idea. I should have done it a long time ago.

> *(Comment: Wife's operant [ploy] was extremely successful. She gauged his interest correctly, and she took him back. Likelihood is that she is supportive. This suggests that the situation is not as bleak as described by the husband and that there are strengths to build on.)*

79. *Worker: How are things with your wife now?*

80. Client: Perfectly all right. *(Pause)* Hmm. Well, it is not exactly right. We are never perfectly right. But they never will be because—wives being wives, my wife thinks that if I'm gone so many hours a day, that I'm gone some place and when I get home, it's work time. I must have been sleeping some place all that time I was gone. So there is a problem there in, uh, our approach to matters.

81. *Worker: Does she expect you to work, help around the house?*

> *(Comment: What are the wife's requirements?)*

82. Client: No. Not really. *(Pause)* She wants me, when I'm home, to spend the time with her and with the children.

> *(Comment: The probe was successful in getting the client to talk about his wife's requirements in his own words.)*

83. *Worker: You don't?*

84. Client: No.

85. *Worker: (Pause) What keeps you from spending time with your children?* [Client remains silent.] *Do you take work home with you?*

   (*Comment: A prompt.*)

86. Client: (*Sigh*) Yes, I do. I take home work to do.

87. *Worker: I see. And she expects you to spend the time at home with her and the kids?*

   (*Comment: His wife has normal expectations. Her deprivation indicates that she likes him and that her efforts to have more of him have resulted in aggression.*)

88. Client: Yes.

89. *Worker: Why do you take work home? Can you tell me about that? Is it necessary for your job?*

90. Client: Well, knowing that I am a marginal individual and always have been, knowing that I am not a very bright fellow basically, it occurred to me a long time ago, uh, the only thing that is quite good enough is my absolute maximum effort. Once I start getting sloppy, I fall flat on my face, so I have to look to get a little ahead and have a little margin.

   (*Comment: His response is typically deprecatory. An alternative explanation is that situational variables are requiring this high output, which he justifies in personally deprecatory terms. As long as he looks at things this way, he will not change the situational variables. The consultant will move into exploring these.*)

91. *Worker: You have to work harder than the next fellow just to get your job done?*

92. Client: I think so, yeah.

93. *Worker: And your wife would like you to spend more time with her?*

94. Client: Yes.

95. *Worker: Do you have the time at the office to read the latest security laws, decisions, and that sort of thing? Is that part of your job? As a lawyer?*

96. Client: No, I don't have the time. It would be ideal if I did, if I could, if I would stay a couple of hours at work, at the end of the day.

   (*Comment: A possible program target.*)

97. *Worker: You are due at nine?*

98. Client: Yes.

99. *Worker: And what time are you finished?*

100. Client: We are finished when we are finished. We are allowed to go and come as we wish. I am, at least. I don't have as much client contact as the others. I do the looking up, the loopholes, the latest laws, and so forth. Actually, I spend a lot of time seeing various lawyers. That part I like.

> (*Comment: Client actually has the opportunity to control much of his environment.*)

101. *Worker: So you hold your own with them?*

> (*Comment: This is a prompt for a more positive statement about himself. Obviously, other lawyers would not be inviting him to intrude on their time on the regular basis described unless he were competent.*)

102. Client: Certainly. I have something they want and they put up with me. And my personality is such that I intend to have them get it.

> (*Comment: Prompt was successful. Client's positive statement will now be reinforced. It should be noted that the reinforcer is a question which extends the discourse.*)

103. *Worker: If you were as dull as you are trying so hard to impress on me that you are, do you think that they would keep coming back to you? Don't they pay you rather stiff fees?*

104. Client: I see your point. I guess I must, I must help them. No, they don't pay me fees. I am on salary. They pay the firm.

105. *Worker: Would you make more money, have more independence on your own, in solo practice, or in a firm of your own?*

> (*Comment: Probe: is the high response cost maintained by a monetary reinforcer?*)

106. Client: Money? Yes, after a while. Independence, hell, I'd never get anything done, I get uptight about seeing clients.

> (*Comment: Apparently, he is an effective lawyer's lawyer.*)

107. *Worker: Do you get uptight about seeing their lawyers?*

108. Client: No, generally not, but then it is a lot of technical talk, no bullshit, I'm not good at that kind of bullshit.

> (*Comment: Other lawyers reinforce his professional behavior, hence his affect is positive.*)

109. *Worker: Have you ever discussed going into solo practice, or your own firm, with your wife?*

> (*Comment: Can his wife be recruited here?*)

110. Client: From time to time. When things get real bad, and I'm swamped, she says that I really don't have to put up with that sort of thing, that I can get lots of jobs.

(Comment: His wife apparently does not share his low opinion of himself.)

111. Worker: Is that true?

112. Client: God, yes! It is a dull kind of life, but it is specialized, not many in it, and even fewer going into it. No young person wants to spend his time buried in a library.

113. Worker: Your wife is behind you then, when it comes to decisions at work? (Pause) Is she?

114. Client: Yes, I'd say that. She thinks I am God Almighty, but only in my work.

(Comment: The client is inviting derogatory inferences about home. Worker resists "biting" for that. Instead, in order to program patterns, he needs specific information about what actually goes on.)

115. Worker: Tell me about your daily routine.

116. Client: I get to work at the office by 9:00, eat lunch at my desk, and sometimes I come home at 5:00. The office gets deserted. Very rarely I stay until 6:00 or 7:00. Not very many evening meetings.

117. Worker: You get home about 6:00 then?

118. Client: Yes.

119. Worker: Then what?

120. Client: I say hello, have a drink, maybe have a sandwich, and then go into my study.

121. Worker: How long do you stay there?

122. Client: Well, again, this is very variable. To say that I go into my study, you are giving me credit for something I don't quite get accomplished. I go in there, and I intend to work, but I often don't.

123. Worker: But you go there anyhow whether you study there or not?

(Comment: Whether anything is accomplished in the study or not, the client puts in his time. This has the effect of separating him from his wife.)

124. Client: Yes, uh.

125. Worker: After supper?

126. Client: After 8:00.

127. *Worker: After 8:00. Tell me what do you do there?*

128. Client: Well, I go in. Sometimes I read new regulations. Sometimes, I check my bank balance. Sometimes I just futz around.

129. *Worker: Until what time?*

130. Client: Maybe 9:00.

131. *Worker: And then?*

132. Client: I go to bed. Sometimes I stay in the study until midnight, but I often go to bed at 9:00.

133. *Worker: And then you get up, go to work. What happens on the weekends?*

134. Client: Conferences in the morning, Saturday morning. Afternoon and Sunday, I am home.

135. *Worker: How much time do you and your wife spend together?*

136. Client: Not much.

137. *Worker: Sounds like she might have some kind of grievance, doesn't it?*

   (*Comment: Wife's behavior is rational; the question is designed to shape positive statements about wife as well as himself.*)

138. Client: Yes.

139. *Worker: OK, let's see. First your wife expressed some annoyance with this state of affairs, yes?*

   (*Comment: The worker is trying to "pin down" what actually happened to bring the client into therapy.*)

140. Client: Yes.

141. *Worker: When she asked you to leave, and filed for divorce, what grounds did she give?*

142. Client: Well, there was a blowup, one night, which precipitated things. She had had the flu for two days and was in bed and claims that I didn't pay any attention to her and she had the flu. This is not strictly true. I asked her more than half a dozen times how she was, what could I get for her.

143. *Worker: Did you take time off from work?*

144. Client: No, I didn't.

145. *Worker: Could you have?*

146. Client: Yes.

147. *Worker: Who was at home with her?*

148. Client: Uh-huh. (*Pause*)

149. *Worker: What do you think bothered her?*

150. Client: Well, I took four days to write a brochure, and she heard that I had these four days off and the thing got precipitated so that the four days were wasted. I had the children with me, and the four days were wasted and . . . she, uh . . . there is such a colossal waste in everything . . . but a divorce suit, for example, lawyers, uh . . . very expensive people.

151. *Worker: Let's see, your wife complains that she doesn't see you enough. She says that she doesn't get enough of you, that she wants more of you.*

   (*Comment: Designed to shape a positive statement about his wife, and to indicate that there are better relations between them; also to continue shaping positive statements about himself.*)

152. Client: Hm-hmm (*pause*).

153. *Worker: You mentioned waste. What did you mean by that?*

154. Client: The waste is my coming home and I have plans. I may even have a list of things to do when I get home, but instead of getting them done, I, uh, sit and worry about the fact that I am not getting anything done.

155. *Worker: Do you waste time at work?*

   (*Comment: The consultant returns to the target of opportunity.*)

156. Client: Well, work is a fairly unusual situation. I keep very busy.

157. *Worker: Is there any wasted time there?*

158. Client: There is waste of time there, but I don't know how to get around that part of it. I have to be close by others, to consult with staff clients. You can't get too far away from it.

   (*Comment: The "stand-by" implication requires clarification. There are procedures to help with scheduling problem.*)

159. *Worker: Do you have your own secretary?*

160. Client: I share one with the pool.

161. *Worker: You are the senior man in your area?*

162. Client: Yes.

163. *Worker: And are you practically a partner in the firm?*

164. *Client: Yes.*

165. *Worker: Wouldn't it be to your firm's advantage to give you your own secretary, a space of her own, to maximize your efficiency?*

166. Client: Yeah, uh, well, I suppose so.

167. *Worker: And haven't you asked for these things?*

168. Client: No.

   (*Comment: Part of the trouble is now evident, and the solution to this part is also evident.*)

169. *Worker: I think that this is something that we can work on. Let's go on to some other area, some other material that we need to know.*

   (*Comment: The fine grain of the work schedule might be difficult to obtain at this time. It should be obtainable from his records. Also, if he gets a good secretary, it may not be necessary for him to acquire the appropriate work schedule. She may do it for him.*)

171. *Worker: (Question 2a) Describe the areas which will not be affected by the program.*

172. Client: It is difficult to say, I'll still be a lawyer.

   (*Comment: Changing his job is not a desired outcome.*)

173. *Worker: Yes, you are accomplished at your profession.*

174. Client: And I would still be married to my wife. I don't want to lose her!

175. *Worker: My guess is that she feels the same way. She dropped a divorce suit when she could have gone through with it. She made therapy a condition. She obviously cares enough for you that she wanted you to get help. She has let you know that she doesn't want you buried in the study, but wants to see more of you.*

   (*Comment: Worker's interpretation contains bases from which to develop further behavior, especially if his wife wants to see more of him. He is a source of reinforcement for behaviors important to his wife.*)

176. Client: Uh, yes, that is so, I didn't think of it that way. I thought that she must be getting tired of me. And the children, they wouldn't change, they would remain the same. They wouldn't exactly, they wouldn't by any means, they would get more attention, which is what they need.

177. *Worker: Then that would change.*

178. Client: And my work would change. I would be doing more, but we have been over this.

179. *Worker: Yes, but we shall return to it. Your profession would stay the same, you would be married to the same woman, the children would be the same except that you would feel that you would give them more attention.*

180. Client: Yes.

181. *Worker: (Question 2b) Your work relationships with colleagues would change, your relations with wife and children would change. Is there any other area that would change?*

   (Comment: A restatement of the more conventional form of this question, namely, "Are there any other areas which will be affected?")

182. Client: Well, just the stuff we talked about earlier, I'd be happier, more efficient, and more confident, and we would go out a lot more.

183. *Worker: You mentioned earlier that you would get more sleep. Is it just the matter of hours you sleep? Rearranging your schedule?*

184. Client: (*Pause*) No. Not really.

185. *Worker: What is it? Is there something you haven't told me yet?*

   (Comment: Specifics are required.)

186. Client: No, not really. It is a situation that is not entirely satisfactory. There is a long drive to work, there is an overextended situation. There are six children at home not getting enough attention, and their father arrives home a little crabby. And this is an argument I have with my wife. If I said "yes," it is perfectly true that I need some therapy, I have known this all of my life.

187. *Worker: (Question 3a) You have started to give information about our next area. About attempts to change. The first question is why start now? What are the circumstances?*

188. Client: Well, uh, I am a middle-aged man, uh, it is about time, and uh, my wife insists upon it.

189. *Worker: How old are you?*

190. Client: Forty-four.

191. *Worker: And your wife?*

192. Client: Well, she is thirteen years younger, she is thirty-one.

193. *Worker: Tell me about your wife. What did she do before marriage?*

194. Client: Well, she's from Belgium; she's not so long in this country.

195. *Worker: How long has she been here?*

196. Client: Eight years.

197. *Worker: And you have six children? Fairly close together?*

198. Client: No, no. Only one is by her.

199. *Worker: I see. They are from a previous marriage?*

200. Client: Yes.

201. *Worker: How did the marriage end?*

202. Client: My wife died. I had four children by her. My current wife had one child, and we had one together.

203. *Worker: How old are the children?*

204. Client: Oldest is in high school, she is fourteen, and twin boys twelve, a girl eleven, and my wife's son eleven, and our son two.

205. *Worker: How long were you married the first time?*

206. Client: Eight years. She died of cancer. I was in Seattle at the time. I advertised for a housekeeper, my current wife answered; we married after that, a year later. She was still married when we met, and her divorce hadn't yet gone through.

207. *Worker: What did she do?*

208. Client: She almost got through secretarial school in Belgium, but dropped out when pregnant. Came to America, worked, and answered my ad.

209. *Worker: How is her English?*

   (Comment: This is an area in which programmed instruction exists.)

210. Client: Oh, she doesn't construct sentences too well; but she is, uh, she gets her messages across. Actually, she doesn't speak English too well.

211. *Worker: How would you describe her?*

212. Client: Not great, but a solid, level-headed person. I guess in answer to your question about starting now, it was her threat of divorce.

213. *Worker: But you had been thinking about doing something about your marital relations. I would say that the way she got you to come here suggests that she is sensitive and understands. (Pause) [Question 3b] How long have you been thinking of some kind of change?*

   (Comment: Client in #212 suggested a natural point to introduce this question. The question reads: "3b: For how long or how often have you considered starting?")

214. Client: Uh . . . I had not really formulated any plans to seek such help because I know this marginal situation. I know these inadequa-

cies and I know that such help could be of benefit but I just think, uh, that more in terms of doing well, to make it somehow without, uh, getting into this kind of program.

(*Comment: The client, as was noted, uses vague terms, wherever he can. The next question was introduced to get at the same material in a more specific way.*)

215. *Worker:* (Question 3c) *When did you first think of getting into this kind of program?*

216. Client: Well, once in law school I went over to a psychiatrist. It was either in the first or second year, I don't remember. I don't recall. I took a battery of tests and took, uh, oh approximately three hours of therapy then, talked to someone.

(*Comment: The specific question produces more specific answers. Questions must be asked very carefully.*)

217. *Worker: What was happening with you?*

218. Client: The conditions were that I was depressed, ineffective. Anyway, I thought that I was in bad shape and at the end of my rope.

219. *Worker: Married then?*

220. Client: Yes, but my problem was not there.

221. *Worker: School?*

222. Client: Well, I was depressed, I felt it was too much effort for what was being accomplished.

(*Comment: A current problem has apparently been encountered before. In the technical terminology of operant behavior, too high a response cost can result in escape, aggression, or other undesirable responses.*)

223. *Worker: You said you went two or three times. What happened? Any results?*

224. Client: Yes, it did a lot of good. I was assigned to a psychiatric resident, and uh, he hardly ever said anything, but listened, he just listened. Which I understood at the time was proper—friends of mine would talk about it and you know how people get kindergarten ideas about, everybody imagines himself a psychiatrist, you know. A cliché in those days was, well, you know, the better the psychiatrist, the less he says. If he says nothing, he must be the world's best.

225. *Worker: Were you satisfied?*

(*Comment: The worker channels the discussion away from the client's digression.*)

226. Client: Yes. Well, there was improvement, I, uh, suddenly faced things that I've never really thought about.

227. *Worker: Like what?*

228. Client: Oh, the fact that physically I'm not what my mother always admired, I don't have a very strong male identity, and I was raised by a bunch of my mother's sisters, uh, and uh.

229. *Worker: Sounds like the psychiatrist said some things.*

230. Client: No, he didn't. I said all this really, but it. . . . I don't know how it will sound, but after I said them, I bought them.

231. *Worker: With regard to the present situation, what have you done to improve it?*

> (*Comment: It will be noted that worker brings the discussion back to the present situation and does not respond to the issue of male identity in the family raised by client in #228. By doing so, he could get more information on this subject, and shape the discussion in this direction. This subject is considered important in other forms of therapy, and might supply information necessary for our programming. If the worker finds later that it is important, he will then ask for it, since the effects of the past and of past programs [explicit or implicit] certainly affect relationships to new programs. An operant approach is not necessarily ahistorical, is not necessarily restricted to the here and now. It will be noted that historical data have been obtained all along. However, historical information which is relevant to current programming aims is being sought. These aims are to prevent further deterioration of the client's life situation and to help him to make changes to improve it.*)

232. Client: Just what I said. Not much really, till my wife brought the divorce action. It was her idea that I come, but I'm really glad, it's *mine* now. I'm not just saying that, she realized I needed the help and now I'm glad she made me come.

233. *Worker: If it were indicated, would your wife come to these sessions too?*

234. Client: Never thought of it. She tries hard in many ways. It never occurred that she might need to come.

235. *Worker: Well, it's too early to tell. Sometimes we see both partners, sometimes we don't. Sometimes it helps speed things up, helps us understand the situation better. It is too early to tell but generally it takes two to make a marital problem. We'll see.*

236. Client: OK.

237. *Worker:* (Question 4a) *Now let me ask you some questions, some further ones, this time about your strengths. We want to know what we*

can build on, what strengths you have, and in what related areas, and other things. What strengths would you say you have in areas related to the problem?

238. Client: My strengths I guess are that I am dependable; I have a certain doggedness.

239. *Worker: And undoubtedly well-placed. What about your wife? What strengths do you have here?*

240. Client: Oh, it's very hard to say.

241. *Worker: She wants you back?*

242. Client: Yeah.

243. *Worker: Anything else?*

244. Client: Well, we have a satisfactory sex life.

245. *Worker: Yes? How often?*

246. Client: More frequently, I would say, than a man my age would average.

247. *Worker: Like?*

248. Client: Oh, say at least three times a week, most likely more.

   (*Comment: An indication that he must be doing* something *right.*)

249. *Worker: And these relations are satisfactory? Pleasing to you both?*

   (*Comment: The answer seems obvious, but the question is asked to get a specific statement of good relations from the client.*)

250. Client: Yes.

   (*Comment: Note the contrast between the number of words spent on positive statements and the number of words spent on "pathological" statements.*)

251. *Worker: What else in relation to your wife?*

252. Client: Well, I'm an inadequate father, but on the other hand I'm not so bad. She has got the son she brought with her to the marriage. I'm not bad with the boy either.

253. *Worker: Well, we're discussing your strengths. Does he respond to you?*

254. Client: Yes, he does. We do things together. He listens to me.

255. *Worker: He responds to you. The other children?*

256. Client: Yes, they do too. I really don't think I should show any partiality among them.

*(Comment: The answers describe a home situation consider-
ably at variance with the initial picture of inadequacies presented. He gets along well with his wife and children—so well,
as a matter of fact, that the family wants more of him.)*

257. *Worker: (Question 4b) What strengths do you have in other
areas? Besides the problem area?*

258. Client: Until very recently, I kept up with my legal reading better
than most people.

259. *Worker: That is awfully hard these days.*

260. Client: Yes.

261. *Worker: OK. Now, leaving aside work and practice and so forth,
what strengths would you say you had in other areas? (Restatement of
Question 4b)*

262. Client: Not very many because uh, oh, I'm a social enough fellow.
We have gone out to dinner with friends. We have had a number of
cocktail parties at my house on Friday nights since we have been here.
In these two years we have had, oh, not a great number, but maybe a
dozen.

263. *Worker: You're describing a fairly active social life, for I assume
you have also gone to other people's parties. Have you enjoyed these
parties?*

264. Client: Yes, very much. As I said before I'd like to enjoy them
more.

265. *Worker: (Question 4d) Let me ask you another question. Have
there been problems, related problems in the past which you have
solved?*

   *(Comment: This question seems appropriate at this point. The
   worker will return to 4c later. Question 4a refers to strengths
   in the problem area; Question 4d concerns problem-solving
   strengths. It implies that the client has the solution to the current problems in his repertoire, and seeks information on
   these.)*

266. Client: Related problems, in the past?

267. *Worker: Which you have solved, and how you solved them.*

268. Client: With my marginal situation, uh, I would have to say, what
relaxes me. Accomplishment does. But since I am not really accomplishing anything, I am a shattered wreck.

269. *Worker: You see yourself on a treadmill?*

   *(Comment: The purpose of this question is to define the prob-
   lem more explicitly.)*

270. Client: Yes.

271. *Worker: Well, in the past, when you were on a treadmill, did you get off, and if so, how?*

   (*Comment: The question, not having been answered in its original form, is restated in a manner specific to the client's repertoire.*)

272. Client: Oh, in the past job situations, I'd go on to a steadily better job and end up way out on a limb.

   (*Comment: This answer has two possible branches. If he goes on to a better job, he must have been accomplishing something at the previous one. He is also reporting inadequacy. Further exploration at this point might involve considerable digression.*)

273. *Worker: We'll discuss this in a minute; but have there been other problems you have solved?*

274. Client: I have a problem with my parents. My mother is in bad shape, severe asthmatic. She is also hysterical and always has been.

275. *Worker: Hysterical? In what sense?*

276. Client: In the psychiatric sense. My real judgment would be that she is schizophrenic.

277. *Worker: Where does she live?*

   (*Comment: The specific question steers him away from psychiatric categorization.*)

278. Client: British Columbia. I know what you are going to ask. I only see her about once a year, or less often, and only when I visit her. She doesn't visit me. I am a wreck after the visits, but they only happen that often, so that is not a pressing problem.

279. *Worker: Is your father alive?*

280. Client: Yes, he is alive.

281. *Worker: How do you get along with him?*

282. Client: Well, in a strange way. He is from a small area in a definite society, in a small-town backwoods Ohio environment. He is a strange fellow, too. He has been a construction worker all his life, didn't get through high school, but mother didn't get to high school either.

283. *Worker: Then college was quite an achievement for you.*

   (*Comment: What the client describes as the poor educational background of his parents suggests an important strength on his part.*)

284. Client: I am told that it is, but if it is, it is nothing an ego will grow on.

285. *Worker: You read, you got good grades in college. What college did you go to?*

>   (*Comment: The assumption of good grades is based upon his having been admitted to a law school.*)

286. Client: The University of Wisconsin in Madison.

287. *Worker: You went to U.W., and got good grades! What did you major in?*

288. Client: Economics.

289. *Worker: Then you went on to law school?*

290. Client: I went to the Columbia Law School.

291. *Worker: You went to these schools, passed difficult bar exams, and you call this marginal achievement?*

>   (*Comment: The client is being asked to evaluate his assets more realistically.*)

292. Client: Well, I don't really *feel* it is an achievement.

>   (*Comment: What the client feels about it is also important, for it helps define the reality to him. The fact that he describes it this way suggests that other contingencies are operating. It may, on the other hand, simply be part of a pattern of self-deprecatory behavior. To explore these now would be too much of a digression.*)

293. *Worker: I believe you, and no amount of argument is going to change that. This is something that we will have to talk about during our sessions. You got good grades. Who paid for your schooling?*

>   (*Comment: Obviously, he did not receive a free ride from his parents.*)

294. Client: Uh, a combination of things. GI Bill was part of it. Some from my father. A lot of loans.

295. *Worker: GI Bill paid for all of this, plus loans?*

>   (*Comment: The GI Bill could not pay for both graduate and undergraduate school. The more the worker knows about the specifics, the better job he can do.*)

296. Client: It ran out. I had weekend [military] reserve money, which was a little bit. Lots of loans, and some of them from my father.

297. *Worker: Did you work too?*

298. Client: Only summers. I needed every moment I had to study.

299. *Worker: You were in the army? When?*

300. Client: 1944 to 1951.

301. *Worker: You said on your application that you were in the Air Force, right?*

302. Client: Navigator. Captain.

    (Comment: There are obviously highly relevant skills available. These skills have been obscured by the presentation of pathology.)

303. *Worker: With the rank of captain. Right out of high school, you went to navigation school, and you obviously did well enough to graduate and navigate. When were you born?*

    (Comment: The purpose of this question will be shortly evident.)

304. Client: September 12, 1927.

305. *Worker: Graduate at seventeen?*

306. Client: Yes.

307. *Worker: Then when you were in the army, with a high school diploma, they sent you to navigation school, where you performed well enough to get your wings and become a captain. You were kept in for seven years, then on the GI Bill went to the University of Wisconsin, got some funds from your father, finished law school, made a pretty good record, for you don't continue in these schools with a mediocre record, and did weekend reserves after studying hard all week. Then you went on to a series of good, or at least from your point of view, pretty high paying jobs. You've had a hard life, working all the way through, and you have succeeded against all kinds of odds. You've made it on your own.*

    (Comment: A statement of achievement.)

308. Client: I guess so, uh, but in the end, where is the success?

309. *Worker: Success is measured partly by where you start from. You have some extraordinary abilities here, which you have not been looking at. What you have been looking at is the problematic side. It seems to me that you have really been working hard and succeeding at it.*

310. Client: Well, it seems also that I've been fooling people all the time.

311. *Worker: How have you been fooling them?*

    (Comment: This may suggest some usable skills. Though "fooling" probably refers to the discrepancy between the obvious esteem with which he is held, and his own reported lack of self-esteem.)

312. Client: Well, I've just barely made it, I'm just . . .

313. *Worker: What do you mean?*

314. Client: I'm a shaky mass of wreckage.

315. *Worker: Well, let's see. You state that you barely made it through navigation school, through college, through law school. You barely made it on these jobs. You know, here I just wonder what is your definition of "barely made it"?*

　　(Comment: Nothing wrong with being argumentative or contrary—if this moves the program to help the client along.)

316. Client: Uh . . . I'm saying that I'm the kind of fellow who got, uh, who is mediocre as hell, who somehow got away with it.

317. *Worker: Really, I don't see how you could have "gotten away with it" in so many places for so long.*

318. Client: Well, I don't either.

319. *Worker: Is it quite possible that you haven't been getting away with anything?*

320. Client: Well, it could be.

321. *Worker: You've been with a lot of sharp people. I don't think these people are readily fooled.*

322. Client: Well, if not, then, I still have to repeat again, if there is something there, it is still lacking.

323. *Worker: Well, I see what you are telling me is that you are not really happy.*

324. Client: Nothing any ego will grow on.

325. *Worker: We will have to find out what that means. Are you saying that, in terms of growth, you don't see much of a future in it?*

326. Client: Well, what I am saying is that I think it's uh, the idea of living is to grow, to develop, yet I'm not developing. I, uh, to develop you have to have a certain amount of ego, and I don't have it somehow. Now this is, these are, my own terms.

327. *Worker: You are, well, I get the message. What you are stating is, the idea of living is to grow and develop and you don't see yourself developing. You don't see a purpose in this of the kind that you like.*

　　(Comment: Purposive behavior is behavior governed by some definable consequence. A possible outcome target of the program is being considered.)

328. Client: True enough.

329. *Worker: You don't see yourself going onward and upward, you see a kind of plateau which isn't very happy.*

(*Comment: Client may be analyzing events in the terms of the social cliché of someone who has evidently spent a great effort in getting ahead and, now that he is there, does not see the point of it. An alternate explanation is that getting there has been worth it, but something about the current contingencies has disrupted behavior. This suggests another examination of the conditions involved in the situation. The fact that the client has been engaged in extraordinary efforts until now indicates that his behavior has been reinforced by his professional rewards.*)

330. Client. True.

331. *Worker:* (Question 4c) *Let me ask, have there been any conditions under which the present problem hasn't been a problem?*

(*Comment: Question provides further clarification and specification.*)

332. Client: I can't think of any in my life. The area is too great.

333. *Worker: Are there any conditions right now in which the present problem isn't a problem?*

334. Client: There are times when I'm accomplishing things and I'm getting things done. And I'm putting these things way back and I feel like I am purposeful, or purposive.

335. *Worker: So occasionally when you are accomplishing things, you feel ok? Right now you don't feel you are accomplishing anything?*

(*Comment: See earlier discussion of contingency analysis of emotions.[2] The implied program for changing his depressed affect is to establish those contingencies which reverse the affect.*)

336. Client: Yeah.

337. *Worker: Let me see if I can make a stab at what goes on. During the day, you are supposed to keep up with changes in laws, the state of the market, deal with clients who come in with problems, consult with staff members from other branches of the law, the solutions to whose problems may have implications in your area. You are very efficient and are constantly called upon by others for consultation.*

(*Comment: The worker is attempting to focus this slow-speaking and self-derogatory client in the interests of time, and in*

[2] Chapter 3.

order to obtain specific information. The worker is "visualiz-
ing" the work situation and trying to check it out, to lead to
contingencies which he infers are competing with the impor-
tant one the client wants.)

338. Client: Yeah, that's right, and not only that, but we also have been getting some law trainees, and I had to devote time to them. They come in at odd times, and I sympathize with them. They've got a heavy schedule, and I make time for them at their convenience. Also, these consultations that I do with other members of the firm are usually done in their office and when their client is there.

339. *Worker: Well this seems to further complicate your "hamburger"*
day. Not only is your time completely chopped up, but the offices
where you spend your time are also chopped up. You run here, run
there, consult this person, talk to that person. If you only could do
something with that time, it would be ok. If you could add it up, by the
end of the day it might add up to something.

> *(Comment: A clear problem is the temporal and spatial ar-*
> *rangements of the client, and a program to rearrange these is*
> *highly feasible. While the client is highly regarded, he does*
> *not have an adequate office; if he had an adequate office,*
> *other lawyers would consult with him there. His secretary*
> *could arrange his time, so that he could do his work at work*
> *and not take it home. The client's depression may be caused*
> *by the contingencies which follow the present disarray or by*
> *the absence of contingencies, important to him, eliminated by*
> *this disarray.)*

340. Client: Yeah, true, true.

341. *Worker: Then, after a day like that, you come home bucking traf-*
fic all the way for one or two hours, your wife isn't too happy, she
hasn't seen you all day, six kids in the house. A woman of thirty-one
years, oldest kid is about seventeen.

342. Client: Fourteen.

343. *Worker: Fourteen—that's pretty much for a woman who would*
like to live and see things. You eat quickly and then you go to your
study and you are unhappy about the day's events, this chopped-up
situation. You sit in your study and it is difficult to sit down and work,
you fritter away up to two hours, feel uneasy and guilty about having
spent your time there. You surface to see your wife at 10 o'clock, 11
o'clock you may have sex and you may not, and then maybe you fall
asleep thereafter and maybe you don't. You toss and turn in your bed,
right? You get a few hours sleep, before you know it there goes the
alarm clock and it's another day and another day and another day.

You carry some stuff home with you for the weekend, right? Your wife makes demands on you and you recognize that these are legitimate. At the same time, there are legitimate demands in regard to work, but if you could keep them separate, if you could do your work, you could enjoy your wife. You waste time. Then the week starts. That's the picture, right?

> *(Comment: This picture, which is "finer grain" than that given by the client, is indeed depressing and may be the "treadmill" which the client said he is on.)*

344. Client: Yes, that's the picture.

345. *Worker: Well, if that's the picture, I don't see how you can feel anything but depressed under these circumstances. You wouldn't be a sensible person if you didn't realize this was fraught with consequences for you as well.*

> *(Comment: The client's depression is stated as making sense—indicating normality rather than pathology.)*

346. Client: Well, if what you say is true, uh, I am much more deeply disturbed than that.

347. *Worker: What I am saying is that you are giving a very accurate assessment of what the situation is. Your emotions don't produce things, your emotions are responsive to events. It is not our depression that makes us work less, it is the fact that we are not doing as well as we could and not accomplishing what is important for us that makes us feel depressed. So your emotions are functioning in a very efficient manner. They are very sensible indicators to what is going on. And I think you would be in serious trouble if you didn't feel depressed.*

348. Client: Well, I'm not prepared for that.

349. *Worker: Well, what are you prepared for?*

> *(Comment: Rather than "reflecting the feeling" in #348, worker changes the sentence from statement of negation [not prepared] to question about affirmation [are prepared] Note effect in #350.)*

350. Client: Oh, I suppose I was waiting to cop some, some sort of sickness later, and flee, I want to rest . . . uh . . . a winter something . . . uh.

> *(Comment: Escape via illness or vacation is one way out, but it would not work in the long run because it would not change the governing contingencies.)*

351. *Worker: What kind of situation is really going on? Is what I am saying plausible?*

352. Client: Yes, it is plausible.

353. *Worker: Basically, as I said, you have every reason in the world to be depressed. Now your wife is miserable, but when she talks about divorce, she isn't trying to get rid of you, she wants you back. But what she is saying is, "I am being disappointed. You have certain things I like, that is what I married you for and I'm not getting enough of them; I don't see you enough."*

354. Client: Hm-hmm.

355. *Worker: Maybe she doesn't say that when she is angry at you, but I think that is the message; she is willing to take you back. And she says if you undergo psychotherapy, she will take you back.*

356. Client: Then why in the hell does it disturb the hell out of a guy to tell him that he is all right?

357. *Worker: I am not telling him that he is all right, I am telling him that he is in a mess of a situation, and that's why he is disturbed. He is tremendously disturbed. (Pause)*

358. Client: (*Client nods his head.*)

359. *Worker: Well, let me summarize so far. I think you need help and some guidance to get out of the present kind of situation or this kind of mess. But what I see, I see you in a depression right now, you have these feelings and as I said, you'd be in serious trouble if you didn't have them.*

360. Client: (*Client nods his head.*)

361. *Worker: (Question 5) Is there anything that we have left out, anything that you consider pertinent which we haven't discussed?*

362. Client: No.

363. *Worker: Anything that you think might have been omitted, or overstressed? Not discussed enough?*

   (*Comment: The same question is rephrased—client has required prompting previously.*)

364. Client: No.

365. *Worker: (Question 6. Smiles and nods.) Is there any information you may want to know about us, anything we can tell you?*

366. Client: Well . . . not really. Can you help me? What are you going to do?

367. *Worker: The first thing is that we shall set up a regular appointment [discussion follows setting time, etc.] Then we'd like you to keep some records, a "log" to get a better, clearer picture of your day, your life. Here is a notebook. We'd like you to write in this log for a week, starting when you get up, at least one entry an hour [describes the*

log].[3] *We shall go over this log, analyze it, and try to find out what is happening in very definite terms, what factors played into what problems and also, which is very important, we want to look at those times when there are no problems, when things are going well, and see if we can analyze those and try to understand the difference between the two. I want to stress to you that these logs are very important; they are the raw material that we will be using when we set up a program. When we look at these logs, we'll set a priority of things to work on, and then we will sign a contract. You are used to contracts, being a lawyer. The contract will simply state what we will work on.*

368. Client: OK. It makes a lot of sense. (*Pause*) I want to thank you very much for seeing me, for seeing me so quickly. (*Client turns and goes to the door.*) Tell me, do all your clients leave here feeling so good?

> (*Comment: The client sees the possibilities of the program, that help is possible and is available.*)

> *End of the initial interview*

ANALYSIS OF THE INITIAL INTERVIEW

This initial interview can be examined for strengths (current relevant repertoires) upon which a program can be built and which may provide guidelines for a program that will take the client, with this current relevant repertoire, to his terminal (target) repertoire. As often happens, especially in involved situations such as this one (and most situations brought to casework agencies are easily as complicated as this one), the signing of the contract did not take place after the first interview. More detailed information was needed.

Current Relevant Repertoire. This client is vocationally and financially successful, an authority in his field. His job requires continual analysis of possible outcomes, the options available to his clients, and assistance to his clients. It should be possible to program the transfer of these abilities from his professional life to his personal life.[4]

[3] The log referred to is a slightly modified form of the Daily Events Log (Goldiamond, 1974).

[4] The fact that the client is a lawyer does not make the task of behavior analysis simpler than if he were engaged in some other occupation, such as teaching,

One of his major assets is that he is a valued member of his firm; thus it may be assumed that if he makes reasonable demands on the firm, aimed at increasing his value, they will probably be met. Another asset is the fact that his wife wants the marriage to continue, provided he meets her terms, which are that she and the children get to see more of him. She has also supported him at work. There are *some* pleasures at home. Although it is a complicated family picture (children from previous marriages of each of them in addition to *their* child), they get along well; he enjoys being with them and handles the children well. The family provides *some* pleasure and support for him, but he does not see enough of them. There are *some* mutually enjoyable social activities, and he does report active, probably mutually satisfying, sexual relations.

He claims to be working inefficiently at his profession, but he does have the ability to put in time. There were many other situations in the past that he has handled well (college, and so on). It is possible to formulate a few possible directions that the program might take. For verification, additional information from his logs and from future interviews will be needed.

Tentative Program Direction. Although it is a bit premature to state them other than tentatively, it seems that the following are potential areas for programming. A major element of the program probably should be: (a) *the establishment of greater control over his own time at work, so that he can allocate the time necessary to finish his work, as well as complete his professional reading there.* If the necessary patterns can be established, he will then be able to spend his time at home with his family. The establishment of appropriate behavioral repertoires at home might not seem to be a problem, for these exist,

---

business, medicine, housewife. Consequences and contingencies are involved in behavior in general. The fact that he is a lawyer, and an efficient one at that, suggests that he be approached with the repertoire that is most familiar to him, namely, law. In addition to his skills in legal analysis, he has considerable skills in record-keeping, spending hours on cases, taxes, and so on. Actually, the client is already "analyzing" his situation, but in terms of pathology, not constructive actions; in psychiatric jargon, not specific, observable, and remediable terms.

provided he has the time. His wife also requires some reinforcement from him for her supportive behaviors. His being at
home and doing things with her are important to her. His work
situation is also important to her, both as it relates to her time
with him and to her evaluation of herself in terms of the qualities of the man she married. Other specific outcomes should
include: (b) *increasing frequency and duration of home-related
behaviors; (c) his establishment of patterns of positive presentation of self;* and (d) *his reinforcement of his wife's behaviors
which reinforce him.* She may be a strong therapeutic ally, and
the program may also include (e) *establishment of behaviors
on his part which explicitly solicit this.*

Ordinarily, the process is to see clients once weekly, although there is no hard and fast rule about this. Sometimes
clients need to be seen or contacted more often, and they may
be seen less frequently, certainly, at least in the termination
process; the process is to "fade out" the therapist. In this case,
the second interview was delayed for two weeks because the
worker became ill.

The client had continued recording during this time. Generally, recording must be shaped and reinforced, especially in
the beginning, on a heavy schedule, every time (CRF). Here,
however, it was less important because record-keeping was not
only part of his repertoire as an attorney, it was essential to his
making a living. His record-keeping may also have been maintained ("motivated") by hopes generated by the initial interview
and the negative reinforcement of his wife's threat to leave him.
Regardless of the cause, the records were unusually good for
the beginning phase of therapy, and they had confirmed the information obtained in the initial interview.

THE SECOND INTERVIEW

The client returned for his second interview on June 10, 1970.
While he was still quite depressed, he was nowhere near so

downcast as he had been at the first interview. He stated that he had had an "up-and-down week" (a favorite expression of his). He stated that nothing different had happened in the past week.

A contract had not been prepared after the first interview because more information was wanted, as well as a better and clearer picture of the client, his day, and his world. Baseline data were needed, not only to assess the progress or lack of progress of the program, but also to obtain more complete information so that the worker might not intervene prematurely and perhaps upon the wrong problems, and thus extinguish further efforts on the client's part. It has been our experience in the clinic that clients often tend to rush things and attempt to make changes on their own initiative. Sometimes the results have been good, but more often than not the interventions have been premature. This is why the therapist initially takes a greater part in the planning.

Mr. Smith's record-keeping was good and more than adequate for this phase of the process. His days tended to fall into two categories: "bad days" and "less bad days" (his terms). Following are the records of two days: June 4 was a "bad day" and June 8 a "less bad day."

The client was praised for his excellent logs. These records were then discussed immediately and thoroughly in the session (one of the strongest possible reinforcers a consultant can provide for record-keeping). The therapeutic purpose of the logs is of primary importance; the research purpose is secondary.

The client's days followed a pattern. Whether or not the day started out "well," he arrived at work frazzled by the traffic, and the workday itself was frustrating because he generally did not complete what he perceived to be a good day's work. After a day at work, marred by constant interruptions and fighting with the secretarial pool and characterized by a lack of assertiveness in setting up the conditions that would make his day easier, he would then get into his automobile and buck heavy traffic on the way home. Once there, he would spend a little time with his wife, then he would bury himself in his home office, where he struggled (generally unsuccessfully) to complete his day's work. He would stay in the study until eleven or twelve at night. On each of these nights his wife would enter the study to get some attention, using the only means she knew, which was essentially an aversive approach. That is, she would interrupt him in his study, demand to know when he was coming out, and an argument would ensue. Negative attention is better than being ignored, and his wife did not want to be ignored. However, on these nights the interaction would end in an argument, and he and his wife either went to bed not talking to each other or, as on June 4, actually sleeping in different rooms. He did not get much work done when he was in his home office because he then brooded about the impending visit of his wife. This pattern occurred in four of the five workdays covered in his records.

One day was an exception. On that day he left work early and, upon arriving home, spent a great deal of time with his wife. He did not work in the evening, but played with his children and, having a good time, decided not to work that evening. He and his wife spent the evening talking and drinking out on the patio. The evening was a very "good" evening (as can be seen in the logs), and that evening he and his wife went to bed happy with each other and had sexual relations.

The difference in pattern between the two days was discussed with the client. He stated that the usual pattern was the day when he buried himself in his home library, although there were occasions such as Monday when he took the evening off. However, he had never realized the relationship between the behavior and the consequences. That is, he had not seen the startling contrast as pointed out during this interview. Technically, his activities were not under proper stimulus control. His office should have been a discriminative stimulus for working, home should have been a discriminative stimulus for enjoying his family and not for doing his office work. This "lack of stimulus control" is an example of the "scrambled eggs" effect noted in Chapter 2. It is common in a great number of behavioral problems.

A familiar example of such "scrambling" is the student who goes to the library to study. After sitting down and

DATE: JUNE 4

	1 *TIME*	2 *ACTIVITY*	3 (setting) *WHERE*	4 *WHO WAS THERE*
T1	7:00 A.M.	Eating breakfast	At home	Wife, 2 yr. old son
T2	8:00 A.M.	Driving	Highway	Self
T3	9:00 A.M.	Mail	At desk	Mr. X. (next desk)
T4	10:00 A.M.	Work	Desk, on telephone	Constant interruption
T5	11:00 A.M.	Same	Same	Same
T6	12:00– 1:00 P.M.	Lunch	Cafe	Was alone
T7	1:00– 5:00 P.M.	Work	Desk, other offices	Co-workers
T8	6:30 P.M.	Finally get home	Highway	Self
T9	10:00 P.M.	At desk	Home office	Alone
T10	10:00 P.M.	Desk	Home office	Wife
T11	11:30 P.M.	Tried to sleep	Bed	Alone; wife in spare bedroom

5 WHAT YOU WANTED	6 (what happened) WHAT YOU GOT	7 COMMENTS
A good day. Peace at home. Things back to normal.	Good breakfast. Was patient with son, conversed with wife.	A good start. I'm optimistic —feel good today.
To get to work	Slow, jams, got there	Damn traffic, but there's nothing I can do about it.
To get mail out of way	Chatter and demands for advice from this young ambitious man	Complied with his request, but seething inside.
Get work done. Get important papers typed.	Delay as no one free in secretarial pool	Frustrated—depressed— work fell off
Same	Same	Just sat at desk shuffling paper.
Relax—have drink	Nothing	Didn't help. Still depressed.
Get work done.	Some of work done	Will have to take work home to catch up.
Get home, relax, catch up on work	Angry at traffic	Finally got home, worn out—had sandwich, spoke with wife, went into office
Get some work done—catch up and possibly be ahead for tomorrow.	Nothing. Sat, shuffled papers—had several drinks	Really discouraged, depressed
To be on good terms with wife	Argument. She wanted to know when I was coming out.	Upset
Wife—good relations, good feeling	Tossed and turned— slept poorly, restlessly.	A typical night after my wife and I have had a fight.

DATE: JUNE 8

	1 *TIME*	2 *ACTIVITY*	3 *SETTING*	4 *WHO WAS THERE*
M1	7:00 A.M.	Breakfast	Kitchen	Wife, 2 yr. old son
M2	8:00 A.M.	Driving	Highway	Self
M3	9:00 A.M.– 12:00	Work	Office	Self, others
M4	12:00– 1:00 P.M.	Lunch	Cafe	Alone
M5	1:30– 4:00 P.M.	Work	Desk	Same
M6	4:00 P.M.	Driving	Highway	Alone
M7	4:40– 6:00 P.M.	Playing with kids, eating	House, back yard, kitchen	Family
M8	7:00 P.M.– 1:00 A.M.	Sitting out- side, talking, eating, and drinking	House, back yard	First kids and wife then wife alone

5 WHAT YOU WANTED	6 WHAT HAPPENED	7 COMMENTS
Eat, leave on good terms	Very nice breakfast. Talked with wife.	A good start—hope things go well after a so-so weekend.
Get to work	Same	Frustrated
Get work done	Same—did much less than I wanted to.	Same goddamned feeling of depression, uselessness. If I were more adequate, I'd get more done.
Eat	Nothing—had a drink.	Don't know which I like less—eating alone or eating with co-worker discussing shop.
Same—get things done	Same—only got part of work done.	Got disgusted—left early— let them fire me if they don't like it.
Get home	Got home quickly— beat the rush.	Came home not feeling frustrated for a change.
Eat, good relations and then go to home office and get work	Ate—had good time— figured "to hell with work."	Change. Good evening so far—I want it to continue.
A good evening— good relations with wife and kids	Got just that—talked with wife, went together to bed—had sex.	Why can't all my evenings, and all my relations be like today?

depositing his books, he divides his time, generally unequally, between looking at his book and gossiping with his neighbor. He then goes out to the lounge for refreshments and more talk. If the student's behavior were under different stimulus control, he would both study and gossip, but study only when in the library and gossip only when in the lounge; the two activities would be separated.

For both the student and the lawyer client, despite the different topographies of the behaviors, the consequences are the same. Behavior that is not under proper stimulus control soon begins to function as a kind of escape and avoidance behavior for what are perceived by the "actor" to be aversive situations. In the case of the student, the aversive behavior is, obviously, studying. While the immediately reinforcing qualities of escaping studies are tempting, the *ultimate aversive consequences* (flunking examinations) are enormous.

With this client, his home situation was marked by quarreling and fighting with his wife. Burying himself in the library had the immediate consequence of escaping aversive contacts with her. However, resultant consequences were even more aversive, escalating into a circular effect that damaged his marriage and lessened his performance at work.

It seemed clear that the immediate choice of intervention, the tactic that seemed to promise the greatest and most immediate relief, was to try to establish, as quickly as possible, stimulus control over each of the behaviors and to assist the client to heighten his stimulus discrimination. This became the goal of the program to establish appropriate (to him) stimulus control over work and home behaviors, separating the office as the place for work from the home as the place for relaxing with his family. Improving the quality of the relationships at both places would be a later agenda item, but for the time being the immediate intervention was to establish this stimulus control.

When the worker applied a similar contingency analysis to his work situation, the recordings in the logs, typified by June 4 and June 8, confirmed the information elicited during the intake interview. Regardless of how well the day started for this client, he soon encountered a series of extinction trials. In operant terms, he was engaging in behavior, often a great deal of behavior, that had no payoff for him. The accompanying lack of payoff often lowered the behavior, but was accompanied by a feeling of depression. Whether the depression caused the extinction or the extinction caused the depression is a moot point. For purposes of intervention programming, they went together, they covaried.

Mr. Smith had to take work home because continual interruptions from the telephone and from his colleagues' "chatter and demands for advice" kept him from completing his work. He did not have a secretary who could serve as a filter. As a result, he reported frustration and depression, resentment, and inability to work.

This interpretation is stated in barest outline. The therapist in this case actually went through a "fine-grain" analysis of the contingencies. For example, he examined the transaction of the intrusion from the point of view of other reasons for the colleagues' "intrusive" behavior (possibly a way of being "social") and what was maintaining it (client's reinforcement) and why (the desire to be considered friendly and sociable, as well as following a norm in his firm of giving advice to younger colleagues).

The therapist also went through a process of weighing other solutions. He examined the client's emotional responses of rage in contrast to reported feelings of anger, in terms of whether or not the client was discriminating properly.

Programming is often very complicated, and good programming requires a great deal of skill and knowledge of human behavior, as well as the behavior of a particular client. There is much more depth to behavior analysis than is usually understood or acknowledged.

SETTING THE CONTRACT

A two-week baseline had been collected, and record-keeping was being shaped. The information received in the initial interview was collated, and a program assessment for Mr. Smith and his family and work situation had been formulated. It was now time to discuss and set the contract with Mr. Smith.

There are priorities in intervention. Situations of immediate importance should be worked on first, but a high priority should also be to provide a situation in which the client can have an immediate success experience. Fortunately, in this case, the immediate target of intervention, the establishment of stimulus control over work and home, fulfilled the requirements of both priorities.

Since therapeutic contracts may be revised, the contract (at this stage) was considered tentative, although this one turned out to be the final contract. The contract had three general target areas (stated nonbehaviorally): (1) to "make work more rewarding"; (2) to improve upon and enjoy a happy home life; and (3) to develop procedures, related to 1 and 2 to achieve these goals. In other words, goals 1 and 2 are terminal repertoires for the client's life; goal 3 is a constellation of program goals that he needed to master in order to achieve goals 1 and 2. The specifics of the contract were as follows:

I. TERMINAL REPERTOIRES

The two major target areas agreed upon by the client and the worker were the following (statements actually written into the contract are italicized):

1a. *Work:* Work is to be made more rewarding; that is, the reinforcers which have maintained the client's behavior up to now are to be continued, but the response cost in obtaining them is to be reduced, so that there is time during the nine-to-five office day to do the work currently brought home. Events which compete with the behaviors appropriate to these goals are to be brought under control. The following specific items are to be included in the contract:

1b. *Specified: Your work situation is to be rearranged so that you will be able to complete your daily work during the working day, including the work you now take home. Further, it will be more enjoyable. Specifically, you will do the following:*

(i) *You are to obtain your own secretary rather than working through a pool. Your schedule is to be arranged through her.*

(ii) *You are to obtain a larger office.*

2a. Home: The client is to devote more time to his wife and family. Currently, the problem is not the nature of his interactions during the few hours he spends with them, but the fact that he spends too few hours with them. The following specific items are to be included in the contract:

2b. Specified: Your evenings and weekends are to be free for you to spend with your family. Specifically, you will do the following:

(i) *You are to spend at least one hour an evening with your wife, giving her your exclusive attention.*

(ii) *You are to spend at least one hour each night with your children, giving them your exclusive attention during this hour.*

(iii) *You are to go out with your wife, without the children, at least two times a week.*

3a. Programming Targets: In order to establish these patterns, records will be required as the basis for their specification: *You are to observe and note events and relations in those areas which you can harness to maintain and extend Targets 1 and 2.*

The client stated goals initially either in such negative terms as "not being a mass of tensions" and "not being scared of people," or in such vague positive terms as being able to handle "aspects of things," "enjoy family," and "improve marital relations." The contract is not concerned with eliminating depression, eliminating work problems, or eliminating marital tensions, and so on. Rather, the contract is stated in terms of constructing or putting together repertoires which already exist and which are to be maintained by the natural reinforcers in the environment. The absence of such reinforcers produces the presenting problems. The client will have to develop or reinstate a variety of patterns which will have cumulative effects, as, for example, speaking to his employers to get a secretary, notifying his colleagues that he is to be on call less frequently and at regular times, and discussing his program with his family. Communication with all concerned should have manifold effects in his relations with them. Each of the patterns will also have to be discussed and programmed. The two sets of target goals are deceptive in that, as stated, they seem simple and narrow.

Two further considerations influence the choice of these targets. They are attainable, and they vary in closeness to present repertoires. This closeness indicates ease of establishment or reinstatement, thus providing fast relief. Accordingly, among them are patterns which can be (a) considered as steps in a program and (b) attained rapidly, thereby reinforcing such programming behaviors as keeping logs, analyzing the data, and meeting appointments. Stated otherwise, the client should rapidly begin to experience success. This should relieve his depression somewhat, and the effects of the depression on his family and colleagues. Note that success would be attained in patterns which are *clearly target-relevant,* hence the importance of consideration (a). The current relevant repertoire, and suggestions for steps in between, will be considered under "current relevant repertoire" and "program notes" respectively.

II. CURRENT RELEVANT REPERTOIRES (ENTRY PATTERNS)

Reinforcers maintain progression through the program to the outcome. Accordingly, the current repertoires must be keyed to the outcome. These repertoires are discussed with the client and recorded on the program worksheets whenever the target outcomes are programmed.

1a. *Background:* Client is a valued member of the firm, and his secretarial and space requirements are necessary for his usefulness to the firm. If this is not already evident to his firm, he should be able to make it so. A question here is: Where do we start?

1*b. Specified:* Client is making extensive use of secretaries in the pool. He has the "ear" of the head of the firm, who relies on him. One of the tasks is to transfer stimulus control of those *assertive behaviors,* which exist elsewhere in his repertoire, to the situations where they are lacking. Such behaviors are in his repertoire; he could not have come this far without them. The pattern of apparently good-natured acceptance of outrageous conditions (inadequate office, no assigned secretary) may have served a function in getting him "up in the world." This pattern is still reinforced, but he is now also being punished by its high response cost and the withdrawal of reinforcers associated with his taking work home, among other consequences.

2*a. Background:* His wife's expulsion of her husband has been interpreted as an operant of desperation on her part, which produced the desired consequence: he went into treatment, which she felt might make him more available to her. Obviously, she still wants him as a husband. The task is to bring them together more. The reinforcers are available.

2*b. Specified:* Client spends some time with his wife and children. He goes out with his wife when they are invited out. They invite others to their home. He and the children do things together and enjoy each other (mutual reinforcement of behavior), as do he and his wife.

3*a. Strategy:* He has the ability to analyze relations, as evidenced by the pathology-oriented analyses of his parents' behaviors and of his own inadequacies. These analytic repertoires can be converted into (or supplemented by) analyses which suggest plans for action toward constructional outcomes. Such constructional analyses are already in his repertoire as a successful lawyer, along with the necessary record-keeping system. It is not necessary to establish new repertoires or even to reinstate old ones. Therefore, the task is to transfer these repertoires to the problem areas.

3*b. Specified:* He analyzes and observes his own behaviors and those of others. He notes consequences and their effects on behavior. As a lawyer, he analyzes cases and laws. He also keeps meticulous records and refers to them.

The outlook is optimistic.

III. CHANGE PROCEDURES

The worker has indicated where he hopes to go and what resources he will utilize or possibly develop on the way. These
are apparent at the outset; undoubtedly, the client will develop
new ones, or they may be suggested in transit. The procedures
are guides which are subject to change.

1. *Work program:* If it becomes necessary to convince the
firm that he should have his own secretary and office, he can
draw up a cost-benefit analysis in advance; as a securities expert, he is familiar with these.

He can discuss these ideas with his wife and colleagues.
By discussing the problem with them, he (*a*) familiarizes them
with the problem (they probably think the changes are long
overdue); (*b*) makes it their cause; (*c*) gets their understanding
and possible support (he has social skills); (*d*) increases communication with them; and (*e*) lays groundwork for changes
listed below.

Assuming that he gets a secretary and office, he should
then work out the scheduling of his time through her. She
should keep his appointment log, and he should not be as
available as he has been.

He should discuss these changes with the office staff and
solicit their advice. He is to instruct his future secretary to
block out for him an inviolable period of time in which to read
his law journals and to do what he now does at home. No one
should interrupt during those periods, and all callers are to be
told he is in conference and she is to take messages.

2. *Home program:* He is to discuss scheduling of time with
wife and children; they will want the family to stay together,
and will want to help him. Perhaps he should see the children
while his wife is washing the dishes. Perhaps he might help
clear the table and wash the dishes with his wife. Perhaps the
children should join in. In all events the discussions should be
a family issue. The conferences should signal a new turn.

In a highly visible place, he is to set up a chart for scheduling time. In the event that the requirements are not met during
one night, owing to some emergency, he is to discuss make-up
time with whoever was involved. The family is to monitor this

chart. It may come in handy later. (When the children start dating and staying out late, they can keep charts.)

When there are to be exceptions to the schedule, such as, for example, possible Saturday conferences at work, these are to be programmed at least three days in advance.

3. *Programming procedures:* He should write out each of the contract items on a legal-sized pad. Each is to be on a different page, and each is to be in a different folder. (These behaviors are in his repertoire.) He might write at the beginning the type of campaign he might institute in each of these areas, and when he might institute them. Any notions he has are to be recorded on the pad. In a separate folder, he can record which of the various folders will have priority, which will be worked on simultaneously, etc. He should bring these materials into sessions for discussion, along with his logs and worksheets.

The client, as a lawyer, is familiar with the fact that favorable outcomes are not obtained immediately and often come stage by stage, in a sequence. This repertoire can be used in the program.

The items proposed may sound artificial and contrived. People should *want* to go out with their wives spontaneously. They should not have to plan it on paper. These criticisms overlook the difference between well-established repertoires and those which have to be established (or reinstated or transferred). People walk spontaneously, and go up stairs, alternating their legs without thinking. The patterns are well-established, or what the psychologist calls "overlearned." However, if you watch a child learning to walk you will see him first switch from moving one foot up a step to meet the other, and later struggle to alternate legs. If driving a car is now spontaneous, try to recall the explicit instructions you were given or developed for yourself.

IV. ENVIRONMENTAL RESOURCES AND REINFORCERS

When the reinforcers required for a program are lacking or are not readily available, special reinforcers may have to be devised or applied, such as points, tokens, words of praise, money, candies, or other special "treats" or "rewards." In such cases, an artificial economy or ecology may have to be constructed. A system should be justified, however, not because it lacks artificiality, but because it has advantages over the alternative contingency systems available. Given the resources and reinforcers readily available to this client, "artificial" contingencies do not seem to be needed here. Early success in attaining some of the steps toward the terminal outcome may be all that is necessary to get this program moving.

1. *Work resources and reinforcers:* The opportunity to engage in his professional behavior has maintained progression through an extensive academic curriculum, and is even maintaining his homework at present. The homework, however, as was already noted, generates problems. The task is to help him eliminate the homework and "unscramble the eggs" into work behaviors at work, and home behaviors at home. The programmer should probably not encourage him to manipulate the professional reinforcers. He can, however, very profitably try to alter the setting of the journal reading.

His superiors and colleagues provide other reinforcers, which might be manipulated indirectly. His supervisors, for example, will probably reinforce assertive behaviors of the types discussed by readily granting them.

2. *Home resources and reinforcers:* The family has the economic means to enjoy family living, and they also treasure the client's presence. His wife has encouraged him, in the past, to get him to assert himself. She is supportive, and an important resource. Her cooperation is critical to the success of the program.

His wife should be enlisted immediately. Her husband is probably the best person to get her involved in this task, by discussing programming aims and developments with her. It is strategic to change the order of the targets in the actual contract, which she may see. She is tired of his consideration of work ahead of everything else. Accordingly, the contract order might be: (1) home repertoires; (2) work repertoires; (3) program repertoires. The success of a program can rest upon such seemingly insignificant procedural details.

3. *Program resources and reinforcers:* Advancement in the program is the reinforcer available from the program consultant. It is generally sufficient, if the program is well-conceived, well-designed, and well-executed.

INTERVENTION PROCEDURES

By the end of the second interview there emerged a fairly clear picture of Mr. Smith's life and the ecology of contingencies that were controlling him and it. There was enough information for baseline purposes. Therefore the contract was proposed, and intervention was initiated with this interview. The weekly worksheet was used (the client worksheet, described in Chapter 3). This form states, in concise, visual presentation, the subgoals for the next week, the repertoires upon which these can be based, and the change procedures whereby the client can progress from his current relevant repertoire to the subgoals for the week. These increasingly approach the terminal repertoire. The following form lists a subgoal on the right, to be accomplished during the coming week, and a strength the client now has upon which he can draw to accomplish this goal, the current relevant repertoire for this particular subgoal. At the bottom is the specific programming aid or assistance to help and guide the client toward the achievement of this goal. The weekly worksheet looked like this:

PROGRAM WORKSHEET: JOHN SMITH, JUNE 17

Current Relevant Repertoire (*Session #2*)	*Subgoal Subterminal Repertoire* (*for session #3*)
1. Has ability to conceptualize and some organizational skills, many legal skills.	1. Arrange schedule so that work done 9–5. Leave materials at work, leave briefcase at work.
2. Can enjoy wife and children if not hassled by work, distractions.	2. At home, spend at least 30 minutes with children (if they wish) and at least one hour with wife alone.
3. Go out with wife at least one time this week.	3. Enjoy each other's company on the occasions that they go out or have time alone.

PROGRAM WORKSHEET: JOHN SMITH, JUNE 17

Current Relevant Repertoire *(Session #2)*	*Subgoal Subterminal Repertoire* *(for session #3)*
4. Has control over certain contingencies, e.g., can set own hours.	4. Analyze work situation and bring in lists of changes that would facilitate goal #1.
5. Is keeping current record exceptionally well.	5. Keep new records.

Program Notes

1. Start out day by *initiating* chat with office mate. Take him into your confidence, tell him you're going to try to complete your work at office. Enlist his cooperation.
2 and 3. Tell kids and wife of resolution; ask for their help.
4. Use legal pads; separate pages for categories.
5. Refer to past records for guides.

One of Mr. Smith's strengths is that he has the ability to conceptualize, and he has some organizational and much legal skill. He is conscientious about work. The first goal is to apply these skills and arrange his schedule so that work can be done from nine to five. The specific suggestion was offered that he leave his briefcase at work. If he did not finish his work on one day, then it was to be done on the next—at the office. This goal is a first step, albeit a large step, to establish stimulus control over work.

The second goal, which was closely linked to the third goal, had to do with relationships at home. It was obvious that he could enjoy the company of his wife and his children under certain conditions. This appeared from his log on Monday, from the conversations during the second interview, and from the data obtained during the initial interview. Therefore "current strength #2" was that he could enjoy the company of his wife and children if the conditions were "right." Therefore, the second subgoal was to spend at least thirty minutes with the children (if they wished and were undistracted by other activities) and at least one hour with his wife alone. This was linked to the third strength, his enjoyment of his wife's company; the subgoal here, for the week, was to go out alone with his wife at least one time without the children.

The fourth strength was the recognition that he could control certain of the contingencies at work. For example, he could set his own hours. Therefore the subgoal for this week (#4) was to analyze his work situation and bring in lists of changes that could facilitate goal #1.

The client was very receptive to the worksheet, especially the Program Guide, in which he himself initated procedures to stop the daily "waste of time."

In the program notes, the second and third entries are related to the terminal goals of "happy marriage" and "happy home life." The fourth explicitly reiterates his professional skills and is designed to have him realize that he is a skilled person in much demand and much more in control than he has realized. The purpose is to make concrete proposals and to try to program toward them.

The next week Mr. Smith brought in further logs. He continued to use the form that is illustrated for June 4 and for June 8, for these provided the client and the worker with enough information to proceed. Going over the written logs, plus any other items the client wishes to talk about, forms the process of the interview. The content of the interview is not restricted to reading and discussion of the logs. Logs are used as a springboard, a starting point for discusssions that will further the client's progress. The client started the interview with, "Well, let's see how well I did" and reported the following progress:

Goal #1. The client was partially successful in the first goal. He kept his work at the office on three of the five workdays. He did take work home on the weekend.

The goal of five days was too high—the step was too large. Making steps that are too large is a common programming error. Shaping should be gradual. All things being equal, it is usually better to make the steps too small, so that they can be achieved, rather than too large, when they will be failed (produce ratio strain). However, the error here was by far overshadowed by the client's apparent delight in achieving the goal on three of the days. He regarded this as a really great achievement, which was seconded by the worker and commented upon most enthusiastically.

Goal #2. This was met on four days. On the days he came

home without his work he exceeded the criterion; that is, he spent more than thirty minutes with the children, and more than one hour with his wife. On the two days that he brought home his office work, and on the weekend days, he repeated the pattern of being in the home office. His partial progress was praised and encouraged, and the next step was planned.

Goal #3. Met. He went out to the movies Saturday night with his wife, and they both had an excellent time. He reported her conversation as animated, and the evening culminated in sexual relations.

Goal #4. Met. The client made a list of changes at work. Client and worker agreed to focus on one, namely, asking for a larger office. This would have immediate consequences in terms of facilitating work.

Goal #5. Met. Excellent records were kept.

The program worksheet made out that week follows. It can be seen that the progress made in meeting last week's subgoals was continued, and that the goals achieved are *now* part of the current relevant repertoire.

A comparison of this week's current relevant repertoire

PROGRAM WORKSHEET: JOHN SMITH, JUNE 24

Current Relevant Repertoire (Session #3)	*Subgoal: Subterminal Repertoire* (for Session #4)
1. Was successful on three days. Worked at home on weekend.	1. (a) Try procedure on all workdays. (b) No work on Sundays.
2. Successful in time with children and wife on four days; on days home without work, exceeded expectations.	2. Try to meet criterion (30 minutes with children and one hour with wife) on all weekdays. Spend all day Sunday with children and wife.
3. Went out Saturday night to movies.	3. Repeat on Saturday P.M. and do one thing together on weekdays.
4. Made a list of changes at work.	4. Ask for larger office.
5. Keeping excellent records.	5. Continue, and soon we'll have graphs as a visible reinforcer.

Program Notes

1. Tell office mate you made it last week on three days and want to shoot for more this week. Also ask him how he'd feel if he had present office all to himself, and explain.

2 and 3. Discuss notion of chart with family.

4. Try to approach head of firm; good list; we'll try them one by one.

5. Try to figure out what to graph on yourself.

with the goals of the preceding week provides an immediate assessment of outcome and program effectiveness. For the next week, he maintained the goals achieved but slowed the "keep work at work" segment down. The worker suggested keeping only Sunday work-free (as compared to last week's goal of the entire weekend). The goal with the children was repeated and was extended to Sundays by mutual agreement. On goal #3, time with wife, the results were so positive that the behavioral requirement was increased to include a "date" during the week. He was asked to consider graphing his behavior—a technique not appropriate for all clients.

FIFTH INTERVIEW: JULY 1

The logs indicated that Mr. Smith succeeded completely in meeting most of the target requirements, as indicated in the program worksheet drawn up that day. The worksheet follows. Mr. Smith succeeded in the goal of not bringing home any work on any weekday and in spending Sunday at home. It was decided to continue this requirement, repeat this task, in order to make it a permanent part of the current relevant repertoire, and to consolidate the gains. The importance of not moving the program too fast cannot be overemphasized.

The client also met the criteria for spending time with his family and achieved the goal of going out alone with his wife two times. They went out to a cocktail party Tuesday night and, although they did not go to the movies Saturday, they went out for a long walk, bought ice cream, and talked. Both found this activity mutually gratifying ("a lot of fun"). It was decided to repeat all three activities the next week (again, to consolidate gains).

He did not meet the fourth task of asking for a larger office. He was afraid of the possible repercussions. It was obvious that in this part of the program the steps were too large. Also, the program was moving satisfactorily on several fronts. It may have been unrealistic to expect movement on *all* targets at the same high pace. However, the feeling of achievement even for a partial success can transfer to other aspects of the program.

PROGRAM WORKSHEET: JOHN SMITH, JULY 1

Current Relevant Repertoire *(Session #4)*	*Subgoal: Subterminal Repertoire* *(for Session #5)*
1. No work taken home on *any* weekday. Sunday spent at home with family.	1. Continue to do all work at work, and reserve time at home for family.
2. Criterion met on all work days and Sunday.	2. Continue to devote stipulated(?) time to wife and children.
3. Went to cocktail party Tuesday night; long walk and ice cream Saturday night.	3. Continue to go out with wife at least twice a week.
4. Had discussions with head of firm, but on matters other than office.	4. Ask for assigned secretary three days a week. Try to figure out ways to get office.
5. Excellent records.	5. Continue records. Start keeping client worksheet.

Program Notes

1.
2. See preceding weeks.
3.
4. Step too great. Let's substitute smaller step as indicated, try to figure out what can be broadened easily and safely.
5. New worksheet is a chance to display your analytic skills, take over programming.
[Note: Therapist missed next session because of illness.]

Success in one area "breeds" success in another area as Mr. Smith had verbalized it the preceding week.

By mutual agreement it was decided to hold off with regard to the office and to switch the target. Mr. Smith was being assigned secretaries on a random basis from a secretarial pool. He agreed that the next step would be to ask for a definite, assigned secretary three days a week, as a starter.

Mr. Smith's records were excellent, and he also agreed that he might start to transfer programming to himself by having him complete the client worksheet.

SEVENTH INTERVIEW: JULY 15

The July 8 session was canceled by agreement, since the worker was ill. Mr. Smith had been asked to fill out a client worksheet for the week of July 1–July 8, and did so. The result follows. The client quickly grasped the manifest purpose of transferring the programming function (control) to himself. He stated the subgoals accurately in his own words; they are not direct copies of targets from program worksheets. While goal #1 had been stated positively by the worker—"Do all work at work, and reserve home time for family"—the client typically made this into the negative: "No work taken home weekdays." While they amount to the same, there is a difference in emphasis and explicitness: the goal of "no work at home" can also be fulfilled by not doing it at office. This can lead to difficulties.

The relations to contracted goals are well stated. In column 3, row 3 is interesting. He could not get tickets to a play he and his wife wanted to attend, and so, as shown in column 4, row 3, he made a decision to avert such problems in the future. All independent programming by clients should be heartily applauded, especially programming that may avoid (prevent) future problems.

The request for a secretary was met; it was "surprisingly easy." Reinforcement of this assertive behavior increased its strength and led to the revival of the goal, "Will ask for larger office" (column 5, row 4). In column 2, row 5, the negative note again: the worksheet will "make [one] less dependent on analyst" rather than "make [one] more self-reliant."

In the next steps (columns 5a and 5b) the client is making very sensible suggestions for the program and future agenda (therapy) topics (#6).

For his coming agenda he wanted to talk about specifics to make his program easier. It will be noted that the client himself began to ask that the amount of record-keeping be cut down. This was a realistic request. While such requests can be interpreted in a variety of ways, they are often a sign that the client is thinking of termination. Indeed, from the success of the program, it was not too early to consider termination.

The logs suggested that he had the office work very well under stimulus control, that he had met the criteria of time with his children, and had gone out three times with his wife. He was given a secretary not for three but for five days! He was told that this was simpler for the personnel office.

Some program changes were made. Mr. Smith was to

IBSW

Mr. Smith

1. Statement of Subgoals	2. Your Understanding of How Stated Subgoals Relate to Contracted Goals	3. Programming Variables: Manner and Extent to Which Subgoals Were Reached; Controlling Variables	4. Comments about Subgoals/Program
1) No work taken home weekdays.	1 and 2) Unscramble "scrambled eggs."	1 and 2) No problems about time. Problems about children. Sometimes want to be off by selves.	1 and 2) Feeling *much* less depressed; in fact, sometimes almost happy! This subgoal easy (so far).
2) 30 min. with children and 1 hr. with wife daily. All day Sunday.			
3) Go out 2 times a week with wife.	3) Better relations with wife.	3) Planned a play, but couldn't get tickets—went to two movies in neighborhood.	3) Wife and I will join theater guild in fall. Will start going to golf driving range.
4) Ask for assigned secretary.	4) Easier working situation.	4) Surprisingly easy.	4) Will ask for larger office.
5) Start keeping this sheet.	5) Help-me program. Make less dependent on analyst.	5) All right. Sheet is more work.	5) None.

5a. Tentative Next Step(s) for Program: Your Suggestions	5b. Justification: Relation to Contracted Goals	6. Tentative Agenda for Coming Session: Your Suggestions:
1) See comment on theater guild and golf range.	1) Better relationship.	1) Home going better, but wife will still not come in. Can we talk about involving her?
2) Try manipulating working hours. Get in at 8:00 and leave at 4:00.	2) Scrambled eggs. Also, avoid agitation of driving delays, and help work and home.	2) Ask for bigger office; discuss more work-related items.
3) Wife and I will join theater guild in fall.	3) Planning activities.	3) Discuss cutting down on amount of record-keeping.
4) Ask for bigger office.	4) Bigger office will make work easier.	

spend ten minutes alone with each of the children, talking about one of the child's particular interests; if necessary, he was to plan something in advance if this could not be done spontaneously. Even though he was going out three times a week with his wife, this was lowered to two, and one of these times was to be with another couple. He was also to ask for a larger office. Client and worker began to change the emphasis from *frequency* of interactions to changing the quality of his relationships with his family and at work. Working hours were to be rearranged from the original nine to five to eight to four. This change would enable him to eliminate the rush-hour traffic in both directions. The particular nature of his law practice made this innovation quite acceptable to his employer, and this was put into effect. The immediate result was alleviation of the hassle of the traffic situation. This might seem to be unusual, but in a surprising number of cases, especially those involving middle-class professionals, manipulation of hours is possible. Most of us are too entrenched in the nine-to-five mentality.

The logs were simplified. In the social interaction log, he was to record time, place, audience, what he said, what other people said, and then comment.

The program worksheet made out during that session follows. The first and second procedures are not combined, as the client has pretty much attained stimulus control over work. The programming notes are very general and nonspecific, for the client knows the details, and he is being encouraged to program on his own.

When he appeared for his next appointment, he had attained all of his subgoals, and the subgoals of the previous week were now the current relevant repertoire. He *had* raised the question of his need for a larger office. He was surprised that the firm had been aware of his needs, but shuffling people around would take some time; he would get a new office the first time someone left or was transferred. Actually, he never *did* get the office, for he left the firm (see follow-up), but in the case of this client, the assertive behavior of asking for the office was almost as great a therapeutic triumph as getting the office itself would have been.

PROGRAM WORKSHEET: JOHN SMITH

Current Relevant Repertoire	*Subgoal: Subterminal Repertoire*
1. No work at home in P.M. or on Sundays.	1. Try procedures 1 (office work), 2 (family) a third week.
2. Met criteria of time with children and wife two weeks in a row.	2. Spend at least 10 minutes *alone* with each child this week, talking about one of *their* interests (*play* with youngest).
3. Went out three times with wife.	3. Go out at least two times; one of times with another couple.
4. Asked for assigned secretary three days; *got full time!* Terrific!	4. Ask for bigger office.
5. Records fine.	5. Change recording procedures, as below.*

Program Notes

1, 2, and 3. Improve *quality* of interaction with children, wife unscrambling the "scrambled eggs" beautifully. Let's keep practicing to make sure.
5. Do social interaction record at home.
5a*. Time   Place   With Whom   What I Said   What They Said   What I Said   Comments

In order to improve the quality as well as the numerical frequency of the interactions, the worker asked the client to change his logs to a simplified social interaction type. The new log proved to be useful in ferreting out remaining problems in his social relations. The following sample "interaction" logs illustrate this type and its utility in this case. The first was with his wife and the second with a fellow worker:

The first interaction was described by the client as a typical interaction. His wife apparently had one thing on her mind (she wanted to talk), and he had another on his mind (he wanted to work). The interaction ended in an argument. It should be noted that the log is deliberately set up in a form that starts and ends with the speech of the client rather than that of the significant other. The intention is for the client to learn both to initiate and to terminate interactions in a positive way (Goldiamond, 1974). In many angry interactions, one partner portrays the other as starting a conversation with a negative remark, himself answering positively, and the partner ending on a negative note. Here the interaction was begun and ended by the other person, and the conversation *did* end on an angry

INTERACTION LOG: JOHN SMITH

Time	Place	With Whom	What I Said	What They Said	What I Said	Comments	Therapist's Comments
10:15 A.M.	Home	Wife		1. Will you clean the garage today?	2. Later. I want to read a brief first.		Wife disappointed. She ended interaction. You end it in future on positive note.
				3. (Angrily) You weren't going to bring work home anymore.	4. (Angrily) I have to get this done. I'll do it later.		
				5. The hell with you (slamming door).		Did not speak with each other for several hours.	
3:00 P.M.	Home	Wife	1. Let's go get ice cream.	2. I have dishes to do.	3. Do them later.	We got ice cream. Did dishes later. Worked out OK.	Fine. You began and ended on a positive note. Also, showed her you would share with her; good, spontaneous programming.
				4. I want to do them now.	5. Leave them for later, and I'll help you with them.		

INTERACTION LOG: JOHN SMITH

Time	Place	With Whom	What I Said	What They Said	What I Said	Comments	Therapist's Comments
9:20 A.M.	Work	Mr. Johnson		1. Can you spare a minute?	2. Yes.	I was busier than hell and had no time to spare.	Don't say "yes" when you mean "no." Related to *conse-quences* of the wrong SD to Mr. Johnson.
				3. He gave a long story about a case, without interruption.	4. I'm busy now. I don't have time to talk.		
				5. Why the hell didn't you say so before I told you about the case?	6. Nothing.	He's right. I should have said something. He went away angry.	He ended the inter-change on a sour note. End (*your* control) on a positive note.
10:30 A.M.	Work	Mr. Johnson	1. I'm sorry I didn't make myself clearer earlier. I'd like to hear about the case now.	2. Told me about the case.	3. Gave my opinion and advice.		
				4. Thanks a lot.	5. It's my pleasure. Ask me again.	I wonder if he believed me.	Act as if he did. You *ended* the conversa-tion on a good note.

note. One therapeutic injunction is to get the client, if he does not initiate the interaction, at least to end it positively, or not contribute to the heat by a further angry comment (which produces another, and so on).

The client described both interactions as typical. He had postponed cleaning the garage, a chore he had promised his wife he would do, and chose to read some work that he had brought home. The interaction took place on a Saturday, a day on which work at his house office was permitted (on Sunday, he was to do no work). He took the work home that Saturday—a kind of "slippage." This was later resolved by including the home on Saturdays as a nonwork site; work on Saturdays was to be explicitly restricted to the office.

However, in keeping with the general therapeutic policy to reinforce positive interactions, the consultant's comment on this interaction was linked with the conversation that took place at two in the afternoon of the same day, when Mr. Smith initiated an interaction with his wife. She reacted as he had in the morning, stating that she had work to do. He persisted and she persisted, but this time he proposed the alternative solution of leaving the dishes until later, when they could cooperate in doing this unpleasant chore. They went out and bought ice cream, talked, and later did the dishes together. The therapist praised both the analysis of the problem and the immediate programming of an alternative solution.

The analysis of the second interaction, that of the interview with a colleague at work, is self-apparent.

EIGHTH TO THIRTEENTH INTERVIEWS: JULY 29—SEPTEMBER 3 (INTERVENTION CONCLUDED)

Mr. Smith came for a total of thirteen visits. The remainder of the contacts focused on the details and quality of interaction at home and in the office. At home, the interaction was at first scheduled, then later replaced by spontaneous activity with wife and children, in both planned and unplanned activities.

Stimulus control, separating work activity from home activity, was maintained throughout these contacts.

A further problem area remained. Mr. Smith had reported that he was extremely awkward in his interaction with personnel at the office. Therefore a program was developed to increase interaction with his colleagues. The contract was amended to add "improved relations with others at work." Modeling procedures were used. Mr. Smith was to observe and record how others in the office interacted with one another around the water cooler and during coffee breaks. He recorded how others approached one another for coffee breaks and invitations to lunch. He continued this observation of others when he lunched in the restaurant where others were lunching. These "small-talk" behaviors (his term) had not been in his repertoire under these conditions, nor did they exist with regard to clients, hence his preference for dealing with lawyers, with whom he could get down to business immediately. However, they were in his repertoire when he was with his wife.

The worker and client together discovered that what was lacking in the client's repertoire was the skill to *initiate* interactions—the kind of introductory small talk which begins interactions, keeps interactions going, and which is topographically different for different groups (baseball in some, political indignation in others, and so on).

The second step for Mr. Smith was to continue to observe and analyze the procedures others used to initiate, maintain, and terminate social interaction, and then to begin to use them himself. The program consisted of his beginning short, work-related conversations with other individuals at *their* desks. Much of this was already within his repertoire: others were eager to share his professional knowledge. If the conversation became burdensome or negative, he could terminate by returning to his own desk.

A third step was for him to begin short, nonwork-related conversations, which were to be no more than two or three minutes long and were to be terminated by Mr. Smith. As a fourth step he began to invite people to take coffee breaks with him and to discuss some business during those breaks. The next step was coffee breaks interspersed with nonwork-related conversations.

In a short time Mr. Smith began to invite others to lunch, and the invitations were reciprocated. By the end of treatment, he was lunching with his colleagues two or three times a week. He regarded this as satisfactory, and he could increase the frequency if he felt the need to do so.

He and his wife had set their vacation to begin in mid-September (their suburban schools started in early October), and termination was scheduled for September 3.

The office situation was under control. He had a secretary of his own, who filtered his contacts.. He was next in line for a new office. Most important, he was able to do his office work at work. He socialized with others—on his terms. At home, things went equally well. Mr Smith was steady, more content, and confident. He had encountered his problems and had overcome them.

FOLLOW-UP

A follow-up six months later, in March, revealed that Mr. Smith had left the firm to become a senior partner in one of his own. The new job not only paid more money but also was closer to his home. Needless to say, he has his own secretary and a large office of his own. Members of his family occasionally drop in, and he shows them off.

Mrs. Smith never did become directly involved in the therapy. However, she did begin to attend evening classes in English. The increasing demands of an enlarging social life (which she found indeed to be quite pleasant) made this a necessity. Relations with the children continued to be on a very high level. In further conversations, first in person and later on the telephone, Mr. Smith reported that he no longer felt so depressed. There were occasional periods of depression, which he was able to analyze and relate to specific contingencies at home or at work. He then tried to program events that altered these contingencies and was hoping to set up others that would prevent their occurrence. At the last follow-up, he reported that things were going well.

five

THE JOHNSON CASE

In the Smith case, we presented an initial interview that used the self control questionnaire in some detail. Therefore, the presentation of the Johnson case will be considerably abridged, and our comments will be restricted to the material that is different.

Mrs. Johnson, a tall, attractive, black woman aged twenty-nine, initially applied for treatment of obesity. She had been referred for help by a former client who had successfully established new eating patterns (the primary goal in obesity cases). It became apparent during the initial interview that Mrs. Johnson's problems of highest priority were marital. Eventually, her husband was also interviewed, and joint and separate programs were developed for them.[1] Mrs. Johnson, who worked steadily in a low supervisory capacity in a laundry, enjoyed her work, but obtained few satisfactions from her marriage, which she felt could be improved. Her husband had had a series of jobs; he was currently in a sales franchise that was bankrupt. He was considering divorce and had told her to leave, precipitating the present crisis. They were heavily in debt.

INITIAL INTERVIEW
WITH MRS. JOHNSON

1. *Worker:* [*Introduces questionnaire and presents question la, client's outcome*]

[1] The interviews have been edited, disguised, and shortened for purposes of presentation.

2. Client: For me, an outcome would be that I would be more at ease with myself; I'd have a loss of weight and be able to understand and cope with my husband.

(Comment: This is a more complicated picture than the client had mentioned to the clerk. However, it is not atypical of some obesity cases. People often use obesity, phobias, or other "behavioral" problems as "tickets of admission" to a behavioral clinic. These must be probed to get a clearer picture and to establish priority of programs.)

3. *Worker: You're having marital problems?*

4. Client: Yes, I am.

5. *Worker: OK. You'd define success by being more at ease with yourself because you would be a different weight, and by understanding and coping with your husband. Let's consider each of these possible outcomes separately. [Question 1b]: Could you be more specific about how someone who doesn't know you would observe that you are more at ease with yourself?*

6. Client: It's a feeling inside me. People aren't able to detect it. No one has reacted, or told me, you know, that I have problems or something like that. But they sense that I feel that I am very tense and very nervous. They don't know that it's because of the way I feel about the problems that I have, and I think, once my situation is eased, then I think I will relate differently.

7. *Worker: Do you have any idea what it is that you do that conveys this to other people? It might be something that you don't do.*

8. Client: Well, I even notice sometimes in my speech. I might say what I really don't mean, or maybe use the wrong word, or I'm talking too fast and the words just don't come out right. And I think it is all because of what is going on inside of me.

9. *Worker: Well, do you have an experience where you don't say what you mean and someone interprets what you did say but . . .*

10. Client: Oh yes. I've had that happen.

11.*Worker: You find yourself in a situation where you are making a lengthy explanation.*

12. Client: Not only a lengthy explanation but feeling kind of stupid.

13. *Worker: In other words, when you'd be "more at ease" with yourself someone who doesn't know you would observe you talking slowly and making sense, and saying things other people react to favorably.*

(Comment: Worker draws the strands together to produce a clearer picture of what "at ease" means.)

14. Client: Oh yes, But right now I'm so anxious I can't think about that.

15. *Worker: With your weight goal, can you specify what kind of weight goal you would like to achieve? In terms of size, or pounds, or something? Compared to now?*

16. Client: Well, I'd say maybe 150. At the time that I got married three years ago, I was weighing 160. And I'd say about 150. Last time I stepped on a scale it was 240, and that was two or three months ago.

17. *Worker: Can you specify any certain size which would be a successful outcome?*

18. Client: I'd say about 14.

   (Comment: Dress size is a positive outcome toward which one can program.)

19. *Worker: With regard to your husband, if someone who doesn't know you now would see you in the future, how would they see that you have a successful relationship with your husband?*

20. Client: With my husband?

21. *Worker: Yes, what would they observe?*

22. Client: I think that my husband and I are really putting on a front when we are out among friends. Here again it is me, but I feel it can be detected, and he has problems that are just about as enormous as mine. I think that that is about the biggest way it can be detected.

23. *Worker: You mean they'd see you communicating in a different way? In what way?*

24. Client: Yes. (*Silence*)

25. *Worker: Well, let's look at it in another way. Could you tell me a little more about the nature of the problem between you? Is it a communication kind of thing?*

   (Comment: Observing and classifying things in a psychiatric framework is not in the client's repertoire [as it was with Mr. Smith]. She does, however, express herself with complaints, so the worker indicates that this is OK. [Complaints are in the current relevant repertoire, behavior analysis is not.] When she did this, as seen below, the floodgates opened.)

26. Client: Yes, it is a communication kind of thing. I think it is the kind of thing where I married my husband, thinking, *knowing* what he was like and I think, blindly, I thought I was going to be able to change him. And I have not been. My husband, when initially he goes on a job he is very enthusiastic, he wants to make a go of it, and then, after

maybe two or three months he is through with that. We have invested some money, a considerable amount of money, which I borrowed and on which I am paying loans on every month, and he sleeps every day. And so, you know, my feelings about that, just seeing him there when I come home from work, gets me angry. I think he looks at me as being, well, we were talking with my girl friend the other night. And he was saying that he *does* think that I carry a superior attitude. It is by no means what I want to convey. I guess it is because I have to shoulder just about all the responsibility and, in terms of his accepting our responsibilities, he does very little. I can usually count on him to pay the rent, and aside from that he does very little, that's it. You know, emptying the garbage, taking the car to the shop, little things, *occasionally* he might do that. And when I get in a bind for money I have no one to turn to and it's . . . just that kind of situation. He is supposed to be a distributor for G—— Products, which is in the way of sales work.

(*Comment: The communication problem, and apparently other problems, are interwoven with problems of financial management. Her shouldering the responsibilities [according to her account] leads to angry accusations, his statements that she considers herself superior, mutual recriminations, and much acrimony. They are certainly communicating with each other, although hardly in a mutually satisfying way. One area of intense, although hostile, communication is over finances. This might be the area of entrance, or highest priority for programming, since a high level of behavior is already there, and the task may turn out to be reprogramming rather than establishing, always an easier task. The programming of financial management seems, at face value, to differ qualitatively from the programming of marital harmony. However, the reader is reminded of the case in which the programming of office assertiveness produced marital harmony. This is a hypothesis. Question 1b has been answered in two areas [ease and eating], and there is a lead in the third [marital]. Worker accordingly turns to questions 1c and 1d. Question 1c seems to have been answered [how things are now], and the worker turns to question 1d.*)

27. *Worker:* (Question 1d, marital) *Could you give me an example? Well, let's say tonight when you go home. You get home—do you have any children?*

28. Client: No. Just the two of us.

29. *Worker: OK, let's say when you get home tonight. What would the situation be like with your husband?*

30. Client: Well, I hate to use tonight. Saturday, he physically abused me, and I feel like I don't even want to see him. I had asked him to

come with me today. This was at the suggestion of my friend who referred me, and I called him this morning and asked him if he would meet me here. And he said to me, "Why did you choose not to tell me?" Well, he had been up all night. He slept all day yesterday, and he was up and when I say up, I mean literally up all night last night. So when I got up this morning, I cooked breakfast, and I didn't have anything to say to him, I didn't want to say anything to him. But I wanted him to come today so I called him and asked him. So more than likely he will ask me what happened today. He is in a state now where anything I say to him upsets him, so rather than be in his presence, I just waited till I got to work to call him.

31. *Worker: You said that on Saturday night he physically abused you. Was this the first time, or has it happened before?*

32. Client: No, it's happened before. You see, my brother goes to the university, and every month my mother sends him a check. I received the check Saturday and my brother had picked it up and gone to the store to cash the check. He had been wanting some boots, so he asked me to let him have the money. You know, usually I don't give him all of the money at one time, so he asked me to give him part of the money now, and he'd give it back on Friday. So I said OK, and he left. He was going downtown and as he pulled off, my husband pulled up and came into the house and asked where my brother was going. I told him he was going downtown to get some boots. And he said, uh, "Why would you give him the money to buy the boots?" So I didn't say anything, because I hadn't told him and I didn't really feel like going into it or anything. So right away he said, "Well, I'm going to tell him to get a job so that he can buy his own boots, and what do you think about that?" And I didn't say anything. And he said, "What do you think about it?" I said I didn't think he should. He said, "Why not?" I said because I think he is doing just about as much as you are, and then he started hitting me. After talking to my girl friend Saturday, Sunday, I found out that he is somewhat jealous of my brother. We don't see him that often, maybe two or three times a week, but he couldn't see why I take so much pains and make sure my brother eats all right, dresses right, does his work at school, and how come I never do that for him? But he's never up. He doesn't have any reason to be up, so why should I have to do that other than on Saturday or Sunday? This has been the first he has physically abused me in quite a while now, and when I say physical abuse, I mean I have a number of bruises on my body. He has occasionally slapped me or hit me, but nothing like the extent that I am now. Let me think. The occasions have all been something that we have argued about. I have known what it was going to lead up to, but tried not to say anything, but when he led me to a point I, you know, said what I felt like. And that leads to this abusing, and like I told my girl friend, when sometimes—like Saturday—a

couple of times when he was hitting me, it was just like he had gone crazy, you know, just for a couple of minutes. Well, I went to the hospital Sunday night, because I have a blood spot on my leg and I was concerned because, you know, I didn't know the extent of the damages. So when I left the hospital, he asked me, "What did they say?" and I said, "You know, I told them that my husband beat me." He asked me if they asked me if I wanted to press charges and I said no. He said, "Well, do you feel better?" I said no, because I am aching. And he has been asking me constantly, "Do you feel better now? Do you want to talk now? Will you forgive me?" Those kind of things. And this is usually the pattern; after an argument he wants to know if I'll forgive him and he is sorry. Usually right after it happens.

33. *Worker: Is there any other problem area with your husband? Other than the situation around his employment, with your brother, the conflict of his thinking that you do more for your brother than you do for him?*

34. Client: No.

35. *Worker: Drinking?*

36. Client: No. Just socially.

37. *Worker: Other women?*

38. Client: No.

> (*Comment: Interchanges #39* [worker] *through #48* [client] *provided information that the Johnsons had been married "three years and two weeks," that they were both the same age, twenty-nine, and her hospital work was in the laundry. These interchanges were as terse as #34. Worker now returns to questions 1c and 1d about eating.*)

49. *Worker: With regard to your eating and dress-size goals, let's assume you had things under control. How would this differ from the way things are now?*

50. Client: The biggest problem I have in terms of my eating habits is that I think it is not so much *how* much I eat as *why* I eat. I eat fattening things unintelligently, I know. I'll say to myself, I'm going to diet, and I might try it for a day or two, I'll try a diet pill—that's how I lost the weight before I got married.

51. *Worker: How about cooking? Do you do much cooking?*

52. Client: Yes.

53. *Worker: Is cooking something you enjoy?*

54. Client: Not really.

55. *Worker: How about eating? Is eating something you enjoy?*

56. Client: Yes, I do.

57. *Worker: We have been discussing possible outcomes and related problems. Obviously, there are many things going for you which will not be affected by our program, and things other than the program areas which are likely to be affected. To differentiate between the areas, the questions are* [reads through questions 2a, 2b, then asks 2a]: *First, what areas of your life will not be affected by our program?*

58. Client: Will not be affected? Hmmm.

59. *Worker: The areas that are going well.*

60. Client: Right now, I can't think of anything that is going well. I think that so many things hinge upon this, upon my situation at home, that I can't think of anything that is going well.

> (Comment: Question 2a concerns areas to be left unchanged. The worker is focusing, trying to ascertain some current effective repertoires, some strengths, and to see which areas need strengthening.)

61. *Worker: Well, there are a lot of areas that you haven't mentioned. How about your job?*

62. Client: Yes, well, I'm very satisfied with that. That's going real well. I like the job. I like the people I work with. (*Pause*) I imagine I'll still be married, but things will have to be more pleasant.

> (Comment: Worker succeeded. Job goes well, and her statement indicates that there are areas in the marriage that are going well, that might be built upon.)

63. *Worker: (Question 2b) What areas other than those for which we program will change?*

64. Client: I can't think of any. Seems to me being at ease, losing weight, and communicating with my husband covers a lot.

65. *Worker: Well, let me make a try. You say a lot of the difficulty with your husband is over financial problems. Would these be changed if you could communicate?*

66. Client: I don't know. Maybe we'd communicate about financial problems. That's part of it, certainly.

67. *Worker: Sounds like it.*

> (Comment: As was noted, they are "communicating" now, but with outcomes which produce emotional confrontations. There is nothing wrong with producing such confrontations per se. The question is: What effect do such patterns and such methods of interactions have on other behaviors and outcomes, which may be more critical to the client? Worker

does not pursue question 2b [areas affected other than pro-
gram areas], because as client has said, "being at ease, losing
weight, and communicating . . . covers a lot." Worker sees
the task as getting data which are more specific and, accord-
ingly, turns to the next question.)

Let's go on to the next series. This concerns attempts to change.
[Reads through 3*a,* 3*b,* 3*c,* and then asks 3*a*]*: Why start now? What are*
the circumstances?

68. Client: Well, I figure in terms of my weight, if I don't start now and
since I'm not able to get any self-control myself, that eventually I'll just
be bursting at the seams. I think that in terms of my marital life that
things couldn't possibly get any worse and that it is time, past time for
that.

69. *Worker:* (Question 3*b*) *OK. For how long or how often have you*
considered starting, and what are the circumstances?

70. Client: Starting the program?

71. *Worker: Well, we realize that you need to begin on your weight*
problem and your marital problem. For how long have you been seek-
ing help?

72. Client: Well, for almost three years, ever since I got married, I've
had marital problems. I have been back to the doctor that I was going
to. The pills that he gave me were sometimes too strong for me to
take, others were too weak, and I'd, you know, eat a candy bar af-
terward. I was referred to a Dr. X., I think.

73. *Worker: Is he a psychiatrist?*

74. Client: Yes.

75. *Worker: Did you go to him?*

76. Client: Yes, just for two visits.

77. *Worker: When did you go to him?*

78. Client: Oh, it must have been in the latter part of 1969. I didn't feel
that I was really being helped. I wanted my husband to go with me
because at the time I thought he should. I didn't see what good it
would do, you know, without his going. And he didn't want to go, and
so I stopped going.

79. *Worker: Have you had any other attempts at starting to get help?*

80. Client: No, I haven't.

81. *Worker:* (Question 3*c*) *When did it first occur to you to make*
changes? And what were the circumstances?

82. Client: It was suggested several times by my girl friend. It was just a matter of my putting it off. She referred me here.

83. *Worker: Why did she refer you here?*

84. Client: I think because she feels very strongly about the program, because she did well here and thought that I would be helped.

85. *Worker: Did you try other ways to help you in your marital problem?*

86. Client: Well, we've tried to patch up things.

87. *Worker: Have you discussed this with other people?*

88. Client: I haven't told my parents, but I think they're aware.

89. *Worker: What about trying to change your weight?*

90. Client: I was on a diet under a doctor's advice.

91. *Worker: Was it in recent months?*

92. Client: No, the only diet I followed under a doctor's care was the weight I lost before I got married. Three years ago.

93. *Worker: Did you lost much weight?*

94. Client: Oh yes. Well, I wasn't as large as I am now, I never have been this large. I lost about thirty or thirty-five pounds.

95. *Worker: Did you see the doctor on this problem, or was it some other problem?*

96. Client: It was for a gynecological problem.

97. *Worker: Do you see him continually for this problem?*

98. Client: No, only when it recurs.

99. *Worker: Do you take any medications or drugs?*

100. Client: I'm taking tranquilizers—it's for this problem, it's a heat treatment that he gives me for this problem.

101. *Worker: Now you say you are on tranquilizers. Are these by prescription?*

102. Client: Yes, right after I got married. Doctor gave me this prescription, four times a day.

103. *Worker: And you have been taking them now for three years?*

104. Client: Yes.

105. *Worker: On this original prescription?*

106. Client: Yes.

107. *Worker: And did you have any side effects to the tranquilizers?*

108. Client: No.

109. *Worker: How often do you take them?*

110. Client: Maybe one every other day. Whenever I feel the need for them.

111. *Worker: Have you ever had tests for thyroid deficiency? Quite often that is the source of excess weight.*

112. Client: No, I haven't.

113. *Worker: Have you been to a regular family doctor or for medical insurance, or, for example, if we asked you to get a complete physical, for this purpose, would that be possible?*

114. Client: Yes.

115. *Worker: Have you had a good medical checkup? In recent months?*

116. Client: No, I haven't.

117. *Worker: When was the last physical checkup you had, Mrs. Johnson?*

118. Client: I'd say in the spring, I think.

119. *Worker: Was that for any special occasion, or . . . ?*

120. Client: Yes, that was for the gynecological problem.

121. *Worker: Regarding the physical, we might be able to get something here at the clinic at Billings [Hospital]. You should have a complete physical. This is something we can talk about later. When you have arguments with your husband, does this affect your eating?*

122. Client: No, I just take more tranquilizers.

123. *Worker: Do they help you get through the day?*

124. Client: Yes. [Client then gave lengthy description of work in laundry, the management of automatic machines. Client stated that she enjoys the job, enjoys working in the hospital, being "part of the team." Client is in charge of ordering supplies, and job entails a certain amount of responsibility and some supervision of other staff.]

125. *Worker: Your abilities here are certainly in line with the next question.* (Reads summary of question 4, strengths.) *We've already touched on some of these things, but let's go through them anyway. Let's start with the first: What related strengths or skills do you now have?*

126. Client: I can't think of any.

127. *Worker: Well, let's look at weight. You know about food values, for example, and you know what carbohydrates and protein are; you*

can read a book on what foods have which value; you'd be able to take a chart that says 4 ounces of meat and apply it. My impression is that you would be able to understand this quite well. And since you obviously have the knowledge to help run the laundry room—all that equipment to oversee, supplies to order, people to get along with, all of which are very closely connected—you obviously have the ability for organization.

128. Client: I can understand what you say, and I think I do have those skills.

129. *Worker: Well, those are the related skills, and there are others, like those we touched on before, like cooking ability.*

130. Client: That's right. A lot of people mention that about me—my organization. Also, it's very seldom that I can say no to someone who wants me to help them and I know that I can, where I've had people to come to me that way.

131. *Worker: You're generous. You often understand what people need without their saying so?*

132. Client: Yes.

133. *Worker: That's good. It means you can figure out what's impor-tant to them, what they're after, and how to help them get it. What other strengths or skills do you have that will help you with your mari-tal problems? Some of them we've already talked about.*

134. Client: I don't know whether you would consider this a strength or not, but a couple of times I've been talking or arguing with my hus-band and I know that he is reaching his breaking point and I wouldn't say anything. Would you consider that a strength?

135. *Worker: Certainly, a very important one, too.*

136. Client: There's something else that I'd like to know and that is, has he really built a fear in me? And I'm not asking this because I fear what he is going to do to me.

137. *Worker: Well the fact is that you can perceive what is bothering another person. You pick up when it is that another person comes under pressure and tension.*

138. Client: Well, I can't perceive this with others as well as I can with my husband because I think I know him better.

139. *Worker: Still, you can do this with your husband. You say he must be feeling this, this, and this, and that something you may be doing may be setting him off. This is a real plus to work with. Another is that you don't have a halo over your head; you don't put yourself always in the right. There are people who are very insensitive to other*

people, and they have a very difficult time in holding relationships. So having the skill is certainly an asset. And I'm sure it is going to benefit us.

140. Client: I hope so. I think so.

141. *Worker: (Question 4b) What strengths and skills in other areas?*

142. Client: Well . . . (*Long pause*)

143. *Worker: One thing that strikes me is that you make a very good personal appearance.*

144. Client: That is something that I have always worked on, and now I don't feel about myself the way that I did when I wasn't weighing as much. My wardrobe is limited, for one thing, because I refuse to buy anything larger, and I find myself wearing the same thing over and over, which bothers me.

145. *Worker: Well, you certainly do present a very good appearance. Um, what other assets?*

146. Client: Seems like you can figure it out better than I can.

147. *Worker: You must be a pretty good organizer to handle all the things you have, your job, and your home, and all that.*

148. Client: Yes, it's a heck of a lot. Especially when I don't think I get the help that I should be getting.

149. *Worker: What other strengths and skills do you have that you don't consider related to your problem?*

150. Client: I can knit, I can sew. I type well. (*Pause*) I don't know why I find it so difficult to talk about myself now.

151. *Worker: What about athletics?*

152. Client: No, but I've always wanted to learn to swim and play tennis.

153. *Worker: How about spectator sports?*

154. Client: I don't really care too much for it.

155. *Worker: How about schooling?*

156. Client: I did real well in high school.

157. *Worker: What school did you go to?*

158. Client: You wouldn't know it. I went to high school in Tennessee.

159. *Worker: How come you went to high school in Tennessee?*

160. Client: I lived with an aunt. Better school, it was integrated. I worked after school. I couldn't afford to go on to college; never really wanted to, if I could have.

161. *Worker: And when did you graduate?*

162. Client: In 1963.

163. *Worker: How would you describe your time in high school? Was it a good time, a bad time?*

164. Client: It was a good time.

165. *Worker: Were you very social?*

166. Client: Yes.

167. *Worker: That's pretty impressive. You got good grades, were social, worked to help support yourself at the same time.*

(Comment: Apparently, the task will be, as it was with Mr. Smith, to transfer stimulus control over patterns already in her behavioral repertoire rather than establish the patterns.)

Did you come to Chicago right away? After graduation?

168. Client: I worked a year and then I came here.

169. *Worker: Have you been working here ever since?*

170. Client: Right.

171. *Worker: So, you've been holding and advancing in your job all these years. What brought you to Chicago?*

172. Client: My girl friend and my husband.

173. *Worker: Oh, you knew them down there?*

174. Client: I came to visit her during the Christmas holidays.

175. *Worker: How long did you know your husband before you were married?*

176. Client: For about four or five years.

177. *Worker: What stood in the way of your marriage?*

178. Client: My husband was away in the service, that was the main thing, I think, and he didn't want to get married then. So I suggested that I come here and work and then he could come back here when he was out of service.

179. *Worker: Where was he in the service?*

180. Client: In Germany.

181. *Worker: What did he do when he got out of service?*

(Comment: Although these questions seem to stray from the program, worker has been trying to evaluate the extent to which husband should be involved in this program. This seems to be a natural point to get pertinent information.)

182. Client: A number of things. We didn't get married right away. We dated for four or five years, first when I was working in Tennessee, then when he was in the service, and then for a while after he got out of the service. He had a lot of jobs, mostly sales. He has driven a cab, he was fired from a job at B. factory; he slept on the job, really slept on the job, he was not doing the job. Kicks around from one to another [more history of irregular employment than detailed explanation of his taking on this franchise operation]. He starts a job, has lots of enthusiasm at the start, and then he loses interest. Right now he really isn't working, and things are the way they are between us.

183. *Worker: Uh-huh. Let's return to the questionnaire.* [Question 4c] *Are there any circumstances under which the current problems aren't problems?*

184. Client: Any circumstances in which the current problems aren't problems?

185. *Worker: Like the diet problem for instance. Are there any circumstances when you don't eat between meals or eat the wrong kinds of food?*

186. Client: No, I eat whenever I feel like it or whatever I want to.

187. *Worker: Are there any times when you and your husband get along well?*

188. Client: Rarely.

189. *Worker: What are the circumstances?*

190. Client: I think mainly when he is working, or when he is trying. It is never anything cut and dried in terms of the distributorship or anything, but when I see an effort. That makes me feel better toward him. I convey that.

191. *Worker: So you are able to convey to him when things are going well? That's important.*

192. Client: There is something that might be a weakness. I don't think that I have given him the help that he wants me to do in terms of the distributorship. We had a close couple in the business, in fact we brought them into the business. The fellow works for the phone company, and his wife and I work together, and they are both working the business on a part-time basis, and here is my husband with nothing to do, and not doing what I think he should be doing. And he sometimes refers to my girl friend and how much support she gives to her husband. And I feel it's like a second job to me almost. It's his job, and I don't feel I should have to give support. That's the way I view it. Because of our investment I wanted to say to my husband, to suggest to him, not in any forcible way, you know, to get back into the swing of

the thing. And I would help him more. But I don't know if I really mean it or whether I would be saying it to get him going and then I wouldn't do it.

193. *Worker: Nevertheless, you have thought about it and thought about the possibilities. What are these financial concerns?*

194. Client: Well, we're in debt to the investment company for $3,000. Also, my husband borrowed from Mutual Finance to pay off the department store to pay our furniture bill and a note that we had at the bank. And we made another loan just recently, and really I think it was just made to get the rent; he didn't have it and I wasn't going to give it to him. Since that time the department store's bill has come to about $300, another is about $600, other bills amounting to a hundred or so. All in all, over $1,000 in bills also.

195. *Worker: (Question 4d) Well, it seems to me that you and your husband are already doing a lot of communicating and it's around the money issue. You may not have solved your money problems but you certainly communicate. Are there any other problems you have solved?*

196. Client: I can't think of any.

197. *Worker: Well, were there some problems involving getting people to do things?*

198. Client: Well, I was finally able to convince my parents·to let my brother go to the university. I'd been planning for that for two years, and got them to agree, and to send him money.

199. *Worker: Where do they live?*

200. Client: They moved back to Tennessee. They come up occasionally.

201. *Worker: What do they do?*

202. Client: My mother was a nurse's aide when they married, and my father went into service right after I was born. Then he got a job as a security officer, and now he's security chief at a college down there. My brother was grown up before he came to Chicago. He's going to college here. He's nineteen.

203. *Worker: Is that the whole family?*

204. Client: Yes.

205. *Worker: Is your brother living with you?*

206. Client: He has a place of his own.

207. *Worker: But you maintain strong family ties, which suggests things went well at home.*

208. Client: Well, my father has an ulcer, my mother is sort of neurotic.

209. *Worker: What makes you say that?*

210. Client: Well, she is easily upset (*inaudible soft talking*) . . . I think she is taking tranquilizers . . .

211. *Worker: (Question 5) Do you want to raise any further issues? Have I left something out that you consider important? Is there anything you consider pertinent that has been omitted, slighted, or overstressed?*

212. Client: No, nothing that I can think about.

213. *Worker: There is one area I'd like to ask you about. You mentioned gynecological problems. How are things sexually between the two of you?*

214. Client: Well, that is a problem. I don't think he is that happy. We sort of, well, we usually don't have sex more than once a week, maybe less, and he starts it. Just gets on top, and that's it. I know he doesn't like it, but he cannot expect me to feel good toward him, when he isn't working and bringing home money, and then he treats me like this, he can't expect me to respond to him.

215. *Worker: Have you ever talked about this, the two of you?*

216. Client: Not really talking. I don't like talking about it. Even now. He starts in, and then I am quiet, don't talk. Sometimes I get angry and then scream at him to let me alone, quit bothering me, and then we don't talk. Yes, this is a problem between us. Wasn't always, especially in the beginning of our marriage. I'm sure that if he ever worked steady, and things were ok between the two of us, this would be ok too. I really don't want to talk about it anymore.

217. *Worker: OK. (Question 6) Is there anything you would like to know about us, our goals, our approach? Any other comments?*

218. Client: No. My girl friend, Mrs. P., told me about you. I think I know about how you work. What do you think?

219. *Worker: Well, I certainly think we can work together to try to help you meet your goals. However, they're your goals and your decision on what and how we do it. One thing you mentioned concerns me. One of your problem areas is a marital one. It would clarify things if we could see your husband. If he agrees, wants to work on this, it might be a lot faster, better.*

220. Client: Yes, that would be wonderful. Would you see us together?

221. *Worker: Sometimes we see couples together and sometimes we see them separately, depending upon what is involved. Right now we are just finding out what's what. Maybe you can suggest to your husband that he can come in to talk about himself, not necessarily to talk about the marital relationship. What do you think about this?*

222. Client: I think that's a good idea. [*This is followed by a discussion of time for meetings, etc.*]

223. *Worker: Why don't you suggest to him that he can call us?*

224. Client: Should I tell him about my conversation today, or . . . ?

225. *Worker: I think you can tell him that you came and you talked, and that you felt he might want to come and talk about himself, too. We're not going to mend anything unless you and your husband want something mended, and then that may not be in the picture, it is still too early to tell. If he wants to come here to talk about himself or if you want us to meet as a group, that can be decided later.*

226. Client: Well, if he asks me if this is in opposition to the two of us coming today, I mean if he thinks you don't want to see him together with me because he didn't come in today?

227. *Worker: You can just say that if both of you are willing, and we think this is the best way, we can see both of you together or we can see you, depending. As for now, since you've already come yourself, maybe he might want to come by himself, at least the first time.*

228. Client: Well, what would we work on?

229. *Worker: You seem to have two immediate problems: your marital situation, which also involves a financial problem, and your weight. I feel we can begin to work with you on both. However, it would be much better if Mr. Johnson could come in and talk to us. Do you think he would?*

230. Client: I'll speak to him tonight about coming in.

231. *Worker: In that case I will hold off asking you to work on something until after you speak to him. If possible we could see him tomorrow. And then see the two of you together soon after and get started right away.*

232. Client: I'll talk to him tonight.

233. *Worker: If he calls, we'll know. If he won't, let us know.*

Interview Ends

Comment: The initial referral problem was obesity; during the interview it quickly became apparent that the most pressing problem was an involved marital problem. The husband not only is involved in the problem situation but in all probability should be involved in the solution [therapy]. The contract or programming decision will be made if he decides to become involved and the situation from his viewpoint may become clear.

Mr. Johnson appeared eager. He called the very next morning. Evidently, Mrs. Johnson had presented the situation to him skillfully. Her skillful handling and his immediate response were both reinforced by setting up an appointment with him that same day. His interview follows.)

INITIAL INTERVIEW
WITH MR. JOHNSON

Mr. Johnson is a very tall, handsome, black man, aged twenty-nine. He appeared the next day. The questionnaire was administered. A condensed report of the interview is presented:

1. *Worker:* [Introduces questionnaire, then asks question 1a] *For you, what would a successful outcome be?*

2. Client: I think, well, uh, my general mental attitude toward, uh, life and my surroundings would be a lot different. Emotionally, I feel.

3. *Worker: Can you tell me more about that?*

4. Client: I think, uh, my attitude toward life, my home, and my wife, and over-all my career and occupation, that I was giving something, that I would be contributing.

5. *Worker:* (Question 1b) *Somebody who didn't know you—how would they be able to look and see? What would they observe that would be different?*

6. Client: I think an increase in activity, a participation in things more. (*Pause*) I think I would be more on the go.

   (*Comment: Client is still vague, refers to "increase, more." These are unobservable. Worker shapes observables.*)

7. *Worker: What kinds of things would you be doing?*

8. Client: Well, for one thing, I would be in business for myself, be in organizations, I'd be taking some kind of leadership in business and in community affairs.

9. *Worker: What kind of business?*

10. Client: One where I wouldn't necessarily have to succumb to the wishes of others. Where I would be in complete control of the situation and not have to take orders from others. Prospering, a self-run kind of thing where I would be boss, in charge, on my own. I would not constantly have to be going back to people, accounting to people. Maybe ask others for resources that I didn't have myself. I think that would be about it. It would be *my* business.

11. *Worker: Have you anything specific in mind?*

12. Client: Well, I've been in a lot of business ventures. I like the arts, maybe some sort of arts novelty store with my own personal touch to it. Be tied in with a lot of leisure things. People have a lot of leisure time, and this would be for them. I have a number of ideas but I don't have the kind of capital needed to generate the business. (*Pause*) I don't have them. I don't know where I'd possibly start.

13. *Worker: You explained you would be more active or more involved with these things. What about the side interests, the volunteer program? What would you be doing?*

14. Client: I'd be a leader in the black community, helping people get started in business . . . looking out for the interests of the community. Working on committees. Maybe active in politics. I'd be happily married, and even if I was no longer married. In that instance, I would hope that we could be very good friends.

15. *Worker: What would this person observe to indicate that you were very happily married?*

16. Client: (*Sigh*) Well, I believe the kind of time we spent together, rewarding to the both of us (*pause*), doing some things that she personally would like, rather than exhibiting some kind of authority in a situation where I say "No" and we might disagree and then we would just never do anything and just feel resentment.

(*Comment: Worker will try to get specific observables in a different way.*)

17. *Worker: (Questions 1c, 1d) Can you give me an example of how it differs from the current state of affairs?*

18. Client: Well, for a long time, carpeting has been an issue in our house. She wants it and I said no. Maybe under more favorable circumstances, at her suggestion, it might just come about, we would go ahead and do that. Uh, I think we are currently, mentally, on the brink of mentally destroying one another. Uh, unless there is an input on both of our parts, personally. I don't think I am contributing to its function because of the way I personally feel about our situation. I let

things go because of my financial responsibilities. I don't put too much thought into it.

19. *Worker: What would the observer be seeing you do together?* (Question 1*b*, marriage, restated. See #15.)

20. Client: We'd be socializing. . . . Well, uh, I don't know, but I'm the kind of person who goes out, likes to be involved with people all the time; my wife is the kind, she likes to sit home. She is not good at social gatherings, although she does like an occasional social gathering.

21. *Worker: You both like it.*

22. Client: Yes, although I like it more than my wife.

23. *Worker: Are you and your wife doing this sort of thing now, this sort of thing, socializing with other people?*

24. Client: Occasionally, not too much. There is sort of a lack of agreement on what my wife would like, like to have in our home. Things she would like to see. She would like the home nice, buy things. I don't think at the moment we can afford it. We might have dinner out occasionally, there are some things we have together. Our weight problems. That's another thing. In terms of our not being happy together, I think that my wife could weigh an awful lot less than she does, look better when we go out. I guess I could weigh less myself, but I'm really more concerned about her looks than my looks. We'd both be more active.

25. *Worker: This is a goal that you both have? To be more active?* [Possible 1*a*, outcome]

26. Client: I think that is a goal that she should have. I really don't know what goals we would have, that's a problem. We haven't worked together like other couples.

27. *Worker: Then this might be another desirable outcome, to have mutual goals that you could work together on. Are you able to talk to each other about things that concern both of you?*

28. Client: Yes, we are, at my insistence. We listen to each other. I'm not so sure we understand each other. I generally voice my opinion. She voices her opinion. Many times I say things and I don't think she understands when I say this to her. She says that I merely want her to repeat what I want her to repeat. But I don't think so. Do you understand what I am saying?

29. *Worker: Yes. Can you tell me something about the current state of affairs in your job and business right now?* [Question 1*c*, business]

30. Client: [Discussion ensues of client's mail order business and distributorship. He started with a great deal of enthusiasm and high

sales, mostly through parties arranged by relatives. However, he has recently put minimal effort into the business, and minimal sales have resulted. He has "disengaged himself" from some of the activities. The business seems to be a franchise operation where an individual invests money, much of which goes to the people owning the franchise. The individual can make money by increasingly involving more people in the franchise. All in all, client is $3,000 in debt to the franchise company, plus other debts. These reports are in complete agreement with his wife's report.] In terms of work, I would like something that is more rewarding, something that I could stick with. I thought this was a business for myself but yet it wasn't. Most of the money goes to the people who own the franchise.

31. *Worker: Have you discussed this business with your wife at all?*

32. Client: We are into it together. We discussed this. We are involved in it, and at this point I think she wants me to continue. She thought I did very well at it, but she thinks I should put more time on the sales end rather than in the top management end, the recruiter, the recruiting of other people to merchandise. I would rather disengage myself from retailing and engage in the recruitment of other people.

33. *Worker: (Question 1c) What was the difference between the time you were doing very well in it, and now?*

34. Client: Uh, what's the difference? Things were happening as the company said they would happen. Success. I had organized a small sales force of my own. I provided a warm atmosphere, a motivational atmosphere, a charged atmosphere, and it seemed to work. [Discussion then indicated that the company had arranged its sales program so that an initial period of success was almost unavoidable. But past a certain point, the individual was left on his own. Client felt that the promises made in the beginning had not been kept, and this discouraged him. Accordingly, income dropped as sales prospects grew increasingly more difficult to locate: he was exhausting his lists of friends and relatives. He considers himself as having been victimized by a "snow" job from a franchise organization of the type currently being investigated by federal agencies.] I really don't know the answer to that, I just became disenchanted with the [franchise] people. They were more interested in the company than in the people they were working with. It wasn't what I thought it was. I thought it was something I could run and it didn't turn out that way. I think the products were good. But the emphasis of the organization was too much on recruiting new people rather than increasing sales.

35. *Worker: Are you still active in the business?*

36. Client: Yes, but very shallow. I occasionally sell a product. I don't really make a living from it.

37. *Worker: Are you planning to drop it?*

38. Client: Well, one of the reasons I don't want to drop it is because it is something to do now. I've gone through a lot and there is also nothing else that seems to be. I borrowed money to go into the business. If I could just get the money to pay off what I borrowed, that would be sufficient. I don't really know about getting out of it. That is part of my problem. I guess I should have had a part-time job while trying it. It was my initial mistake.

39. *Worker: Do you have anything particular in mind as a kind of back-up job or anything you would like to do?*

40. Client: Well, one of the things that·bothers me is that I don't have a skill or a job or a trade.

41. *Worker: That you are interested in going into? What kind of field of work would you like to get into?*

   (Comment: This is a possible outcome to consider.)

42. Client: I don't really know. I see areas where I could really be effective, yet I really can't pin down any vocation. I have a high school diploma. I took a few business courses in college, but I didn't stick with it. I don't know what profession or career. I see sciences some time. I am interested in plants, animals, biology kind of things, but I don't have the training.

43. *Worker: Have you talked to Mrs. Johnson about this?*

44. Client: I think so; at times I do. When I was in service I was active, I was verbal, I was philosophical. The pressure on my mind drove me. For the last few years I don't think I have expressed myself that directly that well. I still feel the pressures, but I don't do it now. *(Pause)* I don't know how to bring it out to explain to her how I feel about what I do. It takes a lot of words sometimes, I want to say it, but in terms of our relationship, I feel it is just better that I keep it to myself.

45. *Worker: What would happen in terms of real relationship if you talked to your wife about this?*

46. Client: Well, there again I just feel my wife doesn't understand what I'm talking about. Then if she were to answer me it would be short and not as involved or interested in what I am saying. I think we have a very peculiar relationship. For the most part of our going together, premarital relationship, I was away from home. I finally decided to come home, and then we got married. We didn't grow up together, we didn't spend two or three years together in the same city, we were constantly around but never really in contact with each other. I don't think we knew each other that well. And yet, I don't know, maybe we did. Maybe things weren't as complex as they are now. *(Long pause)*

47. *Worker: You'd like to be able to talk about these problems?*

48. Client: I would think so and yet maybe we understand each other very well. I really don't know whether I am seeking to understand what goes on between us because I'm not really sure I want the marriage to go on.

49. *Worker: You have some question about this?*

50. Client: Right.

51. *Worker: But if you do, you definitely want things to change.*

52. Client: Right.

53. *Worker: Looks like we're moving right into our next question.* [Reads introduction to question 2. Asks question 2a.]

54. Client: I don't think I understand.

55. *Worker:* (Restates question 2a) *What areas of your life are you satisfied with? And that you are not going to change?*

56. Client: I don't really know that I am satisfied with anything. I have some healthy thoughts about certain types of actions but nothing in activities.

57. *Worker: What about living in Chicago? Are you satisfied with that?*

58. Client: I like Chicago.

59. *Worker: That is one area that has worked well.*

   (*Comment: Worker is "prompting"* [*in programming·terms*] *the client.*)

60. Client: Say that again.

61. *Worker: That is one area of your life that might not be affected. What else?*

62. Client: I don't think my attitude toward (*pause*) how I feel about people in general will change. In terms of how I would like to work. I still believe in being independent.

63. *Worker: Anything else?*

64. Client: (*Long pause*) Really don't know.

65. *Worker: Any outside interests?*

66. Client: I think the way I feel about community organization and programs to be started in the community and under my direction, how some things could be done of group value to people, how those things should be done. Input into something. Being successful.

67. *Worker: You want to change your involvement in it but you're satisfied with your ideas about it.*

68. Client: Yes.

69. *Worker:* (Question 2b) *Now, if we were successful in our program, what areas of your life other than those we have worked on would change? Becoming more involved is one. What other areas?*

70. Client: I'd like to get outdoors, do more, exercise. I don't run as much. Amount of physical activity will be affected.

71. *Worker: What about your general health condition? How good is that?*

72. Client: I've always had excellent health except for the weight now, which is sort of recent. Never really a problem. Joke about it but I'm in good health. I'd like to lose weight. I don't have high blood pressure. Had a physical examination recently for insurance policy. Was fine. Had it for the company. They wanted me to take it because of my weight. Came out OK except for the weight.

73. *Worker: How tall are you?*

74. Client: 6'4".

75. *Worker: And your weight is 260?*

76. Client: No athletic activities now. This would change. [Discussion follows on past athletic activities. Client reports he could have been an athlete, and was good in games.]

77. *Worker: What about relations with your wife?*

78. Client: I made a comment that my attitude toward sex would change in relation to my wife. I'm not satisfied. I think it has a great deal of effect on our relationship. I hope that would change. More a warmer type of thing. I don't think she enjoys that part of it. I don't enjoy that part of it and she doesn't, and I think she has certain assumptions about me, kind of rigid.

79. *Worker: Rigid?*

80. Client: Maybe I have more of that than she but I see myself after her more than she brings to me. I'm always the one that starts it. I'm always the active one.

81. *Worker: Are you able to talk to each other about this?*

82. Client: I've talked to her. I've given her my attitudes about this. She doesn't listen. She becomes very quiet. At certain times I get loud about it. I think that her attitude is that for the most part, she doesn't say anything.

83. *Worker: So it really consists of you making comments and that's the end of it?*

84. Client: Right.

85. *Worker: How about job? You mentioned interest in other areas.*

86. Client: Yes, but don't know what.

87. *Worker: Have you ever considered any positions in the medical field, such as technician?*

88. Client: Yes, but I don't know how one goes about getting involved. Computer fields, too. I have an interest for that. I don't know where one would be or where one ends up. What is it you are destined to wind up in, you know. Courses, curriculum.

89. *Worker: Have you ever had any vocational evaluation or guidance? Or counseling?*

90. Client: Yes, in high school. The state gave it. I took it at the employment service.

91. *Worker: That would be about ten years ago, right?*

92. Client: Right.

93. *Worker: People sometimes have difficulty in choices because they don't know what the opportunities are.*

94. Client: I'd like a venture, something successful, with enough expertise on everyone's part so it would work out. (*Pause*)

95. *Worker: OK. Let's consider the next area: attempts to change.* [Introduces question 3.] *Why start now? What are the circumstances?*

96. Client: I'm pretty close to bankruptcy. Emotionally, I've just about had it. I've got to be involved in something that I can do that I want to do. I always felt that I could start at any point in my life. I guess I'm getting a little fearful. I need some direction. Enough direction to get started. I'm depressed now. Sometimes I think maybe I like being depressed. I really dig it. I'm addicted to depression. Get excuses for not doing things. For the most part I sit around and think. I try to charge myself up sometimes.

97. *Worker:* (Question 3*b*) *For how long have you tried to do something about it?*

98. Client: Don't know what I do, but I must be doing something. Comes on over a period of six months, lasts a week, goes, comes back. What I do is sort of avoid people, get over it. [Told of previous history when in army; he would come out of his room only for duties and for meals, to avoid company of others. This was told in depressed voice, and with very slow speech. Reported that weight gains were related; reported tendencies to eat when depressed. Depression reported as especially great before trying to start new things, and after dropping things.] In terms of my getting involved, starting things, and quitting, it can be traced back to high school. I'd stay in bed, not get up.

99. *Worker: Would you describe yourself as being in that period now?*

100. Client: Yes, most part last two or three months. Unless I'm really involved in something that's what I'm doing.

> (*Comment: The depression appears to be a logical result of the contingencies. When he is "really involved" [behavior is densely reinforced] he is not depressed [#100]. He reports depression before starting and after stopping an activity. This language can confuse us. A sequence of activities and pauses is activity, pause, activity, etc. The postactivity pause and preactivity pause may be in effect the same kind of pause. In long fixed ratios, when an individual puts out a great deal of behavior before reinforcement, he pauses immediately after reinforcement—often for a lengthy period before resuming— and then seems to drag himself back. This is called a "post-reinforcement pause"; there is also a "prebehavior pause." These pauses may be depression. Functionally, such pauses decrease if the behavior-consequence contingency involves a lower response cost, among other procedures.*)

101. *Worker: What do you do when you are depressed? What does your wife do?*

102. Client: She looks at me strange sometimes. Great deal of disgust at a man doing that. I force a lot of responsibility on my wife. I agree to change, yet that's how I respond. I just don't do anything. I agree more to myself than to her. We often don't talk at this time. Often a woman speaks the truth. In this case it is the truth, but I don't accept it that readily about myself.

103. *Worker: (Question 3b) You've been discussing the problem, and considering making changes. For how long have you considered making some changes?*

104. Client: For the last three years.

105. *Worker: It really dates from the time of the marriage?*

106. Client: Yes. Prior to that I was involved in Civil Rights movement, really involved. But it went sour.

107. *Worker: (Question 3c) When did it first occur to you to change?*

108. Client: I don't know when it first started, but the thought of changing has been more pressing the last few months, specially since my wife has been talking of coming here. I get farther behind. I didn't plan to escape this time. Want to regenerate myself in some kinds of activity.

109. *Worker: What do you think your wife thinks about your coming?*

110. Client: She wants me to come. I'm uptight about jobs. I just won't take any job, but I really need the money. I'd like to get involved in a business I could make money with. Driving a cab had a lot of fulfillment for me. I didn't have to worry about the boss. I did very well. I enjoyed the change, meeting new people, learning to talk with them, learned different all the time, being outdoors. I tried to lease a cab before getting into this business. No one would lease one to me. I thought driving a cab would really put me in the place where I could get an income. Put me in another business, go to school. If I had the capital, I might be able to buy one or certainly lease on a long term. I'd like to go back to school. There was a cab number [shield] for me to buy, I could buy the cab, I could get the money from Small Business. That would really be a good solution, but there is no number available at the moment.

111. *Worker: Are you still interested in that?*

112. Client: I like the work. I could generate a lot of money. It would suit me ideally in terms of time. Work at the cab, sell the product in the evening, or the other way around.

113. *Worker: Can you drive a cab as an employee?*

114. Client: I was an employee. I was making money but not getting enough of it. Not too well for myself. I was looking for making more money out of that business. [Detailed discussion ensues on mechanics of buying a cab and cab number in Chicago.]

115. *Worker: This brings us to our next set of questions.* [Introduces question 4.] *What strengths or skills do you have which are related to the problem?*

116. Client: Related to the problem? Would my experience at driving a cab be that?

117. *Worker: Yes.*

118. Client: I can handle it well. I can get people where they want to go fast enough. I'm courteous to people. I know how to handle them. In relation to my [franchise] business, I think I can present myself. Get across the sales pitch. Have people like me. I believe I could be a leader.

119. *Worker: You mentioned you had writing abilities.*

120. Client: Yes, I was good at English composition, getting things down. I can get up in front of a group and speak. I'm a good listener. Is that a strength?

121. *Worker: Yes. It's particularly valuable.*

122. Client: I think I can work hard at something I like. I have worked hard at different times in my life, manual labor, other things. I can

work hard. I paint around the house. I do fixing up around the house. I do work slowly at this kind of thing. I drag it out. But I do get it done.

123. *Worker:* (Question 4b) *What skills in other areas?* [No response] *You are intelligent and you are able to stand back and look at yourself. You can figure out what is going right. You can take an objective look at yourself.*

124. Client: I think that is why it has taken so long to consult somebody independent or unbiased. I thought I'd like to look at myself. It has to come from me anyhow. I wasn't motivated to change before. I have a very vivid imagination. I sometimes express myself to people in words they don't quite understand. Unless you knew what I was thinking about . . . that's why I would like to write, express my feeling.

125. *Worker:* (Question 4c) *Any circumstances under which the current problem is no problem?*

126. Client: There are times when my wife and I communicate. Saturday she fixed something different for breakfast. She never fixed that before. I liked it. I told her that, and we had a nice breakfast together. We talked. We talk a lot sometimes over topics that don't particularly relate to each of us, like other people, or things on the television, but often when it is stuff in the home or it is us, we fight about that. She'll be quiet. That's part of my thing. I'm not satisfied with things we can discuss. We don't sit down and talk about things. My attitude toward how I want to be involved. She doesn't really want me to be a cab driver. What that means to her and what that represents to her is something we just can't get together on. It doesn't have much prestige.

127. *Worker:* (Question 4d) *Have there been any problems in related areas you have solved, and how?*

128. Client: Well, I've been depressed, sometimes I write things down. I started writing things down a couple of months. Quit smoking. Maybe for a day or two. The "stick-to-it kind of thing" I'm not good at. That's one thing I liked about the business. It's goal-oriented toward setting goals. I like that. You know, I'm going to do this, I'm going to do that, I'm going to get better, but I don't do it. I don't follow through with those kinds of things.

> (*Comment:* Every *client has patterns which can be related to programming and contingencies. These are the basis for programming and are made manifest by interviewer asking the appropriate questions.*)

129. *Worker:* (Question 5) *We may have left something out you consider important. Is there anything which we omitted, slighted, or overstressed?*

130. Client: No.

131. *Worker:* (Question 6) *You may want some information about us. Is there anything you would like to know about us, our goals or approach? Are there any comments?*

132. Client: No. What do we do from here? [Worker explains policy and procedures. In many cases, worker said, husband and wife are seen together; in others, separately. Mr. Johnson indicated his preference for meeting together with his wife: "That way, we could be communicating here, at least." The worker agreed with the wisdom of the client.]

> (*Comment: The responses support the statement made by client that he did not know his goals. What he listed as byproducts of the program* [weight, job satisfaction] *seem the most critical outcomes.*)

SUMMARY OF INITIAL INTERVIEW WITH MRS. JOHNSON

Mrs. Johnson is a capable, hard-working woman, black, aged twenty-nine, with a strong sense of values. She has been married for three years. She has held a job as a supervisor in a hospital laundry for over six years. She has been continually promoted and assigned increasing responsibilities.

It seems that she can be very effective in dealing with people. Although she never went beyond high school (where she made "good grades," had a "rich social life," and simultaneously supported herself—she was living with relatives away from home in order to go to a good school), she persuaded her parents to pay her younger brother's way through college. She applied for the weight-control program, but rapidly diverted the discussion to other problems that required solution. She persuaded her husband to call us, within a few hours after returning from the interview, for treatment for himself.

Her husband has a long history of depression. During his upswings, she is highly supportive, and during his downs she is not. She becomes passive sexually. The couple is heavily in debt; she has borrowed money to help him in business, and not only is the investment going down the drain because of his

idleness, but the debt is not being paid off. Although she controls her speech during these periods of depression and gives
him the "silent treatment," occasionally she has "sounded
off." On one occasion, he beat her so badly that she required
treatment in an emergency room. He was then contrite and solicitous.

She seems to be able to analyze situations well and to realize that her behavior is not helpful. However, the debts weigh
heavily on her, and she feels she cannot help herself, or him,
much as she would like to, and therefore tries to hold her
tongue or discuss only neutral issues with him. She would like
to reduce and become attractive again, but at present this is
difficult in view of her other problems. She states that she
would like to stay married to her husband, but be helpful to
him.

MRS. JOHNSON'S CURRENT RELEVANT REPERTOIRES

As can be inferred from the interview and the summary, Mrs.
Johnson seems to have much going for her. She demonstrates
good analytic skills, analyzing her relations with her husband
quite well. Unfortunately, this tends to occur primarily when
things go wrong, but the prospects seem good that in the
course of the program she can learn to analyze contingencies
when things go right. She has skills in recording, and she has
completed previous programs (high school and some current
job training). She seems to be able to schedule her time and
her efforts. Her awareness of budgets and caloric values of
food augurs well for a diet regimen.

Mrs. Johnson's husband is important to her, but his atten-
tions seem to be obtained primarily by aversive means. This
could be changed, and she could be taught to obtain her husband's attention through nonaversive means. For example, she
should be able to transfer her repertoire with her staff and her
other acquaintances to her relations with her husband. To get
her husband to do what *she* wants, she might start examining
what *he* wants. She also uses reinforcement/extinction for his

high/low periods. She might try to reinforce whatever positive behaviors occur during his low periods rather than scolding him for his absence of behavior; such scolding is currently, at best, not working. At worst, it is reinforcing the depressive pattern, since it indicates concern and involvement when this occurs.

She is good at her job at a training hospital, and it may be possible to program some higher education or training that could mean increased status, responsibility, and so forth for her at the hospital, if she wishes.

TENTATIVE PROGRAM DIRECTIONS FOR MRS. JOHNSON

There is currently much communication between Mr. and Mrs. Johnson, mostly centered on their financial problems. It is true that the consequences are often blows, showdowns, and manipulative silences. However, they communicate in a civil manner about inconsequential matters. It seems that a program of working together to solve their financial problems could maintain and sustain positively reinforcing behavior, since the consequences are extremely potent. Such joint effort might transfer to other areas.

When her husband is working toward solution of their joint problems, she reinforces this behavior. It is when he is despondent that she tries to eliminate his depressed affect and his lack of constructive behaviors through withholding reinforcement or applying punishment directly. One aim of the program might be to develop insight on her part into these contingency relations so that she might change them.

Another possible area of program outcomes might be the establishment of new eating patterns. Mr. Johnson also is overweight, and a joint program in which they monitored each other's diet and weight loss might be highly effective; it might also maintain positive interpersonal responses. Other interpersonal targets, such as sexual responsiveness, should await resolution of the two prime target areas.

The fact that so many of their problems are mutual and the

solutions are interwoven seems to indicate that Mr. and Mrs. Johnson, if willing, should be seen together.

SUMMARY OF INITIAL INTERVIEW
WITH MR. JOHNSON

Mr. Johnson is a tall, strong, black man, aged twenty-nine, of impressive appearance and manner. He has a sense of identification with his community and for a while participated in the Civil Rights movement. He has a high school education and served successfully in the army. He is able to articulate his problems and those of others; he reports being able to speak before groups, to understand others, and to write well. He possibly would have had no problems going through college, or through business school, considering his interests in running his own business and his numerous attempts in this direction. He has thus far been unable, given his lack of specialized training, finances, and contacts, to find a vocation that satisfies him and utilizes his talents. His own analysis seems appropriate: he needs "goal-oriented" work, and he considers working "toward setting goals" as important.

He reports profound depressions going back as far as high school. He spends much of his time in bed or in activities maintained by readily available consequences which, since they are not part of a chain leading to the critical back-up consequences, can maintain behavior only for brief periods. New projects initially produce considerable enthusiasm and behavior, but the lack of immediate success extinguishes these and he becomes depressed.

Currently, he is in a franchise business, which he is dropping with a considerable financial loss. He and Mrs. Johnson are heavily in debt, and his current lack of productive behavior naturally concerns his wife more than ever before. She seems unable to avoid making derogatory remarks, and they argue. He has on occasion struck and beaten her. He realistically reports that they are tearing each other to pieces, and he would want to continue the marriage only if they could reverse this pattern. They do get along well (sometimes) when discussing things other than money; they can (on occasion) get along well and be supportive of each other.

Mr. Johnson indicated that one type of work area that he might like is cab-driving, and if a number became available it might even lead to a consequence critical to him: a business of his own. However, his wife, who has strong middle-class values, considers such work demeaning.

MR. JOHNSON'S CURRENT RELEVANT REPERTOIRES

Mr. Johnson has analytic ability, is verbal, and is an astute observer of himself and others. In his business he has had some experience at recording. He has some previous history of successful programs, such as his jobs and the Civil Rights work at college; he can become enthusiastic and maintain behavior when the consequences are important (when it is potentiated for him). He has a high degree of social skill, which indicates an ability to get along well with others, both on an individual and on a group basis. He speaks well before groups.

He seems to get along well with his wife under certain conditions. He has also had some good work experience, for example, driving taxicabs; he knows his way around this field and is enthusiastic about it. He is not content with his weight and lack of physical exercise, and he wishes to do something about them.

TENTATIVE PROGRAM DIRECTIONS FOR MR. JOHNSON

As was noted with Mrs. Johnson, there is currently communication between the two centered on finances. They might work together on solving this problem. Mr. Johnson's driving a taxicab, at least part time, might then become much more acceptable to Mrs. Johnson than it has been, and the program for him might include discussion, rather than argument, about this issue. The eating problem might also be an area of joint discussion, since Mrs. Johnson is also overweight.

More specific programs should await joint discussion with his wife. The primary goals seem to indicate mutual efforts to become financially solvent and to establish better eating programs.

SOME COMPARISONS OF THE SMITH AND JOHNSON CASES

Both cases have some factors in common; they both involve marital problems and depression. In regard to marital conflict, however, they present differences that are crucial from a programming point of view, necessitating different types of programs. For example, in the case of Mr. Smith, it was not necessary to bring Mrs. Smith into the program; changing his work habits could be done in consultation with him alone. In the case of Mr. Johnson, establishing financial solvency would best be programmed in conjunction with Mrs. Johnson, since establishment of consequences critical to Mr. Johnson might also require change in her behavior.

In both cases there is a long history of severe depression in the male, but the programs are necessarily different. In Mr. Smith's case, the critical consequences for maintaining non-depression were available, but other contingencies interfered with their delivery. In Mr. Johnson's case, the critical consequences either had not yet been discovered or, if available, were not effective because of a number of factors, one of which may be the aversive control exercised by Mrs. Johnson.

CONTRACT NEGOTIATIONS

During the joint interview with Mr. and Mrs. Johnson, the case-worker pointed out that they each had many strengths as well as problematic areas. One of their main strengths was that they agreed on what were the problems between them. Although each, of course, differed in his interpretation of his respective role, they agreed on the essential facts. The fact that they had both come for therapy so quickly was a sign that both of them wanted to work on the marriage. The caseworker stated that she felt safe in assuming that, since they were both present in her office rather than in a divorce attorney's office, they both wanted to work to save their marriage.

Mr. and Mrs. Johnson agreed with the worker that there were four areas that could be worked on: (1) The financial problem: the partners are in debt. (2) Communication: Mr. Johnson wants Mrs. Johnson to listen to him. (3) The problem of sex: Mr. Johnson stated that Mrs. Johnson is fat, unappealing, and very cold to him. Mrs. Johnson complained that he is a man who is not working, therefore not a man, so how could she possibly enjoy sex with him? Further, his approach turns her off; he is harsh, cold, and sometimes brutal. (4) The weight problem: each has a weight problem, and they both want to lose weight.

To summarize, at this first interview the caseworker, in determining the contract with the Johnsons, stressed the areas in which they were communicating and explored with them the areas and the conditions during which things went well for them.

The preliminary contract was signed with the following priorities: (1) They would work together to resolve the financial problem. As this was an immediate concern, it seemed to be the area that was most amenable to intervention. (2) They would work on the weight problem. (3) The third phase of the contract was to resolve interpersonal difficulties, but it was agreed that work on this would be delayed until after work on the first two problems. (4) The sexual problem would be considered along with the interpersonal problem.

There was a logic and a rationale to this stating of priorities. The financial problem, including Mr. Johnson's work, had to be resolved immediately. Weight reduction was an area that they could work on together, monitoring each other's diet and exercise. This program would probably give them some immediate success experience, some immediate reinforcement experience, that might maintain the behaviors necessary for the third and fourth problems, the interpersonal and the sexual. These would probably be much harder to work upon.

Since neither partner in this situation had a history of orgasmic or potency difficulties, it was decided not to handle the sexual problem directly, but to hypothesize that, as the frequency of positive interchanges between the Johnsons rose and their relationship improved, sexual relations between them would reflect this change, somewhat like a barometer reflecting improving weather. This assumption proved to be correct. Thus the first items to be programmed were the financial problem and the weight reduction program undertaken concurrently.

The subgoals were designed for the Johnsons to work on together. They were to deal with areas that not only were immediately pressing but also were centered on getting factual kinds of information. These might provide an opportunity for mutual discussion and, it was hoped, a minimum of interpersonal stress. During the interview the Johnsons were advised not to get into the genesis of the debts, but merely to list the facts.

The first subgoal was to compile a list of debts and obligations. The second was to contact the company to see if a settlement was possible on the franchise, and the third was to draw up a possible budget together. This last was possibly more problematic, but it was suggested by Mrs. Johnson with Mr. Johnson agreeing, and it was included as a subgoal for the next week, recognizing that it was a very large step, difficult to accomplish. The fourth subgoal was to arrive at a baseline on the daily food intake; this intake was to be recorded.

The weekly worksheet, made up after the first interview, appeared as follows:

PROGRAM WORKSHEET: MR. & MRS. JOHNSON, DECEMBER

Current Relevant Repertoire	*Subgoal Subterminal Repertoire*
1. Can keep records in own areas.	1. Make a list of debts and obligations.
2. Are already contacting franchise company.	2. Contact franchise company and see if a settlement is possible.
3. Are already discussing finances.	3. Draw up a budget together.
4. Both keep records of other activities.	4. Record daily food intake on forms.

Program Notes

1, 2, and 3 to be done together!
4. Do separately, but check each other's records at the end of the day.

THE PROCESS

When the Johnsons appeared for their interview the next week, they had completed all of the tasks. In addition, Mr. Johnson had, on his own initiative, obtained a part-time job driving a taxicab owned by a friend of his. Mrs. Johnson had approved. Mr. Johnson said that he wanted to explore the possibilities of buying a cab.

The Johnsons had also drawn up a list of debts which, if one excluded the franchise, were not so overwhelming as they had thought. They had been in touch with the company during this week, and, after some complicated financial negotiations, the company agreed to buy back the products, the inventory, and the customer list, together with other aspects of the business, for essentially the amount that Mrs. Johnson had paid for it. However, since they had been paying on a monthly basis, they forfeited the interest on the loan which they paid to the company and which amounted to some $700. The Johnsons agreed they would sell back the franchise. Mr. Johnson acknowledged that the loss was due to his bad judgment, and he agreed to repay it by regular payments into their mutual bank account. He said it was only fair that Mrs. Johnson was to buy furniture or any other household article she would like with this money.

The Johnsons responded immediately to the worker's suggestion that they see a financial counselor to formulate a plan to solidify their situation and gradually discharge their debts. Both Mr. and Mrs. Johnson rejected the idea of bankruptcy. It was possible, for a rather small fee, to obtain the services of a financial counselor attached to a local family agency. The Johnsons were to bring their situation to this counselor for help in reaching some sort of decision about their money problems.

The Johnsons had both kept excellent and complete records of their food intake. The baseline eating patterns indicated that Mr. and Mrs. Johnson were each ingesting about 3,000 calories a day, and their weights were stable. Mrs. Johnson was having the equivalent of small lunches right after waking up at 6:30 (270 calories), upon arriving at work at 8:15 (150 calories), and during a midday work break at 3:30 (270 calories). After her return home, she also nibbled gingersnaps and other snacks from 4:30 to 7:00 (460 calories). This was in addition to a solid lunch and a solid dinner. Mr. Johnson ate less often, but also added extras throughout the day.

The eating patterns were discussed, and it was believed that later in the program Mrs. Johnson could readily cut down to 2,000 calories, and Mr. Johnson to 2,500, if both confined their eating to breakfast and dinner together and a lunch apart. They were told that the aim of the program was to develop enjoyable eating patterns, and they were to enjoy their eating. Neither indicated that the extra eating and nibbling were particularly enjoyable. They were asked to draw a series of parallel straight lines on graph paper, showing 14,000 and 17,500 calories on the ordinate and seven days on the abscissa. These were their ideal cumulative curves. Every day, they were to cumulate actual ingestion. If a point was to the right of the ideal line, they were eating less, and if to the left they were eating more. This is part of an eating program developed by Goldiamond (1974). It will be noted that the program does not stress eating less or dieting, but it does set patterns of ingestion which will result in weight loss if followed and controls conditions that strongly reinforce overeating.

Numerous studies have shown that eating is a "commpounded" affair. Many overweight people eat while watching television, reading, and so on, so that the television becomes a conditioned reinforcer for the eating. One of the chief therapeutic strategies in the behavioral approach is to make eating a "pure" experience and to keep the dieting person concentrating on the food alone. Therefore, a subgoal for the coming week was to select one place to eat in the home and at work. They chose the dining room in their home, and they agreed with the suggestion that they eat sitting down at a formally set table. Mrs. Johnson suggested a brightly colored place setting (stimulus control).

Another subgoal was to continue to record food intake. They then agreed that they would try at first to restrict food intake to 2,000 calories a day for Mrs. Johnson and 2,500 a day for Mr. Johnson. Because of their size and weight, each of them should begin to lose weight even on a diet as high in calories as this.

Recording their food ingestion had one additional function for the Johnsons: they were continually surprised at the amount of food and, in particular, at the amount of "empty" calories they ingested during the day. Records can be an extremely good sensitizing device, and, of course, they put the intervention on a factual, concrete level.

The subgoals for the following week appeared as follows:

1. See a financial counselor to draw up plans to solidify situations.

2. Sell back franchise.

3. Discuss the budget with financial counselor.

4. Start eating in one place; Mrs. J. 2,000 calories daily; Mr. J. 2,500 daily.

5. Investigate the realities of buying a cab.

During the Christmas period, which followed, the Johnsons consulted the financial counselor provided by the family agency, and they had drawn up a financial plan and a budget. They had sold the franchise back to the company for what they had paid for it. They had drawn up and had tried sticking to a budget with limited but promising results. Mr. Johnson had investigated the amount of money needed and had found that he could buy a number (shield) and cab with a down payment of from three to four thousand dollars. He thought that his family might possibly cosign a loan. Investigation of this possibility was to be a subgoal for the next week.

Mr. and Mrs. Johnson kept very good records on their food intake. However, the period covered the Christmas holidays, and their meals at the homes of relatives brought the curves considerably to the left of the ideal curves. They were congratulated on keeping good records, and it was noted that when they were not at the homes of relatives, their curves paralleled the ideal curves. They were told to relax and enjoy their holidays. The programming of their diets had been too fast and somewhat unrealistic in view of the Christmas holidays and the other programming demands. The worksheet for the next period appeared as follows:

PROGRAM WORKSHEET: MR. & MRS. JOHNSON, JANUARY

Current Relevant Repertoire	*Subterminal Repertoire*
1. Financial counselor seen; plans drawn up.	1. Initiate plans.
2. Franchise sold to company; Mr. Johnson begins making payments of interest.	2. Continue payments and renegotiate if cab deal (or full-time job) emerges.
3. Drew up and is sticking to budget.	3. Continue; start grocery shopping together.

Current Relevant Repertoire	Subterminal Repertoire
4. Records excellent; diet not too successful because of Christmas holidays.	4. Continue records. Continue eating one place. Mrs. J. 2,000; Mr. J. 2,500.
5. Mr. J. investigated $ re cab.	5. Arrange for loan, with Mr. J's family as cosigners.

Program Notes

2. Sold back franchise. Lost $700 interest, which Mr. J. is to pay back. Mrs. J. to buy furniture.

3. Discuss all grocery and other purchases together (except for incidentals— $3.00).

4. Christmas too difficult a time to begin dieting. Let's try now; holidays are over and it might be easier.

During the next few weeks, Mrs. Johnson succeeded in losing twelve pounds, and Mr. Johnson lost ten pounds. The weight loss continued to be fairly even, between two and three pounds a week for Mrs. Johnson and about two pounds a week for Mr. Johnson, who had more difficulty sticking to the diet. Mr. Johnson began to participate in the grocery shopping and in some of the minor meal preparation.

CONTRACT RENEGOTIATION

The Johnsons were now in control of their financial program, they were adhering to the eating program, and they were engaged in a variety of mutually reinforcing activities centered on these areas. In the eating program, they had been urged to monitor each other's records, reviewing them each night. They ate breakfast and dinner together almost every day. The eating and shopping activities also provided a variety of topics of conversation and opportunities for mutual activities that were certainly more conflict-free than the areas of sex, affection, and so on.

The worker and the Johnsons agreed that it was time to renegotiate the contract, to put into concrete terms the target area of interpersonal relationships within the marriage. Since "communication" was a mutually defined problem, it was decided to change the record-keeping. The couple was to continue to keep records relating to weight, such as food intake, stimulus control of eating, and so on (including exercises, which were introduced slowly after the program had taken effect). The initial assignment to the Johnsons was to set up interaction logs regarding behaviors related to the other. Since they were already keeping two sets of records, the interaction records were reduced to simple entries; they were to record interactions, outcomes, and how they felt—substantially the same material that appeared in the more standard interaction logs. A new contract was drawn up listing interpersonal communication as a third target. Each of the Johnsons succeeded in recording several interactions. Sample interactions from the records of both Mrs. Johnson and Mr. Johnson are reproduced below. They include both problematic and nonproblematic kinds of interactions:

Mrs. Johnson's Interactions

2/16. I had taken a nap after arriving home from work and immediately upon awakening my husband came into the bedroom and wanted to have sex. I kept insisting that I did not want to. After becoming a little upset, he left me alone.

2/17. Didn't see my husband—was very late when he came home and I was in bed—nothing was said when he got into bed.

2/18. We had been invited to a party at a friend's house. I told my husband that I did not want to go. He asked me a couple of times, and I still refused. He went alone.

2/19. I was awakened to have sex. I resisted somewhat at first, but later we had sex and I enjoyed it.

2/20. My husband asked me to type some resumes for him, and I told him I didn't feel like typing them because it was late and I had to get up early for work. He was very persistent, became very angry to the point where I felt as though he may hit me. He said that he wanted to mail them that night and later changed it until the next day. Because I was afraid of the consequences, I typed them when asked again. He did not mail the resumes until *two* days later.

2/21. Today was our anniversary. After dinner my husband suggested that we have champagne and I agreed. He went out for it, showed up and served it to me. It was delicious.

2/22. I didn't record this on the 22d and I remember vaguely our conversation about my leaving.

2/23. I was asleep when my husband arrived from the Loop with a dress for me. He asked me to get up and try the dress on. I did. I did not like the dress and I told him so. He wasn't too upset about that but told me that it was very difficult trying to buy anything for me because of my size. I did not respond to this.

I was cleaning up the apartment and asked my husband to help me and he refused—watched TV instead. Later asked me to attend church [Christmas Eve] with him that night and I refused because I wanted to finish cleaning. His sister went with him.

2/25. We were to have dinner at my sister-in-law's and my husband told me about 12:30 or 1:00 P.M. that he wanted me to start getting ready soon so we could be on time (3:00 o'clock). When asked again, I started getting dressed.

2/27. My husband had to go downtown to return the dress he bought and asked me to go with him and I agreed to. An enjoyable afternoon together.

2/28. Shortly after arriving home from the doctor, my husband wanted sex and I told him I did not want to. He became very angry, cursed me out and told me what I could do for myself. I said nothing. Later that night, we had sex, and I enjoyed it.

3/1. Didn't record and can't recall what happened.

3/2. My husband was in bed and ask me to look on the back porch and bring him the paper. I looked and told him I did not see it. He asked me if I looked down the stairs and I said I didn't so he hollered at me and asked me to look for it again, so I did and it wasn't there. He asked me or told me to call the news agency to report we had no paper when he was in bed right by the phone. I said nothing, stopped cooking dinner and called.

3/3. My husband had gone to the airport to pick up my brother and I had gone to the grocery store. We arrived home at the same time and I was taking the groceries from the car and stopped to go over and see them. Then we all started in the building with groceries and bags and I went back to the car and my husband hollered at me and told me to come and bring the bags upstairs. I told him I was going back to the car so I wouldn't have to make two trips. He hollered at me again and told me to come and that I needed the exercise anyway.

3/4. My husband started to go out and I asked him to stay. He proceeded to get dressed. I asked him if he felt that his going out would help us stay together and he asked me to answer. I did by replying that I didn't think so. I asked him again what he thought and he never replied—just said that I had answered myself.

3/5. Was asked to type resumes and I replied that I was too tired. He asked again, also inquiring as to why I wouldn't want to do something that would help him to get a job. I again told him I was tired. He left me alone and said nothing else.

3/6. Didn't say too much of anything to each other. I suppose because of the previous evening.

3/7. While writing about relations with husband, my husband came into the bedroom and asked to read them. I refused at first and then gave them to him later. He made a comment that I lied or was this how I remembered a particular day and I replied that was the way I remembered it.

Mr. Johnson's Interactions

3/11. I asked my wife to make peas with the dinner instead of green beans which she was making. She said that she wanted to have beans because they were less in calories, and because we had peas the day before. I again said I wanted peas and suggested that she make peas for me and maybe beans for herself. She said she did not want to make two vegetables but she made the peas but she was not happy about it.

Later I was going out and my wife was sitting in the living room. I stopped and asked her to give me a kiss. She said no. I asked her again and she turned her cheek and I kissed her on the cheek.

3/12. I was sitting in the living room and my wife was going from the bath to the bedroom. I called to her and pulled her toward me saying I wanted to kiss her. We kissed. She started to leave the room and I pulled her back again and kissed her again.

3/15. We were invited out by friends to play poker. My wife said she did not want to go. I told her she was going (I didn't ask her, I told her she was going). She got pissed and we went back and forth like this till finally I said she was ashamed to go out. She said she wasn't. Later that evening she very reluctantly decided to go with me. We went and we had a good time.

3/16. My wife was in the kitchen making some toast for herself. I came in and told her to make me some too. I guess I just started getting loud and called her selfish and then I got very angry and punched her on the arm. I wanted to know why my wife couldn't ask me if I wanted some too since she was preparing some for herself. She answered that she did know. She made the toast for both of us. She was very quiet and I was sort of ashamed of what I did.

3/18. I asked her if she would type some letters for me. She turned and looked at me in a way that meant she didn't want to do it. She didn't say anything. There was silence and I left the room. Later I was watching television in the kitchen and my wife yelled at me to watch the television in the living room because I had it turned up too loud. I ignored her and after a minute or so I turned it down but I cursed at her and then left the kitchen and watched the television in the living room.

Comment on the Interaction Logs. It is obvious to any trained observer, of any theoretical orientation, that it was not lack of communication between the Johnsons that was the problem. There was a great deal of communication, mostly aversive, that went on between the two of them. Both partners said that these were typical of the interaction between the two. There were constant requests made of each other to do services, to relate, to have sex, to do favors, and so forth. A great deal of the interaction was a struggle for control and responding to aversive stimuli. That is, requests were made in an extremely aversive

manner and in such a way that granting them would, in essence, have positively reinforced an aversive request-making
style. In this event it was perfectly natural for each to refuse to
grant the "favor" to the other under the conditions of negative
reinforcement.

Mr. and Mrs. Johnson and the worker discussed these instances at some length. Both partners were quick to grasp the
central factor that, if we consider problems between marital
partners to be interpersonal rather than psychological, then the
therapeutic task is to manipulate transactions and increase the
frequency of mutually positive reinforcing exchanges. If one
wishes to change one's partner's behavior, then one might first
change one's own. Another way to state this technically is that
a different kind of discriminative stimulus (or rule for reinforcement of other) must be given. The Johnsons analyzed each
other's recording, with the worker playing the role of a somewhat passive bystander, intervening only to clarify a point or to
head off nonproductive or nonconstructive interaction between
the two. In essence, the worker made Mr. and Mrs. Johnson
each other's behavior analyst (consultant).

Making them each other's consultant meant that the bulk
of the programming chore went over to the Johnsons. Each
began to suggest situations and techniques for handling problems. One example was the lack of activity on Saturday night.
Mr. and Mrs. Johnson agreed that each would take responsibility for planning alternate Saturday night activities. They
would suggest it to the other a day or two in advance, keeping
in mind their budgetary limitations. If agreed upon a day ahead
of time, Saturday evening, for example, could be spent at home
watching television, although Mr. Johnson had stated in an earlier interview that he wished to go out more. Mrs. Johnson was
not opposed to going out to social events, especially in view of
her increasing physical attractiveness as she lost weight, but
she objected to this being presented to her aversively.

Similarly, Mr. Johnson was satisfied if he felt his wife went
willingly; he wished to go out only one or two times per week,
as the work with the taxicab he had purchased kept him quite
tired. He was working five and sometimes five and a half or

even six days a week. Being in business for himself, the more he worked driving the taxi, the more money he made. He soon proved to be quite a hustler, and Saturday night became the only time for socialization. Sundays, because of Mr. Johnson's fatigue, were generally spent going to church in the morning and visiting relatives or generally relaxing in the afternoon.

After twenty-two interviews the caseworker and the Johnsons began to schedule the interviews every other week, then every third week. Formal contact with the Johnsons was terminated after one year of interviews. Follow-up has been done at six-month intervals since closing the case. At the closing of the case, new eating patterns seemed very well established. Mrs. Johnson was close to her premarriage weight; the weight loss was comparatively less for Mr. Johnson, but still quite marked. Both partners were happy with their progress.

The Johnsons were sticking to the financial plan and by the end of the first year had made a sizable dent in the debt. Mrs. Johnson was seriously considering going into a practical nursing training program at the hospital. This would mean a lowered income while she was being trained, but eventually would mean not only higher professional status but also more money in her paycheck. Mr. Johnson was in favor of her making this move. The training period and lowered income would be made possible by Mr. Johnson's increased earnings as a cabdriver. She now spoke of him as a "self-employed businessman." She was no longer trying to remake him.

six

INTERVENTIONS BASED ON THE PAVLOVIAN AND MODELING ORIENTATIONS

There are a number of behavioral orientations other than those derived from operant principles. These different orientations have produced differing theoretical models and have also produced differing intervention procedures. In actual practice, though, these models are not mutually exclusive but do overlap. There are probably operant consequences to all interventions. Furthermore, even operant therapists may, to differing degrees of purposefulness, incorporate principles of modeling and imitation. Much operant behavior has become so ingrained in the repertoires of individuals that they may seem to be occurring on a reflex, or automatic behavior level. Despite the proliferation of approaches, in this chapter we shall limit discussion to those intervention techniques and applications based on the classical and on the modeling orientations. The discussion will open with selected Pavlovian procedures, or what Kanfer and Phillips (1970) call "behavior modification by control of stimulus-response arrangements."

THERAPIES BASED ON THE CLASSICAL CONDITIONING MODEL

The greatest impact of the classical approach has not stemmed directly from Pavlov's formulations but through the American extension of Pavlov's thought into the classical learning theories as exemplified by Clark Hull (see Dollard and Miller, 1950). The single most influential behavior therapist in the Western world is the psychiatrist Joseph Wolpe, who has pioneered this approach into what has been generally called "behavior therapy."

THE RECIPROCAL INHIBITION THERAPIES OF JOSEPH WOLPE

A prolific writer, Wolpe has expounded his theories at length and in great detail, and has opened his laboratories and exposed his data to qualified investigators. Wolpe works primarily with the neuroses, particularly the various phobias. Until recently he has not done much work with psychotic patients, as he believes that the psychoses are mainly organic in origin (Wolpe, 1958). He defines neurosis, or neurotic behavior, to mean any persistent unadaptive habits. He assumes that neurotic habits are learned and that they can be eliminated effectively only through unlearning. Behavior is classified as adaptive or unadaptive. It is adaptive if it successfully reduces central neural excitation—reduces a drive or satisfies a need—or if it successfully avoids possible damage or deprivation.

The response of anxiety is seen always as a part of the original neurotic learning situation and as a part of the eventual symptom pattern. The therapeutic task, then, is to alter these learned connections between previously neutral situational or response events (stimuli) and these anxiety responses or the unadaptive habits following upon the anxiety responses. Wolpe states that, because of inherent limitations of the nervous system, two contradictory emotional responses cannot exist in the same individual at the same time. That is, a person cannot feel relaxed and anxious at the same time. Thus, he says, "if a response inhibitory of anxiety can be made to occur in the presence of anxiety-evoking stimuli it will weaken the bond between these stimuli and the anxiety" (Wolpe, 1969, p. 15). This formulation is based on Hull's response-termination (drive reduction) principle. If the anxiety response is blocked or inhibited by incompatible response, "and if a major drive reduction follows," the anxiety habit will be weakened. Wolpe's principal therapeutic approach is called "reciprocal inhibition through systematic desensitization" or, more commonly, "systematic desensitization."

To eliminate neurosis, eliminate anxiety. Perhaps oversimplifying, let us imagine a person who is afraid of heights. He reacts to heights, or thoughts of heights, with feelings of anxiety. Therefore, height is a conditioned noxious stimulus. If a patient were to engage in a relaxation response while thinking of being in a high place, then this relaxation would conflict with the anxiety that height generally produced, and being in a tall building would gradually lose its noxious quality. The sense of relaxation will reciprocally inhibit the anxiety response. The main technique Wolpe utilizes is systematic desensitization. The individual is gradually exposed to a very faint form of the noxious stimulus while the patient is relaxed. This faint form produces little anxiety. The noxious stimulus is gradually increased so that he progressively overcomes it more and more. He is "systematically desensitized" to the noxious stimulus; that is, he is (in a sense) almost "immunized" to increasingly larger doses.

Wolpe teaches the client a series of relaxation exercises based on the work of Jacobson, a neurologist (Jacobson, 1938). The exercises enable the patient to relax upon command or upon self-instigation. Then the therapist and the patient construct a "hierarchy" in which the feared object is imagined, from the least to the most threatening situation. In the case of the individual afraid of height, the hierarchy may be in terms of floors from the ground. The first scene might be that of approaching the ground floor of a skyscraper. The client imagines he is before the building, and then indicates (usually by raising a finger) whether or not he is anxious. If he is not anxious, then the next scene might be entering the building, then in the next scene going to the third floor, then the fourth floor, and so forth until he reached the observation tower on, let us say, the ninety-fifth floor, and looked down. At any spot along the way, the client practices the relaxation response until he is able to go on to the next scene.

After intensive intake and admission interviews, which include taking detailed histories and completion of several psychological inventories, the hierarchy is constructed according to the individual history and problems of the client. The number of sessions will obviously vary according to the problem, the individual, and other variables. In a recent report of a sample of patients with phobias, Wolpe reported (1969, p. 149) that the "mean number of sessions per phobia was 11.2, the median 10.0." These were forty-five-minute sessions.

Systematic desensitization has been one of the most widely used and extensively researched techniques in *any* psychotherapeutic approach. The techniques and variations of the techniques have been applied to a number of conditions and problems besides the phobias, and to involved and complicated case situations in which phobias were only part of the problem. Wolpe has been most forthright and direct in reporting his work. The literature and reports of scientific investigations are enormous. A good place for an interested reader to begin is with Wolpe's own writings (especially Wolpe, 1969).

There have been a number of interpretations, other than Wolpe's own, to explain the effectiveness of the procedures, and these interpretations have generated considerable research.[1] Some of these writers question Wolpe's theoretical basis, stating that Wolpe has oversimplified the nature of phobias and that his explanation of a neurological basis for neurosis is not well-founded. As in the vermin phobia described in Chapter 3, phobias can be maintained by the consequences they provide to the client, that is, the payoff. The treatment here would be to help the client get the payoffs through means

[1] The two articles by Gordon Paul (1969) and the article in the same volume by Peter J. Lang provide a good, though slightly dated, overview summary of the research on systematic desensitization. Furthermore, Bandura (1969) and Kanfer and Phillips (1970) present good overviews of the process and results of research. Ongoing research reports may be found in a number of journals, particularly *Behaviour Research and Therapy, Journal of Behavior Therapy and Experimental Psychiatry, Behavior Therapy,* and *Psychotherapy: Theory, Research, and Practice.*

which are less costly to him. If such a phobia is simply removed, the individual must learn other ways to get this payoff, or the phobia will return. It should be emphasized that this is *not* "symptom substitution."

It is to Wolpe's credit that, regardless of the eventual status of his formulations, he has pioneered explicit procedures for intervening in problems which had previously been considered intractable. Furthermore, even those investigators who disagree with him can devise ways to test and compare their procedures and formulations with Wolpe's.

IMPLOSION AND FLOODING

There are techniques which do not introduce the noxious stimulus gradually but in intense but imaginal form. The chief technique, originated by Stampfl and Levis (1967, 1968), is called "implosive therapy" or *implosion.* The theory behind implosive therapy is that "extinction of anxiety can be most effectively achieved by repeated elicitation of intense emotional responses without the occurrence of physically injurious consequences" (Bandura, 1969, p. 402). In implosive therapy, clients who, for example, are phobic about dirt are asked to imagine themselves buried to the armpits in feces, having excreta and other noxious and revolting substances thrown at them, and so forth. A snake phobic client would be asked to imagine that snakes are crawling all over him and biting him.

In another form of this therapy the noxious stimuli (when possible) are presented in real form: the client handles live snakes. This therapy is called *flooding.* The principles behind implosion and flooding are the same; the difference is that in implosion the stimuli are presented in imaginal form and in flooding they are presented in real (in vivo) form.

These two techniques are controversial (Bandura, 1969, pp. 400–405; Marks, 1972) and should be used with a great deal of caution. While repeated exposure may produce extinction of fear in some people, many (if not most) people react extremely negatively when presented abruptly with a feared object. Wolpe believes that systematic desensitization, in which the noxious stimuli are presented gradually, is by far the more humane treatment and that flooding and implosion are treatments of "final recourse" (Wolpe, 1969, p. 189).

The results of comparative research on systematic desensitization and flooding have been inconsistent, and varying results have been explained by differences in the procedures used (Marks, 1972; Morganstern, 1973).[2] Furthermore, it has been shown that exposing an individual to the stimulus (either real or imagined) on a massive basis can heighten his anxiety and exacerbate the situation, providing not a cure but possibly exposing him to needless amounts of concentrated anxiety (Morganstern, 1973). In addition, many clients understandably will not continue treatment under such an extremely unpleasant set of procedures.

IN VIVO DESENSITIZATION

One form of desensitization that appears to hold promise for use by social caseworkers (although possibly in combination with other techniques) is the technique called "in vivo desensitization." This is a procedure whereby the individual approaches the feared object or condition in real life, but his approach to the feared object, unlike flooding, is gradual. The technique has been used, in one form or another, for many years; it is probably familiar to anyone who has tried to overcome a fear of dogs by approaching an animal indirectly.

The technique requires that the individual be comfortable and approach the object gradually. The gradual approach increasingly exposes the individual, and the noxious or fearful object or condition loses its "power" to evoke a fearful, or phobic, response. A description of the technique and its comparison to systematic desensitization, in which the stimulus is also presented gradually but in imaginal form, may be found in Wolpe (1969, pp. 161–66). In imaginal systematic desensitiza-

---

[2] For a rebuttal to Morganstern's criticisms see Levis (1974).

tion the young man who had a fear of heights was to imagine himself higher and higher in the building. In vivo procedures could have been put into practice, either to supplement (carry over to the systematic desensitization) or as an in vivo process in its own right. Here the technique would be for the individual to approach the building and, if he felt comfortable, actually go to the first floor, then to the second floor, and so on, until he felt anxious, at which point he could either terminate the program *for that session* or return to a lower floor. The target floor to be visited could be raised until the young man was actually standing on the observation platform of the ninety-fifth floor.

This technique has been used with great success in the treatment of a number of phobias, as well as other problems of college students (Watson and Tharp, 1972). This technique can also be used with some of the modeling techniques to be mentioned in this chapter. For example, an individual could see a model expose himself gradually to a feared (noxious) stimulus and then, gradually, the individual could expose himself to the same stimulus.

In vivo desensitization is often combined with some sort of consequences or reward for progressive steps, through token economies, as well as with other techniques. There are obvious operant consequences to the procedures.

ASSERTIVE TRAINING

There are a number of complex techniques that may not be easily pigeonholed into any of the three classifications of mediational, respondent, and operant techniques. One which is primarily used for behavioral deficits (when there is either an absence of, or a low rate of, behavior) is the technique or group of techniques called "assertive conditioning" or *assertive training.* Cautela (1969) includes this among the respondent techniques. He believes that people are often inhibited by anxiety from performing a task. Performing the task itself lessens the anxiety.

In such assertive training, the individual rehearses the deficit behavior and then performs the behavior, first in an artificial setting, such as a group or therapy situation. He then may go out and perform the task in a real-life situation, in vivo. The performing of the act lessens the anxiety-act bonds. Obviously, there are consequences to the performance of such acts, so that, upon careful examination of the results (consequences) of assertive training, one might very well make a case that the techniques are, or have, operant consequences as in the case of Mr. Smith, in chapter four.

The ability of the individual to perform these tasks upon his self direction also prompts Cautela to include assertive training and behavior rehearsal among the self control approaches. The self control response is the assertive response, and the response to be controlled is anxiety (Cautela, 1969).

Assertive training has been applied to many unique problems. For example, it has been utilized as a treatment for many New York residents who are "overly anxious about some of the problems of the city." One such action is to ask individuals to go into a luncheonette, ask for a drink of water, and leave without putting down a tip. This requires a certain amount of initiative and courage from a resident of New York City (Wolfe, 1973).

Fensterheim (1972) had marital partners practice desired behaviors and rate each other's performances. Spencer Rathus (1972, 1973) used assertive training in groups, using video tape. He trained women in specific techniques for shaping assertive behavior and reducing fears of social confrontation. He did several control studies showing that these techniques, when used in conjunction with a video feedback system, produced a greater gain in control in those women who underwent the training than in those who underwent other kinds of training. However, assertive training used in this way contains many elements of modeling and thus is a complex, "mixed" technique. Rathus's work has obvious implications for "women's liberation" and the raising of women's consciousness.

Richey found that "women are generally unassertive when interacting with men [and that] women's restricted verbal participation in mixed-sex discussions limits their display of competence and reduces their potential contributions" (Richey, 1973). Richey has devised programs to increase assertive responding, using ingenious systems of self-recording and self-rewarding of assertive actions. Gambrill and Richey have devised manuals and techniques for increasing self-assertive behaviors, and have devised an "assertive inventory" (Gambrill and Richey, 1973).

Assertive training, while placed among the classical learning theory techniques, combines some aspects of modeling with operant and self control aspects. The performance of assertive actions and the filling of a behavioral deficit have obvious payoff and consequences and the assertive actions may be, in fact, supported by environmental contingencies. Thus the technique further merits the classification of a "complex technique" by the addition of operant consequences.

THOUGHT-STOPPING

Some individuals are bothered by persistent trains of thought (obsessive thoughts) that they cannot seem to get out of their minds. One technique, described by Wolpe (1969), is for the patient to think these thoughts. The therapist then yells "Stop!" very loudly. It is pointed out to the patient that the thoughts *did* stop, and that the patient *himself* may utilize this technique, first with practice in the therapist's office and then later by himself. Cautela includes this technique within a reciprocal inhibition framework, but he also states it is a self control technique, since the patient can obviously initiate its use whenever he wishes. Cautela has found the technique helpful in cases of obsessive thinking, hallucinations, and compulsive behavior (Cautela, 1969).

Wolpe (1969, p. 224) classifies thought-stopping as an operant technique, stating that it is the inhibition of a "perseverating train of thought" by positive reinforcement. The positive reinforcement he identifies as the substitution of other thoughts. The technique is maintained by lessening the frequency of the obsessive thoughts.

NEGATIVE PRACTICE

Another technique that might be classified under the "respondent" classification is *negative practice,* in which a behavioral habit, such as a tic, is continually performed and nonreinforced so that, in time, the habit lessens (Yates, 1958). This technique has mixed results, especially with children (Graziano, 1971).

THE TREATMENT OF SEXUAL DYSFUNCTIONING

A set of respondent-related techniques that have proved successful include those used for the treatment of sexual dysfunctioning, such as impotence, frigidity, premature ejaculation, and the like. Wolpe has a chapter on "therapeutic sexual arousal" (Wolpe, 1969); his work was later expanded by Masters and Johnson (1966, 1970), who have generated a whole series of researches and techniques, behaviorally based and oriented, that have made these once-difficult-to-treat conditions amenable to intervention.

THE AVERSION THERAPIES

Basically, the aversion techniques follow this general procedure: an unconditioned stimulus that produces an undesirable effect (electric shock, chemicals, noise, drugs that produce vomiting, or other stimuli) is paired with a neutral stimulus— the unwanted behavior, such as drinking, sexual deviation, and so forth. In time, the unwanted or antisocial behavior comes to elicit the same response as the unconditioned stimulus. An illustration would be found in the work of the late Dr. Joseph Thimann at the Washingtonian Hospital in Boston. An alcoholic patient is injected with a nausea-producing drug and then given a shot of his favorite whisky. The patient, after drinking the whisky, would vomit. After a while, the whisky (a "neutral" stimulus) becomes a conditioned stimulus for vomiting; the whisky acquires the properties of the unconditioned stimulus, the nausea-producing drug (Thimann, 1949).

Thimann utilized a chemical agent as an aversive stimulus; chemical stimuli have been most used in the aversion treatment of alcoholism. Chemicals have also been used in the treatment of sexual deviations; for example, the cross-dressing of the transvestite, when the transvestite was made to feel ill at the sight of ladies' undergarments.

Other aversive stimuli used have been noise, traumatic respiratory paralysis, and electric shock of varying intensities (Rachman and Teasdale, 1969).

There are numerous reviews of the results of aversion therapy (generally chemical aversion therapy) with alcoholics. These reviews are summarized in Bandura (1969), Kanfer and Phillips (1970), Rachman and Teasdale (1969), and periodically in the *Quarterly Journal of Studies on Alcohol.* Rachman and Teasdale state (1969, p. 23) that when chemical aversion treatment is used in well-controlled and well-conducted studies, the abstinence rate one year after treatment is about 60 percent. There is a continuing problem of a high relapse rate, but this, they report, can be reduced with booster treatment. The majority of relapses occur within one year after treatment.

Furthermore, those patients who functioned adequately before the alcoholism (had a stable premorbid personality) and had a cohesive home background will probably respond better than other types. The voluntary and work-oriented patient has a better prognosis than other types of patients. In other words, the "best" patient for the use of aversive techniques is also the "best" patient for other kinds of therapeutic interventions.

However, there are obviously many shortcomings in the use of chemical stimuli. The treatment is unpleasant not only for the patient but also for the therapists. There is also some evidence that chemical aversion treatment brings about increased aggressiveness and hostility on the part of the patients (Rachman and Teasdale, 1969, p. 33). It arouses anxiety and, of course, some of the drugs have dangerous side effects as well as quite serious consequences.

Aversive stimuli, both chemical and electrical, have been used to treat homosexuality, fetishism of various kinds (handbags, women's underwear, baby buggies), transvestism, sadism, compulsive masturbation, and others (Feldman, 1966).

Some simple aversive conditioning techniques utilize a technique designed to produce repugnance as well as sickness and avoidance at the thought and sight of the "forbidden" actions. With such problems as homosexuality, a technique frequently used is called "aversion relief treatment," in which a homosexual might receive an electric shock while looking at pictures (slides) of young boys but not while looking at pictures of attractive young women. Another example is the homosexual patient who received an electric shock in the presence of slides depicting sodomy, flapping wrists, and so forth, while the relief stimuli consisted of heterosexual pictures, such as female breasts, attractive girls, and so forth (Rachman and Teasdale, 1969).

The results of aversive treatment of sexual deviations are mixed. Rachman and Teasdale (1969) state that "chemical aversion therapy appears to be at least moderately successful in treating sexual disorders with the possible exception of homosexuality" (p. 28), while "electrical aversion has been employed with apparent success in the treatment of transvestites, fetishists, homosexuals, masochists, exhibitionists—but the total number of cases reported . . . is still small and there is a need for careful control studies" (p. 70).

Feldman and MacCullough (1972) conclude that aversive treatments for homosexuality seem to have been most effective with those individuals who have in their histories a repertoire of heterosexual activity. In other words, the various aversion therapies do not seem as successful in building up heterosexuality as they seem to be in suppressing homosexuality and thus, indirectly, enhancing heterosexual behavior.

A well-known aversive treatment that uses the respondent paradigm is the various "bell and pad" techniques for treating enuresis. Among the first to use these techniques were Mowrer (1938) and Lovibond (1964). Generally, the first drops of urine complete an electrical circuit which sounds a bell or some other warning device and wakes up the child, thus "catching" him (and also punishing him, not only with the sound of the aversive stimulus but also with lack of sleep). Many investigators have reported success with these devices (see Kanfer and Phillips, 1970, pp. 123–27, for a good and complete review). There has been speculation about whether the successful treatment of enuresis is due to the conditioning process alone, or to the social consequences of parental attention, giving rewards and attention for dryness, and so forth.

In marked contrast are the operant techniques recently developed by Azrin and Foxx (1974) which reinforce "dryness" rather than punishing "wetness." No aversive control is used. They report overwhelming success with nonprofessionally trained parents who use their manual and techniques.

COVERT SENSITIZATION

There is a group of techniques called "aversive imagery" or, as they are better known, "covert sensitization." Here the unconditioned stimulus is not a tangible, "physical" stimulus, such as chemicals or electricity, but one or more imagined events from the person's life situation. The techniques were introduced by Cautela (1967). Cautela assumed that stimuli presented in imaginal form have the same relation to subsequent behavior as do stimuli actually presented physically. In covert sensitization, both the behavior to be modified and the aversive event are presented imaginally (alcoholics imagine drinking and becoming nauseated and then vomit). Cautela states that this technique has many advantages over the use of real stimuli: (1) The procedure is not so unpleasant, and thus there is less premature termination of the therapy. (2) It can be used as a self control technique, since the patient can evoke the scenes at any time. (3) No special apparatus or medical supervision is needed. (4) There are no physical dangers or side effects, as with the use of drugs and electrical stimuli.

For example, with a drinking problem, Cautela divides the treatment sessions into three stages: (1) The subject imagines scenes in which drinking and alcohol lead to change of taste, stomach upset, nausea, and finally vomiting. (2) Scenes are imagined in which the desire to drink and preliminary drinking behavior (opening the bottle, pouring the beer) lead to nausea. In addition, scenes are presented in which the subject imagines he avoids the alcohol (and the resulting nausea) and therefore experiences a feeling of relief. (3) Scenes are presented in which the subject's desire for alcohol leads to nausea and vomiting (these scenes differ from stage 2 as the presence of alcohol is not imagined).

Covert sensitization has been used for a number of conditions, often in combination with other treatments. Stuart (1967) has used the technique in the treatment of obesity. He asked an obese woman to imagine the worst possible event occurring when she reached for a cookie. In one case, it was her husband making love to another woman, rejecting her because of her bulk. Every time she felt tempted to reach for a cookie, she was to imagine this scene. The rate of cookie-eating dropped drastically.

The use of covert sensitization has been reported in cases of sexual deviation, obesity, smoking, and alcoholism, although in small numbers and with mixed reports of success (Agras, 1972). Gold and Neufeld used it to overcome a sixteen-year-old boy's habit of soliciting men in public toilets. Davidson eliminated a sadistic fantasy, and Kolvin treated a fetish and an addiction to the sniffing of gasoline (cited in Wolpe, 1969). Agras (1972) reports that the long-term effectiveness of covert sensitization has not been adequately investigated.

THE AVERSION THERAPIES, PRO AND CON, AND ALTERNATIVES

There is a great deal of controversy regarding the use of aversion therapies. Even the leading writers in this area, Rachman and Teasdale (1969), state that they themselves have mixed feelings about aversion therapy. On the one hand, they are interested in it as a psychological process and as a possibly new and effective therapy, especially for difficult conditioning. On the other hand, they are frank in stating that "it is an unpleasant form of therapy and one which is open to abuse." They state that it is not enough merely to eliminate the undesirable behavior, but that the therapy should also involve the establishment of alternative, prosocial behaviors.

In one study, Corte, Wolf, and Locke (1971) attempted to eliminate the extreme self-injurious behaviors of four institutionalized, profoundly retarded adolescents. These behaviors included face-slapping, face-banging, hair-pulling, face-scratching, and finger-biting. Techniques such as elimination of consequences, positive reinforcement of alternative behaviors, and deprivation of food either were minimally effective or not effective at all, while electric-shock punishment eliminated these behaviors in all four subjects. However, the effects tended to be specific to the setting.

There are, moreover, certain patterns of behavior whose effects can only be described as gruesome. Examples include such self-mutilization as putting one's eyes out, smashing one's head until there is brain injury, or tearing at one's flesh until the bone is exposed (Lovaas *et al.,* 1973). Frequently, the only treatments applied are physical constraints, such as strapping the patient into a straitjacket, or chemical constraints, such as heavy sedation. Such control, of course, merely "freezes" the patient in his present state, and establishes no new patterns of behavior.

Lovaas *et al.* (1973) and others have stopped serious self-destructive behaviors of long duration with a few seconds of intense faradic shock. However, Lovaas, as well as others, ceases to use aversives after the cessation of the self-destructive behavior and immediately begins a training program to establish new patterns using positive reinforcements. Much of the outcry against the use of punishment in such extreme situations is generally made by those who themselves do not undertake the therapeutic responsibility for this kind of client, since their verbal, evocative therapies are inappropriate (or ineffective). Thus these clients are often condemned to what Baer calls a "half-alive" status.

Baer (1970) hypothesized that such procedures maintain pathology since they neither eliminate such behaviors nor do they use programs of positive reeducation. Baer, who is fully committed to positive methods, states (1970, p. 246) that we have "confined [these people] to a small hell in consequence. Can we now refuse that they endure a small number of painful episodes over a short span of sessions, hopefully designed to let them live the rest of their lives awake and untied?" He goes on to say that his examples and arguments are extreme, and he argues that *"not to rescue a person from an unhappy organization of his behavior is to punish him, in that it leaves him in a state of recurrent punishment"* (*ibid.;* italics in original). He concludes that we have a moral obligation to investigate just how punishment may or may not be effective in treating hitherto untreatable conditions and, if possible, to shorten therapies that are now overlong and/or not so effective as they might be.

Baer adds the caveat that punishment is basically a behavior-removing and not a behavior-building technique. To be effective, punishment, as well as all aversive techniques, should be combined with procedures to build or strengthen adaptive (prosocial) behaviors.

Further research and investigations are obviously needed on the conditions for the use of punishment and on procedures which provide positive alternatives. In all events, punishment has little potential use as a procedure in social casework. It is often punishment received that sends the client into treatment, and for the agency which is supposed to provide *relief* from such punishment to *provide* additional punishment raises an obvious ethical question.

THE MODELING APPROACH

Some behavioral theorists, primarily Albert Bandura and his associates (Bandura, 1969, 1971), state that much learning that takes place through direct experience occurs because individuals, either planfully or accidentally, observe and imitate the actions of others. Complicated patterns of behavior, including affective responses, can be acquired and maintained after being modeled by others. Through modeling procedures, one may acquire new behaviors and responses, or extinguish nonadaptive behaviors and responses. The conditions for modeling may be arranged by a therapist, and the modeling situation may make use of a live model (including the therapist) or may utilize audiotape recordings, videotape recordings, films, live actors, and other means, limited only by technological limitations and the imagination of the therapist.

Many terms have been used to describe what is called "modeling." These include "imitation," "observational learning," "identification," "internalization," "introjection," "incorporation," "copying," "social facilitation," "contagion," and "role-playing" (Bandura, 1971, pp. 3–4). The approach has also been called the "vicarious learning" approach.

There is a continuing debate over the theoretical basis of modeling procedures which is part of a greater debate on learning and learning theory. Earlier explanations were based on classical conditioning or associative theories. In this application, a person makes a response which is copied by a second person, and this sets up a circular associative sequence whereby the second person's matching behavior becomes a stimulus for the first person's behavior (Parke, 1969). Bandura (1971) criticizes associative theory by questioning why the theory does not account for some behaviors that are not controlled by stimuli to which the person has been exposed, and he adds that this explanation does not account for the learning of novel responses.

More recent developments, to which we shall return, tend to stress the operant or instrumental consequences of imitated behavior. Led primarily by Baer and his colleagues, this approach (oversimplifying) states that certain responses which are imitated (learned) are differentially and selectively reinforced, thus are maintained in the person's repertoire (are performed). Behavior thus reinforced becomes a discriminative stimulus (a cue, for the time being) for the appropriate future behavior. Bandura questions the Skinnerian A-B-C sequence as an explanation, on several bases. He notes that the actual first performances are often delayed until considerable time has passed, since they were learned through modeling, so that there is not the opportunity for differential reinforcement. Thus Bandura believes that the operant analysis does not satisfactorily explain the acquisition of novel behavior.

Discussion of the various theories of modeling may be found elsewhere (Bandura, 1969, 1971; Kanfer and Phillips, 1970; among others). This section will sample the various possible views of the process.

BANDURA'S VIEWS OF MODELING

According to Bandura, there are three separate effects of the exposure to modeling. The first is that an individual can acquire new response patterns, novel responses that did not previously exist in his behavioral repertoire. The second is that modeling may strengthen or weaken inhibitory responses in observers. The third is that significant others (models) may serve as discriminative stimuli for the observer. The presence of the significant other may be a cue that certain behaviors are appropriate or that certain behaviors are not appropriate. (In operant terms, certain behaviors are likely to be reinforced and certain behaviors are not likely to be reinforced.) The significant other reinforces recently learned behaviors and helps in their generalization to other behaviors in the same class (the "response facilitation effect") (Bandura, 1969, p. 120).

Modeling, in practice, is actually a complex technique. One view is that the imitative rule, like other discriminative control, is established (learned) by consequences attached to behaviors in the same stimulus class, that is, which are similar to the behaviors of the model (Goldiamond and Dyrud, 1967a). The behaviors are maintained by their consequences. Stated otherwise, they are operants. This is the viewpoint of Baer, Sherman, and others.

THE VIEW OF PATTERSON

According to Patterson (1969), the child first responds to the eliciting and reinforcing properties of the behavior of his mother. From this interaction with the mother, training (the response) generalizes to other kinds of social situations. This admittedly oversimplifies, since (1) the process for training for responsiveness is carried out over a considerable period of time; (2) the particular experience the child has with a particular person determines how responsive he will be *through* the behavior; that is, not all significant others are equally potent to serve as models. Finally, there is not a single trait of responsiveness to social stimuli. Patterson suggests (1969, p. 345) that the terms "social reinforcement," "persuasion," and "modeling" are really different operational definitions of the term "social responsiveness." Thus some modeling is related to the eliciting effects of social behavior (persuasion and modeling), and some is related directly to the consequences provided by the behavior of another person (social reinforcement).

BEHAVIOR AS LEARNED BEHAVIOR

What *all* the approaches agree upon—and again over-simplifying—is that imitative behavior is learned and is learned in interpersonal relations, starting in interactions with the parenting figures and then gradually being shifted to peers, and so forth. This viewpoint certainly is in agreement with psychodynamic and developmental theories.

   This process of learning starts early. Parents may try to shape or hand-guide imitative behaviors. Parents may beam and coo at the child's behavior. They may capitalize on available reflexes or set up eliciting conditions for them (a respondent model), and they (or others in the ecology) may attach consequences to the occurrence of the behaviors (an operant model).

   Imitative or observational learning has many advantages over shaping. There are some behaviors, such as learning to drive a car or performing an appendectomy, in which shaping, successive approximation, and trial-and-error learning would be a little impractical if not downright hazardous (Bandura, 1971). However, learning to drive a car, or to cut open a body by observation can be subsumed under instructional or abstractional control (Chapter two), and these are operant formulations. Operant procedures are not restricted to shaping; they also include discriminative transfer and instructional control.

Baer and Sherman (1964) stress the imitative aspects of vicarious learning, but they also state that the permanence of the learning, as well as the learning process itself, can be enhanced by the systematic use of reinforcement techniques.

Kanfer states that the neurotic behavior seen in some clients in the clinic is sometimes related to patterns the client has observed in parents or other models. A child may use a nonadaptive way of coping with stress, perhaps pleading illness. The "illness' may be tolerated and reinforced and thus used on future occasions. Kanfer cites a further example of this type of learning—the delinquent behaviors often picked up by children committed to institutions, who become further delinquent by imitating their friends. This is the "getting an education in jail" phenomenon, and this phenomenon, says Kanfer, can be socially utilized. since "intensive change can even be brought about by deliberately programmed observational learning in psychotherapy" (Kanfer and Phillips, 1970). Goldstein and his associates (1973) provide a good example in their recent experimentation, in which they significantly increased "independence behavior" in two samples of neurotic outpatients and one sample of psychiatric inpatients through the planful use of modeling techniques. Goldiamond and Thompson (1966) distinguish between "doing what I reinforce" (shaping), "doing what I do" (modeling and imitation), and "doing what I say" (instructional control).

APPLICATIONS OF MODELING

The uses of the "social learning" approach, particularly that of Bandura, are many and varied. Krasner (1971) lists usages of modeling in the one-to-one psychotherapy situation, in the training of retarded children, in work with juvenile delinquents, in enhancing the social behavior of isolates, in eliminating phobias of children (regarding dogs, for example), in eliminating phobias of adults (regarding snakes, for instance), and others.

There has also been extensive work in teaching speech to mute or speech-deficient autistic children (Lovaas *et al.*, 1966). In teaching speech to autistic children, the general procedure is for the therapist to model a sound and then encourage the child to repeat, to imitate, the sound. Successful imitation is usually rewarded immediately and, hopefully, reinforced first by primary reinforcers (generally food—often the famous "M & M" candies of the behavior modifier) and later by social or secondary reinforcers, such as praise (Lovaas, 1966).[3]

Nordquist and Wahler (1973) treated a four-year-old autistic child with no verbal repertoire by first teaching him to imitate simple nonverbal tasks. They then trained the parents to work with the child and found that there was effective transfer to the parent of the therapist's role, and that the parents were able to encourage and train this imitative behavior, particularly imitative verbal behavior.

The literature on language learning and training through imitation and modeling procedures is extensive. Much of it also overlaps the literature on training of retarded children, as language training of retarded children through imitation and modeling is currently a widely accepted procedure.

The Use of Modeling with the Mentally Retarded. Although modeling and imitation procedures have been used with a wide variety of cases, one of the most successful has been the training and education of retarded children. Peterson (1968) showed that a severely retarded child was able to learn a series of responses by imitation, such as putting on her hat, clapping her hands, moving the carriage of a typewriter, and other be-

---

[3] A summary of Lovaas's work with autistic children may be found in Bandura (1969, pp. 152–58), although the interested reader is encouraged to look at the original work of Lovaas and his associates (Bucher and Lovaas, 1970; Lovaas *et al.*, 1973).

haviors. These imitations were maintained without reinforcement "when they were distributed among other reinforced imitations."

Furthermore, mentally retarded children will engage in behaviors if they see *peers* reinforced for these behaviors. The observers themselves did not receive any direct reinforcers, thus "the results indicated a vicarious reinforcing effect" (Kazdin, 1973, pp. 76–77).

O'Brien and Azrin (1972) combined modeling with maintenance procedures and reinforcement to train twelve retarded children in appropriate mealtime behaviors. These behaviors were maintained after termination of the training, and the program was easily run by staff in the institution.

Modeling may also be used to extinguish behavior. In one experiment, young children who had fear of dogs were assigned to one of four treatment conditions. One group, in eight sessions, observed a peer without fear engage progressively in more fear-provoking interactions with a dog. A second group of children observed the same modeled performance, but in a neutral context. A third group of children observed a dog in a positive context, but with the model absent. The fourth group participated in positive activities, but were not exposed to the dog or to the model displays. After treatment they were asked to approach and pet a dog, to release her from the playpen, to play with the dog, and finally to climb into the playpen with the dog. The children who observed the model interact fearlessly with the dog exhibited significantly greater approach behavior (Bandura, Grusec, and Monleve, 1967).

Variations of the above procedures were applied by Bandura to other phobias. He found modeling to be effective regardless of the severity of children's phobic behavior, although children with many fears benefited less from a multiple-modeling treatment than those who had fewer fears (Bandura, 1969).

Wolpe has used modeling to eliminate snake phobias. Modeling combined with desensitization seems to be more effective and to have longer-lasting consequences than desensitization alone (Wolpe, 1969).

The Work of Sheldon Rose. Rose has been particularly inventive in utilizing modeling techniques within a social group work context (Rose, 1973, 1974). Rose believes that groups particularly lend themselves to the use of modeling techniques, for there are many "potential models" within the group, new models may be introduced "without seriously disrupting existing social patterns," and the group is a particularly good framework for the use of role-playing and behavioral rehearsal (Rose, 1973, p. 107).

Rose and his colleagues, working with juvenile delinquents in Detroit, utilized a great degree of "model presentation." One model was the worker or peer who sometimes role-played the client under conditions such as applying for jobs, getting along with the police, and so forth. A second type of model was made up of guests who were very attractive or in high status to group members, such as "athletes, disk jockeys, and popular teachers." Rose chose prestigious models of the same race and background, using, for example, a black ex-convict who was a well-known and respected boxer. When group members spoke about "the attractiveness of various delinquent acts," the worker referred back to the model's comments on the consequences of these acts. This is modeling combined with feedback.

Rose also made use of "behavioral rehearsal." Here the youngsters in the group practiced behaviors that later they had to perform in the real-life situation, such as applying for jobs, conducting themselves in various institutional situations, and so forth.

Behavior rehearsal was a second step that followed model presentation and discussion. A third step was a behavioral assignment to perform outside, and the fourth step was feedback to the actor (Rose *et al.,* 1970, p. 227).

Live Models. In their handbook for counselors and psychologists, Krumboltz and Thorensen (1969, p. 113) advocate the use of modeling techniques for counseling in a variety of problems. They state that the clients may understand their problematic behaviors but not know how to behave in other ways. Thus, observing the behavior of someone else in the situation can suggest new and appropriate social behaviors. They state that models should be "prestigious, competent, knowledgeable, attractive, and powerful," and they agree with Rose that there should be some similarity between the model and the observer, but which characteristics and how similar is still a question for further research (*ibid.*, p. 164). Krumholtz and Thorensen suggest a number of formats, such as videotapes, symbolic models, written manuals, films, audiotapes, and live models. The live model is probably the most available and certainly the most familiar.

Counselors, parents, teachers, peers, and others are live models, but in general their use has been unsystematic. There are obvious advantages to using live models, not the least of which is realism; similarity between model and observer can be enhanced. There are, however, some problems. For some people, the live modeling situation can be overwhelming. Subjects often receive many cues; they are often flooded with information; and it is sometimes not certain which behaviors are being modeled and which are not. Of course, it is often difficult for teachers and counselors, as contrasted with therapists in a time-limited, one-hour session, to serve as models, for they too are human and may display some behaviors, such as losing their tempers, that should not be modeled.

Ritter (1969) described the treatment of a forty-nine-year-old widow with a fear of crossing streets. This phobia prevented her from holding a job. She had received both individual and group therapy for a ten-year period; she had also been hospitalized. Ritter had a model first demonstrate the behavior, then used behavioral prompts to encourage the client to repeat the behavior in a real-life situation, and then faded out the model's prompts as the client observer performed more and more of the behavior independently.

A series of tasks was set up (a number of streets in the client's immediate area were selected and ranked according to difficulty), and the first session was in an area close to the client's home. The counselor walked across the narrow street for about one minute while the client watched. Then the counselor put her arm around the client's waist and walked across with her a number of times until the client began to cross the street by herself. First, the counselor walked beside the client and then followed the client. Then she only partially crossed the street, and then finally she let the client walk by herself.

Gradually, these stages were increased with streets that were wider, then with streets with traffic lights, then secondary targets were chosen of sites that the client wished to visit. Gradually, client and therapist went on tours. The sessions lasted a period of forty-seven days, and the client's street-crossing inhibitions were successfully treated.

Ritter in this case actually used a combination of methods besides modeling, particularly a variation of in vivo desensitization, which is a gradual exposure of the client to the feared state of affairs.

Sarason and Ganzer (1969, p. 179) worked with adolescent delinquent boys who observed modeling situations related to their vocational planning, to their motivations and interests, to their attitudes toward work and education, and to the utility of socially appropriate behavior. The models were four clinical psychology graduate students who were informally acquainted with the boys. Scripts were written on situations such as "how to interact appropriately with the police," "how to behave during a job interview," "how to handle negative peer pressure," "how to make a good impression," and so forth. The four models practiced the roles and, utilizing tape recordings, ran sessions from twenty to thirty minutes in length. They involved models and observers in a great deal of physical activity and replaying of the roles. There was a high emphasis on nonverbal acting because of the limited verbal ability of these lower-class delinquent boys. Feedback was also utilized.

Their preliminary research results (the work is still in progress) suggest that "boys who have received the modeling conditioning become more personally dissatisfied with themselves as their stay at the institution proceeds" (Sarason and Ganzer, 1969, p. 191). Boys in experimental groups showed more changes in attitude and behavior than matched control boys. Follow-up indicated that much of the behaviors imitated and observed remained in the repertoire of the youngsters upon follow-up.

Filmed Models. One disadvantage to live presentation is the difficulty in controlling the model's behavior. Films can present important auditory and visual clues that can be structured precisely in accordance with what is to be modeled. (This is also true of videotapes.) In addition to the flexibility and utility of filmed models, the films can be used over and over again in a variety of settings.

Hosford and Sorenson (1969) worked with fourth-, fifth-, and sixth-grade students who did not participate in class. They made a film which presented a shy elementary-school student talking with a counselor (a doctoral candidate). The film was shown in classes; it was explained that this boy had the same problem and, after talking with the counselor, was able to speak up more. A follow-up questionnaire showed that students had become involved with the film, and that over 90 percent of them (both boys and girls) indicated that they had used some of the ideas. Showing the film twice, a week apart, significantly improved recall of the film.

Nixon (1969) utilized a film to reduce hyperactive behaviors. He made a film showing ten scenes of children in task-oriented situations and five scenes of distractible hyperactive behavior. The hyperactive sequences were interspersed with task-oriented scenes. When an observer identified a youngster engaging in task-oriented behaviors, a small light would be activated, and a reinforcer (an M & M or a penny) would be given to the children viewing the film. Nontask-oriented sequences were shown and just identified by a verbal comment to indicate that the subject had correctly identified the scene. There was no praise or enthusiasm voiced.

There were marked changes in the behaviors of youngsters in the classroom. The study demonstrated the feasibility of using filmed social models in combination with instructions and reinforcement procedures. Nixon emphasizes, however, that the observer often needs to be trained in what to observe. That is, just providing him with a model is not enough; one often has to specify just *which part* of the performance should be imitated.

Audiotapes have been used by Smith (1969) to help students schedule their time better, and by Beach (1969) to help underachievers acquire better study habits. Audiotapes are useful but are, of course, limited by their use of only audio material and the omission of the very important nonverbal aspects of communication.

COMBINATION OF MODELING AND REINFORCEMENT PRINCIPLES

Important inputs into the use of modeling and imitation, combining these techniques with reinforcement principles, have been made by Baer, Bijou, Patterson, Sherman, Peterson, and others. Sherman and Baer (1969) stress the importance of imitation for the development of complex behavior. After observing and imitating behaviors of a model, children will begin to match *new* behaviors of the model even though they are not reinforced for these new behaviors. These new, unreinforced behaviors will be maintained for a long period of time—as long as other imitated behaviors are reinforced.

Sherman and Baer (1969) state that modeling is especially good when there are behavioral deficits. They first establish a general imitative skill and then use modeling to generate new behaviors. They believe that it would "seem possible to develop a wide variety of new behaviors without the necessity of extensive shaping procedures for each new response" (*ibid.,* p. 200).

For example, Baer and Sherman (1964) established three imitative responses—head-nodding, mouthing, and strange verbalizations—by social reinforcement from a puppet. They found that a fourth imitative response (bar-pressing) increased in strength when reinforcement followed the other three imitative responses. This indicated that a generalized similarity of responding between puppet and child could be a reinforcing stimulus in the child's behavior. Baer and Sherman theorize that, given similarity of situations of stimuli, the stimulus of similarity between behaviors may become discriminative for reinforcement. The stimulus that is discriminative for reinforcement becomes secondarily reinforcing in its own right; responses which reduce similarity between behaviors would therefore be strengthened. This is some of the rationale for the child's becoming "imitative."

MODELING AND PSYCHOTHERAPY

The traditional psychotherapeutic interview contains elements of modeling. In a provocative article, Ullmann (1969b) states that he views modeling as prompting, and that prompting and fading, as operant as well as modeling concepts, constitute a large part of the "learning" that takes place in psychotherapy. As Ullmann puts it, "whether called modeling, imitation, vicarious reinforcement, or observational learning, there is a teachable skill that may be used to alter a behavior and that has been shown to be effective in experiments conducted in a laboratory and clinic. The questions then become what behaviors should be modeled, i.e., selection of a behavior, and how modeling may be used, that is, guidelines for applications" (ibid., p. 177).

Ullmann believes that modeling is only part of the therapeutic process, especially in dealing with behaviors and situations outside the therapy room, where the data for examination are the client's verbal reproductions of reality. Here the therapist's reaction to verbal accounts, in addition to having obvious reinforcing or punishing aspects, acts as a cue to the client about what behavior is acceptable, and therefore is an indirect kind of modeling. Ullmann further states that in this sense "the concept of modeling is so large as to subsume nearly all learning and thus becomes less useful" (Ullmann, 1969b, p. 175). He believes that the task is so great that the only real alternative is to teach others to be their own therapists, a view expounded earlier by Goldiamond (1965c) and reflecting the model proposed in this book. This teaching of the skills of self-analysis, teaching the client to be his own therapist, is "by definition . . . a behavior a therapist can and does model" (Ullmann, 1969b, p. 178).

Although the social work literature abounds with articles on role theory, role-modeling, and the like, only one contemporary casework theorist has given modeling (by that name) a prominent role in her system. McBroom, in her approach which she calls a "socialization model," deliberately suggests that the social worker provide a model for clients to emulate, stating that the "social worker's function as model for his client has not received full attention in theory" (McBroom, 1970, p. 339). She calls upon the worker to "demonstrate specific acts of social competence for and with the client" (p. 340) with possible extensions of the technique and approach for the teaching of parenting behaviors and the like.

This chapter completes our presentation of the three main "branches" of behavioral thought, with emphasis on the operant. We have presented an operant self control model in depth and have illustrated its application with a detailed presentation of two cases. In the last chapter we shall explore the ethical and practical questions for social work that were raised throughout the book about the utility of this self control approach for social casework.

seven

THE BEHAVIORAL APPROACH
AND SOCIAL CASEWORK TODAY

This book has presented a model for casework practice that stresses teaching the client the logic and the techniques for analyzing and increasing his control over his own behavior. "Self control," so defined, can provide an enhancement of the client's self-determination, which has long characterized social casework practice. This philosophical orientation provides hope; by focusing on environmental contingencies that can be made explicit rather than on internal forces which are implicit, it offers a greater possibility for change and for the development and evaluation of procedures for change.

This book focuses on the behavior analysis model developed by Goldiamond and interprets the model into social casework. The casework process in the model in this book is based on an interpersonal relationship. The transactions, as in all casework, are a meaningful encounter between human beings. There are, to be sure, caseworkers (and psychotherapists) who lack warmth and empathy and cannot really form meaningful relationships or give support to a client. Their practice would be considered mechanistic regardless of the theoretical system to which they gave allegiance. Yet a widely held misconception of the behavioral approach is that it is cold and mechanistic, that it ignores the whole man and atomizes him into small component parts (Bruck, 1968). That is far from the truth. The operant view does indeed see the "whole man," the individual within the total set of his ecology. It views and assesses the person in the situation but selects specific goals and terminal repertoires—it "partializes," in the words of the psychoanalytically oriented caseworker. The therapeutic intervention of the applied analysis of behavior necessitates an interpersonal relationship, but relationship is a necessary, but not a sufficient, condition or factor in changing human behavior. The emphasis upon change, the burden for the change within this theoretical context, lies upon the *program.* The responsibility for the effectiveness of the program lies ultimately with the *therapist,* although there is mutual planning and, in many ways, mutual responsibility.

This is not to deny that the relationship factors that are ''pressing'' in other therapeutic relationships are not as pressing here. For example, transference and countertransference reactions, although less emphasized and certainly not deliberate targets of intervention, also occur within this orientation. Clients in behavior analysis can fall in love with their therapists. Some therapists like certain clients and do not like other clients. Some therapists are effective with one kind of client and not effective with another kind of client. Some therapists can handle some conditions, can program some sets of contingencies, but cannot program other sets of contingencies. There are therapists who are effective in some situations with some people, but are ineffective in some situations with other people and other problems and conditions.

Liking for the client, respect for the client, and an investment in seeing that the client attains his terminal repertoire are all characteristics of the ''good'' operant social worker, just as they are all typical of the ''good'' psychodynamic therapist or therapist of any persuasion.

In short, relationship factors play a critical part in the operant approach. However, because of the specificity of the techniques, the specificity of the program, and the over-all observable nature of the interaction, there is less emphasis on nonobservable process variables that characterize the more traditional approaches. The respect of therapist and client for one another is enhanced by the nature of the process, which is open, manifest, overt. Moreover, the process lends itself to examination by interested others. In the operant literature, some cases reported are cases of therapeutic failure; there are also cases of success. This is a reflection of the empirical orientation of the approach. There is careful investigation of the specified therapeutic outcomes, both successful and unsuccessful.

There is heavy emphasis upon not repeating unsuccessful interventions and upon the constant devising of newer, more parsimonious and humanitarian methods of intervention.

MISCONCEPTIONS AND POPULAR "MYTHS" ABOUT BEHAVIOR MODIFICATION

There are misconceptions about behavior modification. Some are based on serious ideological differences; some are based on an essential lack of knowledge about the approach; some are based on the rigidities and vested interests of individuals preserving their own therapeutic status quo. Few are based on experimental or data-based conclusions. Bruck (1968), for example, has criticized behavior modification on a number of charges, such as making unsubstantiated claims, considering men only "in parts," ignoring emotions, and being indifferent to "client's random introspective comments." Most important, he has accused behaviorists of being interested "entirely in the manipulation of stimulus-response connections to change maladaptive behavior to more adaptive behavior." Carter and Stuart (1970) replied that Bruck used criteria for operant work that were not applied to other approaches. For example, he decried the absence of large-scale studies which demonstrated the effectiveness of behavioral methods, but did not emphasize the absence of such evaluations of the more traditional methods, even though there has been more time for such tests. Bruck also did not take into account either the differences in research strategies or the numerous research studies that were based on single organism designs.[1] Furthermore, Carter and Stuart appropriately pointed out that Bruck (at that time) not only was outdated but was attacking interventions based primarily upon Pavlovian approaches (in particular, Wolpe and his

[1] For an excellent statement of single organism design, the reader is referred to Sidman (1960). For applications to social work, see Stuart (1971) and Howe (1974).

associates), while ignoring the fact that the majority of the field is oriented along Skinnerian and operant lines. In addition, most behaviorists *do* take into account "internal factors"—the "private events" of Skinner (1953), and the cognitive and emotional aspects of the self control approach, which we are setting forth in this book.

Morrow and Gochros (1970) further summarize the criticisms of the operant approach—that it is "not validated, [is] mechanistic, atomistic, manipulative and unethical, inconsistent with 'the' casework approach, limited in applicability, and not really new." They state that each criticism bears "a grain of truth but involves misconception," and they rebut the "unvalidated" claim by citing the mass of research that has utilized a single-organism approach. They state that the operant approach is not mechanistic but is highly individualized. Certainly the model in this book is not atomistic; it is based primarily upon considerations of the individual in the ecology of his contingency relations rather than as a passive participant in some stimulus-response relationships. They deny that the operant approach is any more manipulative or unethical than other approaches. In fact, because of the public, overt nature of the behavioral contract, the operant approach is a great deal less manipulative or unethical than approaches that proclaim "self-determination" and "freedom of choice" yet shroud their procedures in mystery and are vague, not only in their treatment goals, but also in the criteria used to determine whether or not these goals are met.[2] Furthermore, the approach is not

[2] A recent joint committee report by the American Psychiatric Association (1973), *Behavior Therapy in Psychiatry,* states that "when psychoanalytic therapy was first introduced it raised the spectre of unethical authoritarian control" (p. 23), that all behavior is controlled, and that therapy is no exception. The authors cite the ethical responsibilities all therapists have to examine the nature of the control they exhibit over clients, and they conclude by stating that "behavior therapists tend to face the issue of control more directly than do some psychotherapists . . . [and] to engage in influences that are overt, explicit, and planned, whereas many psychotherapists exercise influences that are covert." They go on to say that part of the fear that behavioral techniques are manipulative stems from the fact that, "when behavioral techniques are effective, they can be quite powerful indeed, and may work with striking rapidity," while in psychoanalysis these "changes may also occur, but . . . generally develop gradually over three, four, five or more years" (*ibid.,* p. 24).

"inconsistent with the casework approach," for there are *many* casework approaches; the idea of "the" casework approach is a myth (see the numerous variations of "the" approach listed in Roberts and Nee, 1970).

The Bruck, Carter and Stuart, and Morrow and Gochros debates are, unfortunately, still current and still widely quoted. Such debates may be inevitable when new treatment approaches and philosophies conflict with older approaches and philosophies. Yet the issues would be better resolved by research and empirical investigation than by debate and rhetoric.

THE SELF CONTROL MODEL, THE BEHAVIORAL CONTRACT, AND SELF-DETERMINATION

The most serious objections raised to behavioral approaches do not apply to the self control model; that is, the idea that the behavior approaches are manipulative, achieve high success by exercising high control, achieve success at a high cost of diminishing individual freedom of action; or, in other words, that behavioral approaches violate the client's essential right to self-determination. On the contrary the overt, contractual nature of the approach can be seen to heighten the client's control over his own life, his self control, and thus heighten his self-determination in a context of dignity and respect.

"Self-determination" is a concept central to the practice of social work and vital to the humanistic basis and orientation of social work. If the operant and psychoanalytic orientations share any commonality, it is in the fact that they are both, in differing senses, deterministic systems. One is a kind of biological determinism; the other is a kind of social determinism. According to Biestek (1957, p. 103) self-determination is

the practical recognition of the right and need of clients to freedom in making their own choices and decisions in the casework process. . . . Caseworkers [must] respect that right . . . activate that potential for self-direction by helping the client to see and use the available resources of the community and his own personality.

The client's right to self-determination, however, is limited by the client's capacity for positive and constructive decision making, by the framework of civil and moral law, and by the function of the agency.

The central element in Biestek's definition of self-determination, and in most definitions of self-determination, is the degree to which people can affect their own lives, their present, and their future. The recent rediscovery of the environment in social work thinking, which parallels and might even be credited to neobehaviorism, has resulted in a severe questioning of the inner aspect of self-determination and has put more emphasis upon the external controls, the contingencies that govern man's behavior.

That self-determination is a concept more honored in the breach than in the observance is attested in Helen Perlman's famous and moving essay in which she discusses the limiting determinants of man's ability to change his contingencies and in which she states that "self-determination is nine-tenths illusion, one-tenth reality" (Perlman, 1965, p. 410). Furthermore, a British writer has stated that "the concept has so many limitations that a serious re-examination of its position in professional social work ideology is essential" (Whittington, 1971, p. 293). Whittington points out the contradiction in the profession's emphasis upon client self-determination and the seeming paradox of the worker's often setting goals, working through resistance, and other "games" (her term) that, in essence, mean that the worker, in an overt or a covert way, is trying to influence the client, is trying to get the client to go along with the worker.

Any relationship involves mutual influence, and a therapeutic relationship is no exception. Therapists *do* influence their clients; even Truax's analysis of Rogerian "nondirective" therapies showed a systematic reinforcing of some kinds of client verbalizations, in a long-term (eighty-five interviews) case carried by Rogers himself (Truax, 1966). Haley has said that a therapist cannot avoid influencing his clients, and the issue here is to make the mutual influencing as manifest, as overt, and as honest as possible (Haley, 1963).

The behavioral contract is a direct statement of the intentions of the worker and the intentions and desires of the client. The contract functions to make overt both the goals and the process by which these goals are to be met. The debate about whether self-determination is an illusion or a reality, the debate about whether man is controlled or is free, the debate about whether man is responsible or merely a passive player in the scene—these are all interesting questions but are, in the final analysis, untestable and almost unanswerable. The practical implications are that, if the worker joins the client in making the *procedures,* the *expectations,* and the *process* as overt as they can, they are, in a direct and forthright way, proclaiming commitment to the dignity of the client and the worker. That is, they will *jointly* analyze and then manipulate the contingencies, affecting rates of behavior, controlling variables, and so on. The client and the worker jointly set the contract, which neither can change unilaterally. As stated above, while control is initially often the therapist's, the purpose of the training in the relationship is to transfer this control to the client as he gains knowledge and competence.

This commitment to self-determination, as operationally defined, presents some difficulties in the conduct of a case in the operant as well as in *all* interpersonal helping situations. As Briar and Miller trace the concept as it is rooted in our Western democratic ideals, they state that, "as an abstract concept, the principle of self-determination has much to offer—as an operating principle it generates considerable difficulty" (Briar and Miller, 1971, p. 40).

In Briar and Miller's discussion of self-determination (one of the most relevant and well-reasoned recent discussions), they state that the concept has been used in three ways: one, as a value, as a goal, and they state (agreeing with Perlman) that "self-determination . . . is not an assumption about human behavior; it is an act of faith" (Briar and Miller, 1971, p. 58). In the second usage, behavior is held to be self-determined. This is the old "free will versus determinism" argument that has already been discussed. The third usage adopts the principle that "casework will be effective to the extent that the client participates actively in treatment" (*ibid.*). This last view of self-determination, as a *principle,* is explicit in the approach presented in this book.

One goal in this approach is to relieve the client of his stress by helping him to expand his repertoire of constructional behaviors. Another goal is to teach him to be his own behavior analyst; in other words, to equip him with a set of analytic tools, a set of carry-over procedures, that he will be able to use in other situations, both problematic and nonproblematic, in his life. In the course of operant casework, the burden of analysis and programming shifts from the worker to the client; thus control is shifted from worker-client sharing to client control. The philosophical orientation, the procedural approach, and, most important, the outcomes suggest that the operant approach—with its emphasis on open procedures, contracts, and the like—does more than merely avow its commitment to self-determination as a guiding principle and therapeutic technique. It can be demonstrated. What seems to be a deterministic approach, allegedly mechanistic, actually heightens client participation, client self-direction, and client control within the framework of a social work intervention. In the operant approach, self-determination is not only a philosophical principle to be verbalized but is also a central therapeutic technique.

SELF-DETERMINATION, CONTROL, AND DETERMINISM

Within both the operant analysis and the Freudian analysis behavior is viewed as controlled. Control, as used by both, is simply the understanding and utilization of the functional relationship between man's behaviors and his environmental contingencies. Given certain contingency relationships, certain end states will occur. This is another way of stating that under certain conditions our behavior is controlled by the contingencies and that our behavior is then determined. By "determinism" we mean that, given these functional relationships, under specified conditions the outcome is predictable. The outcome is "controlled."

Determinism is not the same as fatalism. (Skinner, 1955; see also Shaw, 1972). Determinism means that, given certain environmental contingencies, certain behaviors are bound to follow. In a fatalistic view, there is the belief that "whatever one does, Y consequences will follow" (Shaw, 1972, p. 162). In fatalism, the contingencies cannot be changed. "Man is a helpless piece of driftwood in the tide of Fate" (ibid., p. 162.). The two concepts are often incorrectly equated and used interchangeably. As Skinner points out in *Beyond Freedom and Dignity* (1971), man is continually changing his contingencies. He is changing his environments through many ways, the developments in technology being a prime example. We control our future by changing our environments, our contingencies.

The two psychotherapeutic approaches most considered to be at opposite poles, the psychodynamic and the behaviorist, are both based on a philosophy of determinism. The determinism of Hollis and the psychoanalysts is based on the biological determinism of Freud, as developed through the later additions of the ego psychologists, although tempered somewhat by Hollis's increasing attention to the environment. The behavioral model, and the behavioristic approaches in general, posits a kind of environmental determinism, which some critics say downplays the internal, or motivational, factors. Nevertheless, the main orientations in casework (with the possible exceptions of the approaches based on the humanistic or existential philosophies) are deterministic, and they adhere to a view of control as has been discussed.

To debate control versus no control is pointless. The task is to investigate the nature of that control. This is admittedly a complicated problem, for the overly simplified "free will versus determinism" arguments previously have downplayed the variability of man and have not given extensive enough attention to individual-environment feedback loops. Again, our knowledge base is weaker than we would like; the "science of behavior" that Skinner declares as a desideratum is a possible future goal, not a current reality (Skinner, 1971).

The aim of the model is to teach the client to be his own behavior analyst—a goal of self control rather than therapist control or professional control of the process and, eventually, of the client's life situation. This statement is repeated because one of the main charges against behaviorist interventions is that they seek not to liberate men but to enslave them, to control them. In spite of the evidence, in spite of the safeguards and the overt discussion of the nature of operant interventions, the charges persist. This is indeed a paradox, for, in the operant approach, man is viewed as an entire human being, "operating" on his environment, manipulating his contingencies, and continually developing his competence. The more man increases his competence, the greater his options and the greater his freedom (Goldiamond, 1965b). This increased potential for action is the *real* meaning of freedom and the *real* humanism, a design for action.

INSIGHT IN THE BEHAVIORAL MODEL

A frequent point of disagreement between dynamic and behavioral approaches centers on insight as a necessary condition for behavior change, with the behaviorists seemingly downplaying its importance. The problem here is really that the term "insight" is used by many people in many ways. In an excellent essay, Yelloly (1972) states that the term "insight" may be used in at least four different senses, such as "empathic understanding," a client's understanding of the nature of the problem and its consequences, or a sudden grasp of a solution to a problem, or (and this is the most frequently encountered sense of its use) as an "understanding of unconscious intrapsychic conflicts and their infantile origins" (*ibid.,* pp. 126–27).

Recent researchers, such as Reid (1967) and Mullen (1968), found that only a very small part of the actual casework process is spent in helping the client to develop awareness in the sense of insight as defined above. Davis (1973) confirmed their observations and stressed the fact that clients desired and responded very favorably to direct advice. As Yelloly has stated, the emphasis on insight was a reaction against the early paternalistic, authoritarian "charity giving" that characterized the early stages of social work, a reaction heightened by the influx of psychoanalytic thought and its pervasive influence on social casework. Furthermore, not only is the concept ill-defined, with attendant confusion about its usage, but there is even more disagreement about the process by which insight is supposed to precede behavioral change (Yelloly, 1972, p. 143).

Bandura (1969, p. 94) states that "reports that clients have achieved self-awareness generally mean, in behavioral terms, that clients have learned to label social stimulus events, past and present causal sequences, and their own response in terms of the predilections and language of their therapists."

The process of intervention operates on more than just the conscious level, as witness the use of the word "insight." Moreover, how often in casework and most contemporary psychotherapy is "insight" used in its old sense of "viewing-in" to the unconscious? In reference to the unconscious, the operant practitioner *does* accept the existence of variables which are unknown to the patient, or rejected by him, and which govern his behavior. These variables include past history as well as present environment. This is called by some the "unconscious"; perhaps a more appropriate term is Freud's original German word *Unbewusst,* the "unknown." The existence of something inside the skin is acknowledged, although it is not the skin that is the boundary, but lack of access to the external reinforcing community (Skinner, 1953). Of course, phenomena accounted for by the unconscious exist, for all of us dream, make slips of the tongue, and have *déjà vu* experiences. While behaviorists differ among themselves, most behaviorists prefer to utilize concepts that are a part of a more testable system. Perhaps such explanations of these phenomena must await advances in science, be these advances in brain chemistry, physiology, or psychology.

The self control model is an educational model, educational in that it teaches insight into the behavior-contingency (man in his situation) relations. We agree with Marmor that "what we call insight is essentially the conceptual framework by means of which a therapist establishes, or attempts to establish, a logical relationship between events, feelings, or experiences that seem unrelated in the mind of the patient" (Marmor, 1962, p. 290). When the client learns the rationale of the approach and becomes his own behavior analyst, he is equipped with carry-over procedures.

SUPPORT

A concept similar to insight and one generally not associated with a behavioral model is the concept of *support.* Briar and Miller (1971) state that the supportive function of the diagnostic school is also not a technique but is part of the relationship process. In this sense, since the model we presented here is also used within an interpersonal relationship, support may also be said to be as integral a part of the relationship as the other "soft" process factors that we have discussed, such as warmth, acceptance, and so on.

Another interpretation of the concept of support is that support is selective and that all caseworkers emphasize and reassure the client in some areas and ignore or pay less attention in other areas. In this way the worker supports or assists the client in working out solutions to various difficulties. The process described is obviously related to, if not directly analogous to, the procedure of *differential reinforcement.* Selectively reinforcing some areas, and not others, is part of the general process of *shaping.* In the self control model, this shaping process is done deliberately, consciously. The successive approximations are to some goal, some target behavior, that is either part of the terminal repertoire or a subgoal which is part of the terminal repertoire.

In the process of differential reinforcement and shaping, the self control model enhances support as, through the programming of successive approximations of small steps, the worker maximizes each step (subgoal) as a support—or, in a sense, a building block—for the next step. As the client more and more "successively approximates" the steps toward the end state (the terminal repertoire), he is accumulating strengths that enable him to take the next steps. Thus, in supporting the client, the worker is strengthening the client to take the next steps and is assisting him to build his own strengths, his own supports. This support is reminiscent of what William Schwartz (1961) calls "lending a vision," as the building and expansion of the current relevant repertoire make once-impossible goals seem more and more probable and achievable. Since the therapist takes the ultimate responsibility for the success of the program, and thus minimizes the client's responsibility for possible failure, what could be more supportive?

SYMPTOM SUBSTITUTION

No volume proposing an operant approach to treatment would be complete without a discussion of the phenomenon called "symptom substitution." The debate about symptom substitution has been increasing with the popularization of behavioral treatment. There are exhaustive summaries of these discussions in the literature, two of the most comprehensive being by Cahoon (1968) and Bandura (1969). Basically, the argument is that behavioristic approaches merely attack specific behaviors, considering the behaviors themselves to be the problem. The psychodynamic approach states that the behavior problems are merely the outward manifestation of a more serious underlying problem (analogous to fever merely being the outward manifestation of an underlying infection). If one treats the fever, and ignores the underlying infection or disease process, then there are serious consequences for the patient, for he is still sick. Generalizing to psychological and behavior problems, the argument is that, if one treats only the behavior (for example, stuttering) and ignores the underlying problem (what "caused" the client to stutter), then the stuttering may stop, but the client is not cured, and he will break out into another set of symptoms—perhaps a serious tic or some other kind of conversion symptom (stuttering, in the classical scheme, is a pregenital conversion disorder). At the extreme, the dynamic people state that the phenomenon is inevitable if the underlying problem is not "worked through," and the behaviorists state that the phenomenon does not happen, that there is little evidence other than the clinical (and hardly unbiased) data of the psychodynamic practitioner. The psychodynamic argument is related to the "limited energy" formulations of Freud, who, operating within the framework of nineteenth-century Newtonian physics, was not aware of the concepts of open and morphogenic systems. The interesting point here is that both sides are, in a sense, correct. If one restricts one's attention, as did the early Pavlovian-oriented behaviorists, to eliminating the behavior and not taking into consideration the consequences of that behavior, then the individual might very well substitute other possibly equally problematic behaviors as *new ways to get that consequence.* The psychoanalyst might say that this is a symptom substitution. However, we believe that the phenomenon may be better explained by the simpler, more manifest operant analysis.

Thus whenever possible the client is helped to learn to obtain, in other, nonproblematic ways, the consequences (attention) he has been receiving as a result of his problematic behavior. This is done within the same ethical and humanitarian limitations that exist in the whole of the field of social work. Thus, "treatment" or programming should involve an awareness of the antecedent and consequential conditions.

Another way of stating the symptom substitution argument, in program terms, is to say that achieving the target implied by the presenting problem (the behavior) is not sufficient. More complex and differential programs, or analysis, on different "levels," including covert or nonapparent (mentalistic, internal) levels are often needed. For example, a child's obesity can be seen as a problem in eating (nutrition), but the obesity may also be an operant which produces parental attention.

What is being questioned here is the persistence of the symptom substitution argument at its present simplistic, mechanistic, and reductionistic level, especially in the absence of empirical—as opposed to theoretical—justification. Bandura (1969) states that the phenomenon known as symptom substitution cannot be tested, for lack of agreement on what is "symptom" and what is "underlying cause" (some behaviorists even deny their existence). However, he believes that, even if there were agreement that the phenomenon occurs, its occurrence could be avoided if the program were to include procedures that removed the reinforcing consequences of the behavior and provided either for social and personally acceptable consequences or for more adaptive ways of attaining the consequences.

In short, the notion of symptom substitution has little or no value in its own right, but is worth while if it serves to focus the attention of the therapist on the "whole patient," that is, the A-B-C (antecedent-behavior-consequences) sequence of causation and the awareness of the individual within the total ecology of his social contingencies—the "person-in-the-situation."

The symptom substitution argument necessitates the introduction and brief mention of the controversy over the medical or disease or illness model of behavior problems.

THE MEDICAL AND OTHER MODELS

The newer models of analysis and treatment of problems are known by a number of names. Most of these newer approaches stress the social, the learned aspects of behavior and behavioral problems. They stand in seeming juxtaposition to the more traditional model which has been called the "medical" model or the "disease" model, or to models that postulate the existence of mental illnesses with a direct analogy to physical illness. The newer models have been called "behavioral," "educational," "preventive," "environmental," "learning," "psychological," "social," and so forth.

The polarizations posed by these terms is not so real as it appears at first glance; for while many of these new terms *do* describe approaches which stress the social over the organic or biologically determined, each of these terms has, at some point, been applied to the discipline of medicine—for example, we have social medicine, preventive medicine, and so forth. (Goldiamond, 1974). The point here is that there are a number of medical models, and to speak of "the" medical model is equivalent to choosing one approach of social work and calling it "the" social work model.

There are, however, genuine and valid differences between approaches to problems. Perhaps a clearer statement of the dichotomy is the identification of the classic or disease model with a *pathological* approach and the newer approaches, as exemplified by the self control model, with a *constructional* model. Pathologically based interventions seek to eliminate or alleviate distress and its causes, and constructionally based interventions seek to establish new repertoires. The question might be put to a client: "Do you want fewer troubles or do you want more happiness?"

Behavior therapists and the behavior modifiers belong to both schools, and the conflicting approaches characterize a number of disciplines. The approaches obviously can help influence the way problems are seen. Much of the present conceptualization of problems is based on the pathological models. We often classify mental illness by the deficits and by the patterns of behavior that produce distress for others. But is mental illness disturbed behavior or is it behavior that is disturbing?

A constructional approach would focus on the development and increase of repertoires which expand the current relevant repertoire, to build "healthy" behavior rather than to eliminate "sick" behavior.

The above statements are admittedly overdrawn and oversimplified, to make a point. The issue is complex, and at our current state of knowledge we often do not know which approach should be used, and with whom, and for what problems. Even though most practitioners utilize both approaches in the clinic, in practice (what they *do* as contrasted to what they *say* they do), the current emphasis still remains on the pathological, on what is wrong or what is lacking. The client's often considerable strength and resourcefulness are over-looked. He is often regarded as a bundle of unresolved problems. Indeed, he often considers himself pathological, designates himself as "sick," and this self-labeling becomes accepted by the patient himself; the resultant lowered self-esteem becomes a self-fulfilling prophecy that makes it more difficult for him to begin to work on solving his problem.

Scheff (1966) defines most problematic behavior as "deviant" behavior, and considers it deviant because it has been labeled as such. Furthermore, the labeling of social problems as medical problems has serious consequences for therapy (Taber *et al.*, 1969). According to Taber (and again oversimplifying), the disease model is the application of the belief system of medicine to what are essentially social problems, problems that are socially defined and have social as well as personal consequences. Social and learning models have been proposed which reject the transfer of the medical concepts of pathology to the interpersonal sphere; that is, that "pathology is the belief in an illness process within the organism, persisting over time" (*ibid.,* p. 351). Moreover, the belief system of pathology is not confined to medicine but is also found in sociology ("sick society," "disordered social systems"). The issue is that problems requiring constructional solutions cannot be resolved by eliminating what is wrong, since this supplies no guarantee of replacement by what is right. The task here is to find out what to do rather than what not to do.

Closely related is the issue of causality. A behavior therapist who produces a satisfying outcome by changing repertoires, and who maintains these changes by changing real-life contingencies, is often accused of not having dealt with *the cause* of the problem. Close to two thousand years ago, Aristotle gave four different definitions of cause, and etiology is only one such definition.

In actuality, the issue is one which should be determined by research and technology rather than by argument or philosophic fiat; for what is impractical to change at one time may become practical at another.

THE PROBLEM OF CARRY-OVER OR TRANSFER

The operant approach in general, and the self control model in particular, have implications beyond the office or institutional setting. When asked where there is the most payoff for our work, certain shortcomings become apparent about that medical model when a patient comes for treatment by an expert in a consulting room or office. For many years, the operations of many child guidance clinics were based on the model in which the psychiatrist saw the child to work on "inner," "deep" problems, while the social workers saw the mother (and, infrequently, the father) to work on "guidance," "environmental manipulation," and the like (Hamilton, 1947).

What happened is that the most meaningful work frequently went on with the mother. In operant terms, what went on was the examination of the social contingencies, and the conditions maintaining (reinforcing) problem behavior, and the like. Work with the mother often involved, for example, differential reinforcement and discrimination training. Gradually, the profession came to realize that what took place in the office was almost exclusively verbal behavior. The "good" therapy hour tended to consist of the client's utterances and the therapist's reinforcement of verbal behavior (Auerbach and Luborsky, 1968). There often was little carry-over from the office to the home. Professionals then began to make home visits to see, first, couples, then entire families. Innovative procedures have included seeing families intensively over a short period of time, with good follow-up results (MacGregor *et al.,* 1964). The emphasis on therapy began to shift out of the office and into the natural environment, such as the home and the school. Although most therapeutic work still goes on in the office or the institution, present trends point toward the future development of intervention techniques in which the locus of intervention will be the natural environment, and the focus of the intervention (if this is not a contradiction in terms) will increasingly be on education, not remediation, on prevention rather than on treatment.

THE SELF CONTROL MODEL AND THE CONTEMPORARY CASEWORK SCENE

A close look at both the practice and the theory of the most widely used casework approaches shows that while there are some real and profound differences among the various models, there are also some great similarities. There is often even closer resemblance when one looks at what practitioners actually do. Furthermore, all therapeutic approaches—no matter how bizarre they may appear—help *some* clients under *some* conditions. The contention within the field obscures the reality that no *current* model (including this model) can be expected to be comprehensive enough to accomplish *all* the goals of the multitudinous targets of social work intervention, especially in view of the rapid political and societal changes and the rapid explosions of information and technology. The scope of social work's activities, the enormity and the essential impossibility of fulfilling these requirements, cannot really be appreciated until one has skimmed the table of contents of a recent issue of the *Social Work Encyclopedia.*

Perhaps the greatest irony is that there is much in the operant approach that is compatible with current models. Translations are possible and are desirable for the construction of some future model or models. The operant assessment of terminal repertoire, current repertoire, and programming, the assessment of the individual's strengths and current problems, parallels processes now described as "diagnosis." The old "study-diagnosis-treatment" triad parallels the operant "study-assessment-programming." Operant work does stress observables, and here there is a difference that has already been discussed. Operant work also stresses specificity of outcome expectations. The specification is stated in terms of "goals," a term common to all social work endeavors. This specificity parallels the partialization or limited goals that characterize the problem-solving approach of Perlman, the time-limited approaches of Reid and Shyne, the tasks of the task-centered approach of Reid and Epstein, and, we believe, is more the "tone" of the practice, as contrasted with the theory of Hollis's psychosocial approach.

Even two supposedly polar positions, such as the operant and the psychosocial of Hollis, do not stand in stark juxtaposition, for Hollis, especially in her most recent work (Hollis, 1972), increases her focus on the "social" in the "psychosocial." In an earlier but still recent work, Hollis (1970, pp. 35–36) states that

the psychosocial view is essentially a system theory approach to casework. The major system to which diagnosis and treatment are addressed is the person-in-situation gestalt or configuration. . . . The person to be helped . . . must be seen in the context of his interactions or transactions with the external world; and the segment of the external world with which he is in close interaction must also be understood.

The concept implicit in the above discussion, that of "increasing the social functioning of the client," is ubiquitous in the social work literature.[3] This recent reaffirmation of the individual-environment interchange, the "person-in-the-situation," is a restatement of the reality that in the practice situation the attention given to the environment is far less than that given to intrapsychic factors, that more often than not mere lip service is given to the environment, to the reality problems faced by the client. Grinnell (1973), who summarizes social work's neglect of the environment, attempts to provide a beginning classification of the "environment." He states that, while the "psyche" has been analyzed, fragmentized, intellectualized, and so forth, the environment has been treated as monolithic and constant. Grinnell urges a conceptualization of the environment at least as thorough as that of the intrapsychic. A similar reflection of the growing importance of the role of the environment or, perhaps more accurately, of the growing

---

[3] The concept of social functioning is prominent in the definition of casework formulated some time ago by Perlman (1957, p. 4), which states that "social casework is a process used by certain human welfare agencies to help individuals to cope more effectively with their problems in social functioning." The model in this book is in conceptual agreement with this definition.

awareness of the complexity of the environments (a single individual has many environments), is the approach of Germain, whose argument for an "ecological casework" is another way of stating that the intrapsychic has been overstressed at the expense of the examination of the environment (Germain, 1973).

Bartlett, in documenting the changing use of the concept of social functioning within social work practice, finds greater potential for social casework if social work "can be thought of as more than the behavior of individuals and can be extended to include their active and exchanging relationships with their environment along with the feedback and consequences to both flowing from that active relationship" (Bartlett, 1970, p. 116). Bartlett conceives of social functioning as being essentially theoretically neutral and not dependent upon any specific theory of personality development, deviance, and so forth. What is essential, however, is the relationship of man to his environment, the importance of the interplay of the two. The social functioning of the client is the focus of all social casework approaches, even though each "school" places different emphasis on different aspects of the "man-in-his-environment," of the individual-environment interchange.

FUTURE DEVELOPMENTS IN SOCIAL CASEWORK: FROM TREATMENT TO PREVENTION

Throughout this book the stress is that the goals of social work intervention should be defined functionally, whether they are individual or societal goals. In relation to the behavior itself, the conditions under which behavior occurs should be examined, as well as the consequences of that behavior. The intervention goals are not merely to remediate problems and adjust the individual to the status quo, but to work against the recurrence of problems and to work for the bettering of what we may call the human condition. In the old social work lingo, the planning of strategies is here applied to individuals as well as to societies.

Currently, most social work is not only remedial but is done on a one-to-one basis, or with small groups. There is a marked dichotomy between work with the individual (generally intrapsychically oriented) and work with the larger system groupings, which is generally more theoretically oriented toward the social factors (the contingencies). This dichotomy is artificial. The system and the individual are not separate inhabitants of distinct places on this planet, but are in constant interaction, in constant interplay.

This idea is certainly not new to the profession, although it bears repeating and retelling. As Gordon states, "the central focus of social work traditionally seems to have been on the person-in-his-life-situation—a *simultaneous dual focus* on man and environment" (Gordon, 1969, p. 6).

While the focus of much of social work practice has been on working with the individual to ameliorate the influence of the environment, little attention has been paid to that environment itself, to *how* that environment shapes, governs, and, in the long run, determines the choices people have, determines the parameters of their life styles. That environment, in many ways, determines the destinies of people.

In addition to the dichotomy of theory and practice concerning the "individual-systems" difference, most social work is still being done within the offices of agencies and by professionals. The principles and the applications of behavior analysis have now been sufficiently developed and empirically tested so that they can be increasingly applied to settings outside the office, to the natural settings. This application will help resolve some of the questions that are usually raised about the conditioning processes in individual psychotherapy, specifically the question about whether the effects generalize from the office to the natural setting. The implications of the recent work on modeling, for example, or of the various kinds of contingency management done in the classroom, show how new behaviors, previously learned in the isolation of the agency office and then tried out in the natural setting (the home, the classroom), may also be learned in the natural environment. Where better to learn how to relate to one's child (or parent) than in the home, in one's real-life situation? It is apparent that the less artificial and laboratory-like the setting, the more likely the behavior is to be retained, to be reinforced by the significant others in the natural environment, or, more technically, to come under the control of these natural contingencies.

Further, if one is working with a child in a classroom, or working with a teacher concerning her behavior with one child, then the principles that may be learned will have relevance to other children and to other situations. Once these behaviors become part of a teacher's (or parent's) repertoire, they are more likely to be applied in the future *before* a problem situation arises. In other words, the principles learned have potential not only for palliation and remediation but also for prevention. A logical extension of the work of the caseworker is the expansion of his role from remediation to prevention; in particular, that the principles learned in the operant laboratory and applied in the real-life setting have increasing utility for prevention.

The increasing functioning of the social worker in prevention as well as in remedial work raises ethical questions that must be considered in addition to the questions of efficacy. These are the same questions that social workers deal with when they get into the issues of planning and when they deal with larger social groupings such as community organizations. Does planning necessarily mean the loss of freedom or the imposition of controls? One could review the previous discussions of freedom and control. Perhaps this is a question of the ends and the means; relevant is the comment by Kunkel that we should delay this discussion until we define exactly what we mean by *ends* and exactly what we mean by *means* (Kunkel, 1970).

If certain applications of, for example, principles of reinforcement will help a social worker to help a teacher teach a class of nonreading children how to read, then a future social worker might help her to set up, let us say, a token economy. This application is remedial, but the worker might also utilize the operant principles in nonproblematic areas, for example, to help a teacher with a limited goal (teaching reading to a class of beginners), but a limited goal that has enormous payoff. The situation itself, the teaching of reading, unlike the focus of most current school social work efforts, is not defined or labeled as problematic, as pathological, as "sick." In other words, the social worker of the future might find himself working more and more with situations in which the applications of the principles are used in prevention rather than in remediation, much like the well-baby clinic, the pediatric checkup. The social worker of the future in, let us say, a school might be called, not a social worker, or a social caseworker, but by a title such as "educational consultant." Indeed, this process has already begun when graduates of the program at the University of Chicago have been hired for similar positions previously slated for other disciplines.

The potential for this model goes far beyond the limits of the classroom. More and more principles are discovered that are applicable to matters such as child rearing, for example, more and more groups of parents of nonproblematic children may meet and discuss issues with the idea of prevention or, perhaps more appropriately, constructive education. Such groups already exist, in one form or another. If the highest goal of therapeutic intervention is to teach people to be their own therapists and planners (to teach them the principles of self control as stated here), then it is logical that the extensions be made from the clinic to the natural environment, from the remediative to the preventive, and in a variety of settings from the school to the home, and so on. In fact, some extremely creative applications have already been made in such diverse areas as decreasing the dumping of litter in a national park (Clark, Burgess, and Hendee, 1972), increasing the self-help activities of welfare recipients (Miller and Miller, 1970), enhancing the utility of economics (Kagel and Winkler, 1972), and in many other social applications (Goodall, 1972).

Parents trained to work with their own children can work with other people's children. Indeed, this work is already under way (Tharp and Wetzel, 1969; Kozloff, 1973). The opportunity to increase the potential pool of helping people is enormous. The literature contains descriptions of successful training of parents, housewives, fellow patients, schoolteachers, ghetto residents, cottage parents, college students, and many others, in the principles of applied behavioral analysis. In fact, because of the previous success in training nonprofessionals or paraprofessionals, one of the main and future roles of professionally trained social workers will be that of educator and consultant.

In view of the above, we believe that some future reorganization of the social work curriculum seems inevitable for a number of reasons, such as the paucity of evidence of the effectiveness of current social work intervention efforts and the high cost of social work education. The fastest growing programs are those at the bachelor's degree level. In fact, there is a proliferation of programs on the junior college level, generally going under the rubric of "human services." People are being taught to do the tasks of a social work technician at the junior college level (AA degree or high school plus two years, a total of fourteen years as opposed to the eighteen required for the MSW). There is increasing questioning of the MSW as the appropriate degree in social work precisely because of these cost and time factors (Katz, 1973), and in the future perhaps there will be a hierarchy of social work statuses directly related to the degree of preparation. For example, the tasks might be done by junior college graduates, much of the programming might be carried out by individuals at the bachelor's (BSW) level, with the MSW used for social work programming and innovation, and an increasing limitation of the DSW (Ph.D.) for research, teaching, development, and so forth. Rather than being a utopian proposal, this already appears to be the reality. In northern Illinois alone there are over forty human services programs at the two-year junior college level. Increasing the pool of potential helpers, or training people to be their own therapists, is once again a negation of the idea that the operant or behavioristic approaches are antidemocratic. In fact, by recognizing the reality that people are generally the best authorities on their own lives, this view veers more closely to current existential views than to traditional psychodynamic thinking.

Furthermore, in the recognition that individuals have the capacity to program for themselves and for others there is also a recognition of the reality that varying degrees of training are needed for tasks of varying difficulties, that no one training orientation or plan is adequate. This means that future developments of the model, moving toward prevention rather than remediation, will mean further weakening of the model in which the client sees the "expert," and a heightening of the individual's ability to arrange his contingencies in such a manner as he wishes or, in the words of Maslow, to actualize his own potential. When people are equipped with the skills and the techniques to do so, both their power and their freedom are heightened. This increased knowledge of techniques means a democratization of the treatment relationship problems, with the worker in the role of technician to help the client attain the goals that the client himself has chosen (Katz, 1973).

The move from remediation to prevention has obvious social policy implications, the closest being the focus on prevention rather than remediation. The issue of planning is too broad to go into here, and the reader is aware that there is an enormous literature reflecting the many controversies about the issues of planning, social engineering, freedom, and self-determination. These concepts are complementary rather than mutually exclusive.

The change from remediation to prevention will probably occur in phases. For example, a school social worker might move from helping a teacher with an aggressive child to helping that teacher plan and implement a reading program, by breaking the program into steps, by indicating occasions (and methods) for reinforcing partial successes, and so forth.

The moves toward prevention will necessitate changes in many aspects of the society in general, and in the field of social work in particular. Certainly some of these changes are already in motion, but further system changes will have to be made. Some of these have been anticipated, for example, by Thomas (1970), who commented that there will have to be some agency change to accommodate the new, behaviorally oriented, specific problem-oriented approaches.

The approach presented in this book and elsewhere (Goldiamond, 1974) has applications for macrosocial as well as microsocial problems. In reference to some social problems on the macro scale, in devising methods of problem solution for larger groups of people, the same sets of questions might be asked: What is the terminal repertoire? What should the "end-product" (defined in specifics) be? What is the current relevant repertoire? What is there to work with? What are the assets and liabilities (advantages and problems)? What is the program through which, starting with the current relevant repertoire (the current social situation), one can work forward to the desired end state, the terminal repertoire? What maintaining consequences (payoffs) can be utilized or developed?

This application of the model will certainly mean that there will be new roles for social workers, such as that of social broker and of social advocate (Briar and Miller, 1971). There will have to be new forms of organizational arrangements for the delivery of social services. Most important of all, there will be new areas into which application of the operant principles, now undergoing testing and revision, will serve a preventive rather than remedial function.

In this book we have presented a model that, at its present stage of development, is primarily constructional in nature. Although developed primarily for the traditional worker-client, the one-to-one or one-to-family, modes of intervention, we believe that the model has the potential to move from the office into the natural environment, the home, the school, the community, and so forth. Indeed, the model is currently being applied and revised for use with larger groupings. Future developments will show that such models, based on teaching and enhancing the individual's use of self control procedures, have applicability for community and social planning, and can be applied and utilized by many people in addition to those professionally trained. They can be applied to problems of prevention as well as remediation, and to new areas of concern, thus expanding the potential influence and effectiveness of social caseworkers.

REFERENCES

AGRAS, W. S. 1972. "Covert Conditioning." *Seminars in Psychiatry* 4:157–64.

AMERICAN PSYCHIATRIC ASSOCIATION TASK FORCE ON BEHAVIOR THERAPY. 1973. *Behavior Therapy in Psychiatry.* Washington, D.C.: American Psychiatric Association.

AUERBACH, A. H., and L. Luborsky. 1968. "Accuracy of Judgments of Psychotherapy and the Nature of the 'Good Hour.'" In *Research in Psychotherapy: Proceedings of the Third Conference,* ed. J. M. Schlien, pp. 155–68. Washington, D.C.: American Psychological Association.

AVIRAM, U. and S. P. Segal. 1973. "Exclusion of the Mentally Ill: Reflections on an Old Problem in a New Context." *Archives of General Psychiatry* 29:126–31.

AYLLON, T., and N. H. Azrin. 1965. "The Measurement and Reinforcement of Behavior of Psychotics." *Journal of Experimental Analysis of Behavior* 3:357–83.

—— 1968. *The Token Economy: a Motivational System for Therapy and Rehabilitation.* New York: Appleton-Century-Crofts.

AZRIN, N. H., and R. M. Foxx. 1974. *Toilet Training in Less than a Day.* New York: Simon and Schuster.

AZRIN, N. H., and W. C. Holz. 1966. "Punishment." In *Operant Behavior: Areas of Research and Application,* ed. W. K. Honig, pp. 380–447. New York: Appleton-Century-Crofts.

BAER, D. M. 1970. "A Case for the Selective Reinforcement of Punishment." In *Behavior Modification in Clinical Psychology,* eds. C. Neuringer and J. L. Michael, pp. 243–49. New York: Appleton-Century-Crofts.

BAER, D. M., and J. A. Sherman. 1964. "Reinforcement Control of Generalized Imitation in Young People." *Journal of Experimental Child Psychiatry* 1:37–49.

BANDURA, A. 1965. "Behavioral Modifications through Modeling Procedures." in *Research in Behavior Modification,* eds. L. Krasner and L. P. Ullmann, pp. 310–40. New York: Holt, Rinehart and Winston.

—— 1969. *Principles of Behavior Modification.* New York: Holt, Rinehart and Winston.

BANDURA, A., ed. 1971. *Psychological Modeling: Conflicting Theories.* Chicago: Aldine-Atherton.

BANDURA, A., J. E. Grusec, and F. L. Monleve. 1967. "Some Social Determinants of Self-monitoring Reinforcement Systems." *Journal of Personality and Social Psychology* 5:449–55.

BANDURA, A., and R. H. Walters. 1963. *Social Learning and Personality Development.* New York: Holt, Rinehart and Winston.

BARTLETT, H. M. 1970. *The Common Base of Social Work Practice.* New York: National Association of Social Workers.

BEACH, A. L. 1969. "Overcoming Underachievement." In *Behavioral Counseling: Cases and Techniques,* eds. J. D. Krumboltz and C. E. Thoresen, pp. 241–48. New York: Holt, Rinehart and Winston.

BENEKE, W. M., and M. B. Harris. 1972. "Teaching Self-Control of Study Behaviour." *Behaviour Research and Therapy* 10:35–41.

BERKOWITZ, B. P., and A. M. Graziano. 1972. "Training Parents as Behaviour Therapists: a Review." *Behaviour Research and Therapy* 10:297–317.

BIESTEK, F. P. 1957. *The Casework Relationship.* Chicago: Loyola University Press.

BIJOU, S., and D. Baer. 1961. *Child Development, I: A Systematic and Empirical Theory.* New York: Appleton-Century-Crofts.

BOREN, J. J., and A. D. Colman. 1970. "Some Experiments on Reinforcement Principles within a Psychiatric Ward for Delinquent Soldiers." *Journal of Applied Behavior Analysis* 3:29–37.

BRIAR, S., and H. Miller. 1971. *Problems and Issues in Social Casework.* New York: Columbia University Press.

BRIERTON, D. 1969. "The Valley View Project: an Introduction to Existential Method in Corrections." Training Manual No. 3. Mimeographed. St. Charles, Ill.: Valley View Training School.

BRUCK, M. 1968. "Behavior Modification Theory and Practice: a Critical Review." *Social Work* 13:43–55.

BUCHER, B., and O. I. Lovaas. 1968. "Use of Aversive Stimulation in Behavior Modification." In *Miami Symposium on the Prediction of Behavior, 1967: Aversive Stimulation,* ed. M. R. Jones, pp. 77–145. Coral Gables, Fla.: University of Miami.

—— 1970. "Operant Procedures in Behavior Modification with Children." In *Learning Approaches to Therapeutic Behavior Change,* ed. D. J. Levis, pp. 36–64. Chicago: Aldine.

BURCHARD, J. D. 1967. "Systematic Socialization: a Programmed Environment for the Habilitation of Antisocial Retardates." *Psychological Record* 17:441–76.

CAHOON, D. D. 1968. "Symptom Substitution and the Behavior Therapies: a Reappraisal." *Psychological Bulletin* 69:149–56.

CANTRELL, R. P., M. L. Cantrell, C. M. Huddleston, and R. L. Woolridge. 1969. "Contingency Contracting with School Problems." *Journal of Applied Behavior Analysis* 2:215–20.

CARTER, R. D., and R. B. Stuart. 1970. "Behavior Modification Theory and Practice: a Reply." *Social Work* 15:37–50 (Jan.)

CAUTELA, J. R. 1967. "Covert Sensitization." *Psychological Record* 16:459–68.

—— 1969. "Behavior Therapy and Self-Control." In *Behavior Therapy: Appraisal and Status,* ed. C. M. Franks, pp. 323–40. New York: McGraw-Hill.

CHAIKLIN, H. 1973. "Discussion and Comment." In *Current Ethical Issues in Mental Health,* eds. M. F. Shore and S. E. Golann, pp. 39–43. Rockville, Md.: National Institute of Mental Health.

CHRISTOPHERSON, E. R., C. M. Arnold, D. W. Hill, and H. R. Quilitich. 1972. "The Home Point System: Token Reinforcement Procedures for Application by Parents of Children with Behavior Problems." *Journal of Applied Behavior Analysis* 5:485–97.

CLARK, R. N., R. L. Burgess, and J. C. Hendee. 1972. "The Development of Anti-Litter Behavior in a Forest Campground." *Journal of Applied Behavior Analysis* 5:1–5.

CLEMENTS, C. B., and J. M. McKee. 1968. "Programmed Instruction for Institutionalized Offenders: Contingency Management and Performance Contracts." *Psychological Reports* 22:957–64.

COHEN, H. L., and J. Filipczak. 1971. *A New Learning Environment.* San Francisco: Jossey-Bass.

CORTE, H. E., M. M. Wolf, and B. J. Locke. 1971. "A Comparison of Procedures for Eliminating Self-injurious Behavior of Retarded Adolescents." *Journal of Applied Behavior Analysis* 4:201–13.

DAVIS, I. P. 1973. "Caseworker's Use of Influence in Counseling Parents." Unpublished doctoral dissertation, School of Social Service Administration, University of Chicago.

DOLLARD, J., and N. E. Miller. 1950. *Personality and Psychotherapy: an Analysis in Terms of Learning, Thinking, and Culture.* New York: McGraw-Hill.

FAIRWEATHER, G. W., D. H. Sanders, H. Maynard, and D. L. Cressler. 1969. *Community Life for the Mentally Ill.* Chicago: Aldine.

FELDMAN, M. P. 1966. "Aversion Therapy for Sexual Deviations: a Critical Review." *Psychological Bulletin* 65:65–79.

FELDMAN, M. P., and M. J. MacCullough. 1972. *Homosexual Behavior: Therapy and Assessment.* New York: Pergamon Press.

FENSTERHEIM, H. 1972. "Assertive Methods and Marital Problems." In *Advances in Behavior Therapy: Proceedings of the Fourth Conference of the Association for the Advancement of Behavior Therapy,* eds. R. D. Rubin *et al.,* pp. 13–18. New York: Academic Press.

FERSTER, C. B., and M. K. DeMyer. 1962. "A Method for the Experimental Analysis of the Behavior of Autistic Children." *American Journal of Orthopsychiatry* 32:89–98.

FERSTER, C. B., and M. C. Perrott. 1968. *Behavior Principles.* New York: New Century.

FERSTER, C. B., and B. F. Skinner. 1957. *Schedules of Reinforcement.* New York: Appleton-Century-Crofts.

FESTINGER, L. 1964. "Behavioral Support for Opinion Change." *Public Opinion Quarterly* 28:404–17.

FIXSEN, D. L., E. L. Phillips, and M. M. Wolf. 1973. "Achievement Place: Experiments in Self-Government with Pre-delinquents." *Journal of Applied Behavior Analysis* 6:31–47.

FLESCHER, J. 1970. *Childhood and Destiny: the Triadic Principle in Genetic Education.* New York: International Universities Press.

FRANKS, C. M., ed. 1969. *Behavior Therapy: Appraisal and Status.* New York: McGraw-Hill.

FULLER, P. R. 1949. "Operant Conditioning of a Vegetative Human Organism." *American Journal of Psychology* 62:587–90.

GADBOIS, C. B. 1972. "Contract Programming." Unpublished manuscript, St. Cloud State Prison, Minnesota.

GAMBRILL, E. D., and C. A. Richey. 1973. "Assertive Inventory." Unpublished manuscript, School of Social Welfare, University of California at Berkeley.

GARFIELD, S. L., and M. Wolpin. 1963. "Expectations Regarding Psychotherapy." *Journal of Nervous and Mental Disease* 137:353–62.

GERMAIN, C. B. 1973. "An Ecological Perspective in Casework Practice." *Social Casework* 54:323–30.

GOLDIAMOND, I. 1962. "Perception." In *Experimental Foundations of Clinical Psychology,* ed. A. J. Bachrach, pp. 280–342. New York: Basic Books.

—— 1965a. "Stuttering and Fluency as Manipulable Operant Response Classes." In *Research in Behavior Modification,* eds. L. Krasner and L. P. Ullmann, pp. 106–56. New York: Holt, Rinehart and Winston.

—— 1965b. "Justified and Unjustified Alarm over Behavioral Control." In *Changing Concepts in the Behavior Disorders,* ed. O. Milton, pp. 237–61. New York: Lippincott.

—— 1965c. "Self-Control Procedures in Personal Behavior Problems." *Psychological Reports,* Monograph Supplement 3-V17, 17:851–68.

—— 1966. "Perception, Language and Conceptualization Rules." In *Problem Solving,* ed. B. Kleinmuntz, pp. 183–224. New York: Wiley.

—— 1969. "Applications of Operant Conditioning." In *Current Trends in Army Medical Psychology,* ed. C. A. Thomas, pp. 198–231. Denver: Fitzsimmons General Hospital.

—— 1970. "A New Social Imperative: Positive Approaches to Behavior Control." In *Confrontation: Psychology and the Problems of Today,* ed. M. Wertheimer, pp. 300–306. Glenview, Ill.: Scott, Foresman.

—— 1974. "Toward a Constructional Approach to Social Problems." *Behaviorism* 2:1–84.

—— 1975. "Coping and Adaptive Behaviors of the Disabled." In *Socialization in the Disability Process,* eds. G. L. Albrecht. Pittsburgh: University of Pittsburgh.

—— *A Contingency Analysis of Emotions.* Forthcoming.

GOLDIAMOND, I., and J. E. Dyrud. 1967a. "Reading as Operant Behavior." In *The Disabled Reader: Education of the Dyslexic,* eds. J. Money and G. Schiffman, pp. 93–115. Baltimore: Johns Hopkins University Press.

—— 1967b. "Some Applications and Implications of Behavioral Analysis for Psychotherapy." In *Research in Psychotherapy,* Vol. III, ed. J. Schlien, pp. 54–89. Washington, D.C.: American Psychological Association.

GOLDIAMOND, I., J. E. Dyrud, and M. D. Miller. 1965. "Practice as Research in Professional Psychology." *Canadian Psychologist* 6a:110–28.

GOLDIAMOND, I., and D. Thompson. 1966. "The Functional Analysis of Behavior." Unpublished manuscript.

GOLDFRIED, M. R., and M. Merbaum, eds. 1973. *Behavior Change through Self-Control.* New York: Holt, Rinehart and Winston.

GOLDSTEIN, A. P. 1973. *Structured Learning Therapy.* New York: Academic Press.

GOLDSTEIN, A. P., J. Martens, J. Hubben, H. A. Van Belle, W. Schaaf, H. Wiersma, and A. Goedhart. 1973. "The Use of Modeling to Increase Independent Behaviour." *Behaviour Research and Therapy* 11:31–42.

GOODALL, K. 1972. "Shapers at Work." *Psychology Today* 6:53–63, 132–38.

GORDON, W. 1969. "Basic Constructs for an Integrative and Generative Conception of Social Work." In *The General Systems Approach: Contributions toward an Holistic Conception of Social Work,* ed. G. Hearn, p. 6. New York: Council on Social Work Education.

GRAZIANO, A. M., ed. 1971. *Behavior Therapy with Children.* Chicago: Aldine-Atherton.

GRINNELL, R. M. 1973. "Environmental Modification: Casework's Concern or Casework's Neglect?" *Social Service Review* 47:208–20.

GUERNEY, B. G., ed. 1969. *Psychotherapeutic Agents: New Roles for Nonprofessionals, Parents and Teachers.* New York: Holt, Rinehart and Winston.

HALEY, J. 1963. *Strategies of Psychotherapy.* New York: Grune and Stratton.

HAMILTON, G. 1947. *Psychotherapy in Child Guidance.* New York: Columbia University Press.

—— 1951. *Theory and Practice of Social Case Work.* 2d ed. rev. New York: Columbia University Press.

HERSEN, M. 1971. "Resistance to Direction in Behavior Therapy: Some Comment." *Journal of Genetic Psychology* 118:121–27.

HOLDEN, C. 1972. "Nader on Mental Health Centers: a Movement That Got Bogged Down." *Science* 177:413–15.

HOLLAND, J. G., and B. F. Skinner. 1961. *The Analysis of Behavior.* New York: McGraw-Hill.

HOLLIS, F. 1970. "The Psychosocial Approach and the Practice of Casework." In *Theories of Social Casework,* eds. R. W. Roberts and R. H. Nee, pp. 33–76. Chicago: University of Chicago Press, 1970.

—— 1972. *Casework: a Psychosocial Therapy.* 2d ed. rev. New York: Random House.

HOMME, L. E. 1965. "Perspectives in Psychology—XXIV: Control of Coverants, the Operants of the Mind." *Psychological Record* 15:501–11.

—— 1969. *How to Use Contingency Contracting in the Classroom.* Champaign, Ill.: Research Press.

HOSFORD, R. E., and D. L. Sorenson. 1969. "Participating in Classroom Discussions." In *Behavior Counseling: Cases and Techniques,* eds. J. D. Krumboltz and C. E. Thoresen, pp. 202–7. New York: Holt, Rinehart and Winston.

HOWE, M. W. 1974. "Casework Self-Evaluation: a Single-Subject Approach." *Social Service Review* 48:1–23.

HUNT, G. M., and N. H. Azrin. 1973. "A Community-Reinforcement Approach to Alcoholism." *Behaviour Research and Therapy* 11:91–104.

JACOBSON, E. 1938. *Progressive Relaxation.* Chicago: University of Chicago Press.

JEHU, D. 1967. *Learning Theory and Social Work.* London: Routledge and Kegan Paul.

JEHU, D., P. Hardiker, M. Yelloly, and M. Shaw. 1972. *Behaviour Modification in Social Work.* London: Wiley-Interscience.

KAGEL, J. H., and R. C. Winkler. 1972. "Behavioral Economics: Areas of Cooperative Research between Economics and Applied Behavioral Analysis." *Journal of Applied Behavior Analysis* 5:335–42.

KANFER, F. H., and J. S. Phillips. 1970. *Learning Foundations of Behavior Therapy.* New York: Wiley.

KASSORLA, I. C. 1969. "A New Approach to Mental Illness." *Science Journal* 5:69–74.

KATZ, D. 1973. "Behavioral Technology: Issues and Implications for Social Work Practice and Education." Paper presented at the Annual Program Meeting, Council on Social Work Education, San Francisco.

KAZDIN, A. E. 1973. "The Effect of Vicarious Reinforcement on Attentive Behavior in the Classroom." *Journal of Applied Behavior Analysis* 6:71–78.

KAZDIN, A. E., and R. R. Bootzin. 1972. "The Token Economy: an Evaluative Review." *Journal of Applied Behavior Analysis* 5:343–72.

KELLER, F. S., and W. N. Schoenfeld. 1950. *Principles of Psychology.* New York: Appleton-Century-Crofts.

KOZLOFF, M. A. 1973. *Reaching the Autistic Child: a Parent Training Program.* Champaign, Ill.: Research Press.

KRASNER, L. 1962. "The Therapist as a Social Reinforcement Machine." In *Research in Psychotherapy,* Vol. II, eds. H. H. Strupp and L. Luborsky, pp. 61–94. Washington, D.C.: American Psychological Association.

—— 1971. "Behavior Therapy." *Annual Review of Psychology* 22:483–532.

KRUMBOLTZ, J. D., and C. E. Thoresen, eds. 1969. *Behavioral Counseling: Cases and Techniques.* New York: Holt, Rinehart and Winston.

KUNKEL, J. H. 1970. *Social and Economic Growth: a Behavioral Perspective of Social Change.* New York: Oxford University Press.

LANG, P. 1969. "The Mechanics of Desensitization and the Laboratory Study of Human Fear." In *Behavior Therapy: Appraisal and Status,* ed. C. M. Franks, pp. 160–91. New York: McGraw-Hill.

LENT, J. R., J. LeBlanc, and J. E. Spradlin. 1970. "Designing a Rehabilitative Culture for Moderately Retarded, Adolescent Girls." In *Control of Human Behavior,* Vol. II: *From Cure to Prevention,* eds. R. Ulrich *et al.,* pp. 121–35. Glenview, Ill.: Scott, Foresman.

LEVIS, D. J. 1974. "Implosive Therapy: a Critical Analysis of Morganstern's Review." *Psychological Bulletin* 81:155–58.

LIBERMAN, R. P. 1970. "Behavioral Approaches to Family and Couple Therapy." *American Journal of Orthopsychiatry* 40:106–18.

LOVAAS, O. I. 1966. "A Program for the Establishment of Speech in Psychotic Children." In *Childhood Autism,* ed. J. K. Wing, pp. 115–44. Oxford: Pergamon Press.

LOVAAS, O. I., J. P. Berberich, B. F. Perloff, and B. Schaeffer. 1966. "Acquisition of Imitative Speech by Schizophrenic Children." *Science* 151:705–7.

LOVAAS, O. I., R. Koegel, J. Q. Simmons, and J. S. Long. 1973. "Some Generalization and Follow-up Measures on Autistic Children in Behavior Therapy." *Journal of Applied Behavior Analysis* 6:131–66.

LOVIBOND, S. H. 1964. *Conditioning and Enuresis.* New York: Pergamon Press.

McBROOM, E. 1970. "Socialization and Social Casework." In *Theories of Social Casework,* eds. R. W. Roberts and R. H. Nee, pp. 313–52. Chicago: University of Chicago Press.

MacGREGOR, R., A. M. Ritchie, A. Serrano, and F. Schuster. 1964. *Multiple Impact Therapy with Families.* New York: McGraw-Hill.

MARKS, I. 1972. "Perspective on Flooding." *Seminars in Psychiatry* 4:129–38.

MARMOR, J. 1962. "Psychoanalytic Therapy as an Educational Process: Common Denominators in the Therapeutic Approaches of Different Psychoanalytic 'Schools.' " In *Science and Psychoanalysis,* ed. J. Masserman, 5:286–99. New York: Grune and Stratton.

MASTERS, W. H., and V. E. Johnson. 1966. *Human Sexual Response.* Boston: Little, Brown.

—— 1970. *Human Sexual Inadequacy.* Boston: Little, Brown.

MILBY, J. B., Jr. 1970. "Modification of Extreme Social Isolation by Contingent Social Reinforcement." *Journal of Applied Behavior Analysis* 3:149–52.

MILLER, L. K., and O. L. Miller. 1970. "Reinforcing Self-Help Group Activities of Welfare Recipients." *Journal of Applied Behavior Analysis* 3:57–64.

MILLER, L. K., and R. Schneider. 1970. "The Use of a Token System in Project Head Start." *Journal of Applied Behavior Analysis* 3:213–20.

MORGANSTERN, K. P. 1973. "Implosive Therapy and Flooding Procedures: a Critical Review." *Psychological Bulletin* 79:318–34.

MORROW, W. R., and H. L. Gochros. 1970. "Misconceptions Regarding Behavior Modification." *Social Service Review* 44:293–307.

MOWRER, O. H. 1938. "Apparatus for the Study and Treatment of Enuresis." *American Journal of Psychology* 51:163–66.

MULLEN, E. J. 1968. "Casework Treatment Procedures as a Function of Client Diagnostic Variables." Unpublished doctoral dissertation, Columbia University School of Social Work, 1968.

NEURINGER, C., and J. L. Michael, eds. 1970. *Behavior Modification in Clinical Psychology.* New York: Appleton-Century-Crofts.

NIXON, S. B. 1969. "Increasing Task-oriented Behavior." In *Behavioral Counseling: Cases and Techniques,* eds. J. D. Krumboltz and C. E. Thoresen, pp. 207–10. New York: Holt, Rinehart and Winston.

NORDQUIST, V. M., and R. G. Wahler. 1973. "Naturalistic Treatment of an Autistic Child." *Journal of Applied Behavior Analysis* 6:79–87.

O'BRIEN, F. O., and N. H. Azrin. 1972. "Developing Proper Mealtime Behaviors of the Institutionalized Retarded." *Journal of Applied Behavior Analysis* 5:389–99.

O'LEARY, K. D., and W. C. Becker. 1967. "Behavior Modification of an Adjustment Class: a Token Reinforcement Program." *Exceptional Children* 9:637–42.

PARKE, R. D., ed. 1969. *Readings in Social Development.* New York: Holt, Rinehart and Winston.

PATTERSON, G. R. 1969. "Behavioral Techniques Based upon Social Learning: an Additional Base for Developing Behavior Modification Technologies." In *Behavior Therapy: Appraisal and Status,* ed. C. M. Franks, pp. 341–74. New York: McGraw-Hill.

PATTERSON, R. L., and J. R. Teigen. 1973. "Conditioning and Post-Hospital Generalization of Non-delusional Responses in a Chronic Psychotic Patient." *Journal of Applied Behavior Analysis* 6:65–70.

PAUL, G. 1969. "Outcome of Systematic Desensitization, I: Background Procedures and Uncontrolled Reports of Individual Treatment; II: Controlled Investigations of Individual Treatment, Technique Variations, and Current Status." In *Behavior Therapy: Appraisal and Status,* ed. C. M. Franks, pp. 63–104, 105–59. New York: McGraw-Hill.

PENDERGRASS, V. E. 1972. "Time-out from Positive Reinforcement Following Persistent, High-Rate Behavior in Retardates." *Journal of Applied Behavior Analysis* 5:85–91.

PERLMAN, H. H. 1957. *Social Casework: a Problem-solving Approach.* Chicago: University of Chicago Press.

—— 1965. "Self-Determination: Reality or Illusion?" *Social Service Review* 39:410–21.

PETERSON, R. F. 1968. "Some Experiments on the Organization of a Class of Imitative Behaviors." *Journal of Applied Behavior Analysis* 1:225–35.

PHILLIPS. E. L. 1968. "Achievement Place: Token Reinforcement Procedures in a Home-Style Rehabilitation Setting for 'Pre-delinquent' Boys." *Journal of Applied Behavior Analysis* 1:213–23.

PHILLIPS, E. L., E. A. Phillips, D. L. Fixsen, and M. M. Wolf. 1971. "Achievement Place: Modification of the Behaviors of Pre-delinquent Boys within a Token Economy." *Journal of Applied Behavior Analysis* 4:45–59.

PREMACK, D. 1965. "Reinforcement Theory." In *Nebraska Symposium on Motivation: 1965,* ed. D. Levine, pp. 123–80. Lincoln: University of Nebraska Press.

RACHMAN, S., and J. Teasdale. 1969. *Aversion Therapy and Behavior Disorders: an Analysis.* Coral Gables, Fla.: University of Miami Press.

RATHUS, S. A. 1972. "An Experimental Investigation of Assertive Training in a Group Setting." *Journal of Behavior Therapy and Experimental Psychiatry* 3:81–86.

—— 1973. "Instigation of Assertive Behavior through Videotape—Mediated Assertive Models and Directed Practice." *Behaviour Research and Therapy* 11:57–65.

REID, W. J. 1967. "Characteristics of Casework Intervention." *Welfare in Review* 5:11–19.

—— 1970. "Implications of Research for the Goals of Casework." *Smith College Studies in Social Work* 40:140–54.

REID, W. J., and L. Epstein. 1972. *Task-centered Casework.* New York: Columbia University Press.

REISINGER, J. J. 1972. "The Treatment of 'Anxiety-Depression' via Positive Reinforcement and Response Cost." *Journal of Applied Behavior Analysis* 5:125–30.

REST, E. R. 1973. "Rehabilitating Offenders through Behavioral Change." In *Social Work Practice and Social Justice,* eds. B. Ross and C. Shireman, pp. 74–84. Washington, D.C.: National Association of Social Workers.

RICHEY, C. A. 1973. "Female Assertiveness through Self-Reward." Unpublished paper, School of Social Welfare, University of California at Berkeley.

RISLEY, T., and M. Wolf. 1967. "Establishing Functional Speech in Echolalic Children." *Behaviour Research and Therapy* 5:73–88.

RITTER, B. 1969. "Eliminating Excessive Fears of the Environment through Contact Desensitization." In *Behavioral Counseling: Cases and Techniques,* eds. J. D. Krumboltz and C. E. Thoresen, pp. 168–78. New York: Holt, Rinehart and Winston.

ROBERTS, R. W., and R. H. Nee, eds. 1970. *Theories of Social Casework.* Chicago: University of Chicago Press.

ROSE, S. D. 1969. "A Behavioral Approach to the Group Treatment of Parents." *Social Work* 14:21–29 (July).

—— 1973. *Treating Children in Groups.* San Francisco: Jossey-Bass.

—— 1974. "Group Training of Parents as Behavior Modifiers." *Social Work* 19:156–62 (March).

ROSE, S. D., M. Sundel, J. Delange, L. Corwin and A. Palumbo. 1970. "The Hartwig Project: a Behavioral Approach to the Treatment of Juvenile Offenders." In *Control of Human Behavior, II: From Cure to Prevention,* eds. R. Ulrich, T. Stachnik, and J. Mabry, pp. 220–30. Glenview, Ill.: Scott, Foresman.

SARASON, I. G., and V. J. Ganzer. 1969. "Developing Appropriate Social Behaviors of Juvenile Delinquents." In *Behavioral Counseling: Cases and Techniques,* eds. J. D. Krumboltz and C. E. Thoresen, pp. 178–93. New York: Holt, Rinehart and Winston.

SCHEFF, T. J. 1966. *Being Mentally Ill.* Chicago: Aldine.

SCHWARTZ, A. 1970. "PPBS and Evaluation Research: Problems and Promises." In *Planning, Programming, Budgeting Systems and Social Welfare,* ed. E. E. Schwartz, pp. 35–41. Chicago: School of Social Service Administration, University of Chicago.

SCHWARTZ, W. 1961. "The Social Worker in the Group." In *The Social Welfare Forum, 1961,* pp. 146–71. New York: Columbia University Press.

SHAW, M. 1972. "Ethical Implications of a Behavioural Approach." In *Behaviour Modification in Social Work,* eds. D. Jehu et al., pp. 161–72. London: Wiley-Interscience.

SHERMAN, J. A., and D. M. Baer. 1969. "Appraisal of Operant Therapy Techniques with Children and Adults." In *Behavior Therapy: Appraisal and Status,* ed. C. M. Franks, pp. 192–219. New York: McGraw-Hill.

SIDMAN, M. 1960. *Tactics of Scientific Research: Evaluating Experimental Data in Psychology.* New York: Basic Books.

SKINNER, B. F. 1948. *Walden Two.* New York: Macmillan.

—— 1953. *Science and Human Behavior.* New York: Macmillan.

—— 1955. "The Control of Human Behavior." In *Transactions of the New York Academy of Sciences,* Series II, 17, No. 7, 547–51.

—— 1957. *Verbal Behavior.* New York: Appleton-Century-Crofts.

—— 1971. *Beyond Freedom and Dignity.* New York: Knopf.

—— 1974. *About Behaviorism.* New York: Knopf.

SMITH, J. E. 1969. "Encouraging Constructive Use of Time." In *Behavioral Counseling: Cases and Techniques,* eds. J. D. Krumboltz and C. E. Thoresen, pp. 234–41. New York: Holt, Rinehart and Winston.

SMITH, J. M., and D. E. P. Smith. 1966. *Child Management: a Program for Parents.* Ann Arbor, Mich.: Ann Arbor Publishers.

STAMPFL, T. G., and D. J. Levis. 1967. "Essentials of Implosive Therapy: a

Learning-Theory-Based Psychodynamic Behavioral Therapy." *Journal of Abnormal Psychology* 72:496–503.

—— 1968. "Implosive Therapy: a Behavioural Therapy." *Behaviour Research and Therapy* 6:31–36.

STUART, R. B. 1967. "Behavioural Control of Overeating." *Behaviour Research and Therapy* 5:357–65.

—— 1971. "A Three-dimensional Program for the Treatment of Obesity." *Behaviour Research and Therapy* 9:177–86.

—— 1971. "Research in Social Work: Social Casework and Social Group Work." In *Encyclopedia of Social Work,* II, 1106–20. New York: National Association of Social Workers.

SULZER, B., and G. R. Mayer. 1972. *Behavior Modification Procedures for School Personnel.* Hinsdale, Ill.: Dryden Press.

SULZER, E. 1962. "Reinforcement and the Therapeutic Contract." *Journal of Counseling Psychology* 9:271–76.

TABER, M., H. C. Quay, H. Mark, and V. Nealey. 1969. "Disease Ideology and Mental Health Research." *Social Problems* 16:349–57.

THARP, R. G., and R. J. Wetzel. 1969. *Behavior Modification in the Natural Environment.* New York: Academic Press.

THIMANN, J. 1949. "Conditioned-Reflex Treatment of Alcoholism, I. *New England Journal of Medicine,* 241:368–70.

THOMAS, E. J. 1968. "Selected Sociobehavioral Techniques and Principles: an Approach to Interpersonal Helping." *Social Work* 13:12–26 (Jan.).

—— 1970. "Behavioral Modification and Casework." In *Theories of Social Casework,* eds. R. W. Roberts and R. H. Nee, pp. 181–218. Chicago: University of Chicago Press.

—— 1971. "Social Casework and Social Group Work: the Behavioral Modification Approach." In *Encyclopedia of Social Work,* II, 1226–37. New York: National Association of Social Workers.

THOMAS, E. J., and E. Goodman. 1965. *Socio-behavioral Theory and Interpersonal Helping in Social Work.* Ann Arbor: Campus Publishers.

THORESEN, C. E., and M. J. Mahoney. 1974. *Behavioral Self-Control.* New York: Holt, Rinehart and Winston.

TRUAX, C. B. 1966. "Reinforcement and Nonreinforcement in Rogerian Psychotherapy." *Journal of Abnormal Psychology* 71:1–9.

ULLMANN, L. P. 1969a. "Behavior Therapy as Social Movement." In *Behavior Therapy: Appraisal and Status,* ed. C. M. Franks, pp. 495–523. New York: McGraw-Hill.

—— 1969b. "Making Use of Modeling in the Therapeutic Interview." In *Advances in Behavior Therapy, 1968,* eds. D. R. Rich and C. M. Franks, pp. 175–82. New York: Academic Press.

ULLMANN, L. P., and L. Krasner, eds. 1965. *Case Studies in Behavior Modification*. New York: Holt, Rinehart and Winston.

ULRICH, R., T. Stachnik, and J. Mabry. 1966. *Control of Human Behavior,* Vol. I. Glenview, Ill.: Scott, Foresman.

—— 1970. *Control of Human Behavior,* Vol. II: *From Cure to Prevention*. Glenview, Ill.: Scott, Foresman.

UPPER, D., and D. S. Goodenough, eds. 1971. *Behavior Modification in Outpatient Settings: Proceedings of the Second Annual Brockton Symposium on Behavior Therapy*. Nutley, N.J.: Roche Laboratories.

WAHLER, R. G. 1969. "Oppositional Children: a Quest for Parental Reinforcement Control." *Journal of Applied Behavior Analysis* 2:159–70.

WATSON, D., and R. Tharp. 1972. *Self-directed Behavior: Self-Modification for Personal Adjustment*. Monterey, Calif.: Brooks-Cole.

WATSON, L. S. 1967. "Application of Operant Techniques to Institutionalized Severely and Profoundly Retarded Children." *Mental Retardation Abstracts* 4:1–18.

WEISBERG, P., and P. B. Waldrop. 1972. "Fixed-Interval Work Habits of Congress." *Journal of Applied Behavior Analysis* 5:93–97.

WHITE, G. D., G. Nielsen, and S. M. Johnson. 1972. "Time-out Duration and the Suppression of Deviant Behavior in Children." *Journal of Applied Behavior Analysis* 5:111–20.

WHITE, O. W. 1971. *A Glossary of Behavioral Terminology*. Champaign, Ill.: Research Press.

WHITTINGTON, C. 1971. "Self-Determination Re-examined." *British Journal of Social Work* 1:293–303.

WILLIAMS, G. D. 1959. "The Elimination of Tantrum Behavior by Extinction Procedures." *Journal of Abnormal and Social Psychology* 59:269.

WINCZE, J. P., H. Leitenberg, and W. S. Agras. 1972. "The Effects of Token Reinforcement and Feedback on the Delusional Verbal Behavior of Chronic Paranoid Schizophrenics." *Journal of Applied Behavior Analysis* 5:247–62.

WOLFE, L. 1973. "Practical Help for Frightened New Yorkers." *New York,* March 5, 1973, pp. 33–40.

WOLPE, J. 1958. *Psychotherapy by Reciprocal Inhibition*. Stanford, Calif.: Stanford University Press.

—— 1969. *The Practice of Behavior Therapy*. New York: Pergamon Press.

YARROW, M., J. Campbell, and R. V. Burton. 1964. "Reliability of Maternal Retrospection: a Preliminary Report." *Family Process* 3:207–18.

YATES, A. J. 1958. "The Application of Learning Theory to the Treatment of Tics." *Journal of Abnormal and Social Psychology* 56:175–82.

YELLOLY, M. 1972. "Insight." In *Behaviour Modification in Social Work,* eds. D. Jehu *et al.,* pp. 126–49. London: Wiley-Interscience.

NAME INDEX

SUBJECT INDEX